Building I

CW01391555

Building Inclusion: A Practical Guide to Equity, Diversity and Inclusion in Architecture and the Built Environment is just that – a manual to support and provide essential guidance to the profession on these key issues. Acknowledging that the existence of EDI procedures does not necessarily ensure their use, it focuses on demonstrating behaviours that help create, implement and enforce policies, procedures and practices to deliver inclusion.

Written by Marsha Ramroop, former inaugural EDI Director at the RIBA and award-winning EDI strategist, the book targets the pain points of talent attraction and retention, public sector procurement, community engagement and inclusive design. It utilises case studies from organisations across the sector and the world with successful EDI practices, as well as testimonials of lived experiences of discrimination which provide important insight to the reader. The book takes an intersectional approach, considering not just the separate identities of race, ethnicity, nationality, age, gender and sexual identity, disability, neurodiversity and class but the overlap of these.

Clearly written and accessible, with key points at the end of each chapter, this book is essential reading for those in the profession seeking to implement EDI practices in their work and workplace.

Marsha Ramroop is a globally award-winning inclusion culture strategist, working across sectors but with a mission to drive change in the built environment and engineering professions, believing these two pillars create our societies, and that if she can influence those sectors to be inclusive, she can influence a more inclusive world. She does this through her business, Unheard Voice Consultancy Ltd. She has also been working as Executive Director of Equity, Diversity, and Inclusion at Building People CIC, a network of networks for equity, diversity and inclusion in construction and the built

Source: Photograph by Malcolm the Photographer.

environment. Marsha was the inaugural Director of Inclusion and Diversity at the Royal Institute of British Architects, before which she had a 30-year career in broadcasting and journalism, including 20 years at the BBC.

She's a Life Fellow of the Royal Society of Arts, a Fellow of the Institute of Diversity and Equality Professionals and has been appointed to the International Advisory Council of the Institute of Business Ethics.

Marsha lives in Derbyshire with her husband and two daughters. To find out more about her work visit: www.unheardvoice.co.uk

"A thoughtful and thought-provoking book that educates and inspires. With her personal experience and pragmatic approach Marsha offers us an opportunity to make meaningful change to the culture of the profession; by taking personal and collective responsibility for our behaviours. She acts as a critical friend throughout and as such this book is essential reading for all in the sector. I was reminded that however much we think we do, we can all do more. I was motivated and determined to do exactly that."

—**Professor Sadie Morgan OBE**, Founding
Director, dRMM

"An excellent, practical handbook to help the sector do better when it comes to EDI – both in terms of how it operates and the spaces it creates. Marsha's engaging style draws the reader in with a blend of her and others' practical experiences, meaningful context and powerful quotes. It lays open the challenges, but also provides practical tools and advice to help empower those that want to make a change. A valuable guide for anyone seeking to embrace the opportunity a diverse, inclusive workforce can unlock."

—**Sarah Chilcott**, Managing Director, Planning Portal

"As Marsha rightly notes, inclusive change in the Built Environment is not optional – it's a personal and leadership obligation. This outstanding and practical guide provides insight and solutions encouraging us to embrace equity, diversity and inclusion as an opportunity and a challenge. We must accept this invitation to get to work, become agents of change and to take responsibility for enabling equitable outcomes we'd like to see embodied within the Built Environment we create."

—**Warren Stapley**, Solicitor and award-winning
Diversity, Equity and Inclusion strategist

"The global majority has never needed a more important, insightful book than this one. Marsha you truly smashed it, 'The Elephant in the room' talking about experience, discrimination and the much needed ACTIONS to make sure that Architecture and the Creative professions reflect the 'Global Majority'. People that look like us. Please read this book or miss out on its valuable insights."

—**Neil Pinder**, Founder of HomeGrown Plus; Head
of Architecture at Graveney School; Hon Professor
Bartlett School of Architecture; Hon RIBA Fellow

"What does inclusion have to do with architecture? You won't have to wait more than a couple pages into this book to find out. Drawing on her brilliant communication skills, her leading expertise in cultural intelligence, and her insider knowledge of the world of architecture, Marsha Ramroop has written a groundbreaking book that is not only overflowing with practical ideas, it's a riveting read. Even people working outside architecture will benefit from reading this."

—**David Livermore**, PhD, Author and leading
authority on cultural intelligence

"Marsha Ramroop's *Building Inclusion* is both compelling and provoking. Her vantage point as an outsider is unique. The holistic, 360-degree perspective adopted within, reflects my approach to inclusion. Systemic factors and processes are addressed in addition to individual behaviour. Filled with practical advice and a strategy for change, it is a must read for any practice leader or individual seeking to build their knowledge and acquire tools for informed action."

—**Dr Teri Okoro**, FRIBA Architect, founder, inclusion
strategist and non-executive director

"The built environment affects us all fundamentally and yet those charged with stewarding it do not represent society at large, nor regularly seek to understand lived experiences beyond their own. This essential guide provides the insight and tools we must all embrace, to not only understand this issue, but also to take the necessary action to create truly inclusive practices."

—**Alasdair Ben Dixon**, Co-author, *RIBA Ethical
Practice Guide*; Co-founder, Collective Works;
Steering Group, Architects Declare

"Marsha's done an exemplary job providing you with a powerful roadmap about why making inclusivity a primary goal is crucial to our survival. If lack of inclusivity is evil, then we don't have any excuse for doing nothing. In the end it's all our responsibility. I encourage you, in fact I challenge you, to take the first step, read this book, and be the change – make a difference now!"

—**Annette Amanda Oyèkúnlé Fisher**, Former
RIBA Vice President; Partner FA Global; Co-Chair,
Unionne; Chair, Let's Build

MARSHA RAMROOP

Building Inclusion
A Practical Guide to Equity, Diversity and Inclusion in Architecture and the Built Environment

Routledge
Taylor & Francis Group

LONDON AND NEW YORK

Designed cover image: © Getty Images

First published 2025
by Routledge
4 Park Square, Milton Park, Abingdon, Oxon OX14 4RN

and by Routledge
605 Third Avenue, New York, NY 10158

Routledge is an imprint of the Taylor & Francis Group, an informa business

© 2025 Marsha Ramroop

The right of Marsha Ramroop to be identified as author of this work has been asserted in accordance with sections 77 and 78 of the Copyright, Designs and Patents Act 1988.

All rights reserved. No part of this book may be reprinted or reproduced or utilised in any form or by any electronic, mechanical, or other means, now known or hereafter invented, including photocopying and recording, or in any information storage or retrieval system, without permission in writing from the publishers.

Trademark notice: Product or corporate names may be trademarks or registered trademarks, and are used only for identification and explanation without intent to infringe.

British Library Cataloguing-in-Publication Data
A catalogue record for this book is available from the British Library

Library of Congress Cataloging-in-Publication Data
Names: Ramroop, Marsha, author. | Lari, Yasmeen, writer of foreword.
Title: Building inclusion : a practical guide to equity, diversity and inclusion in architecture and the built environment / Marsha Ramroop.
Description: Abingdon, Oxon : Routledge, 2025. |
Includes bibliographical references and index.
Identifiers: LCCN 2024006987 (print) | LCCN 2024006988 (ebook) |
ISBN 9781032564852 (hardback) | ISBN 9781032564838 (paperback) |
ISBN 9781003435747 (ebook)
Subjects: LCSH: Architectural practice—Social aspects.
Classification: LCC NA1995 .R36 2025 (print) | LCC NA1995 (ebook) |
DDC 720.87—dc23/eng/20240423
LC record available at https://lccn.loc.gov/2024006987
LC ebook record available at https://lccn.loc.gov/2024006988

ISBN: 9781032564852 (hbk)
ISBN: 9781032564838 (pbk)
ISBN: 9781003435747 (ebk)

DOI: 10.4324/9781003435747

Typeset in Joanna
by codeMantra

For my mother, Omatee, on whose strong shoulders I have always stood, but not acknowledged enough, empowering me to say:

Do Náiomi agus Teamhair,

Tá súil agam go bhfágfaidh mé domhan níos fear do bhur todhchaí ná an domhan inar rugadh mé féin.

A new type of thinking is essential if [hu]mankind is to survive
and move toward higher levels.
—**Albert Einstein**

Contents

CREATE 185

ENGAGE 233

xii **Contents**

QR Codes

Notes and Disclaimers

This is a book about inclusion, and to that end the intention is to be inclusive in the language. Where I miss the mark, please get in touch to let me know, and I will rectify for future editions. I share personal stories not to shock or trigger, but to allow the opening up of conversations about shared experiences which are, too often, stigmatised or unbelieved.

LANGUAGE USE GENERALLY

The terms and definitions used in this book are continually in flux. What may be appropriate today, may not be tomorrow, and yet reclaimed later. I would urge you to consider the purpose of a term and what you wish to achieve with it, rather than the current standing of a particular word at a given time. What is the impact you wish to make and how can you create inclusion?

TERMINOLOGY AROUND SEX AND GENDER

When I reference men and women, this pertains to gender and I am including all who identify by those particular labels. This is not to exclude those who do not use these terms.

While female and male can equally be applied to gender, when I reference female and male this pertains to the extremes of binary sex assigned at birth, cognisant that there are other sexes including intersex and other identified sexes. In many countries sex is assigned in a binary manner, in some places, however, there are more assignment choices.

I realise these matters are still not widely understood and more education is needed. The context may still change during and after the publication of this book.

There is no intention of judgement in the use of these terms, they meant to be descriptive and serve as adjectives, and I would request leniency if you infer any judgement.

EDI AND DEI

Equity, Diversity and Inclusion (EDI) is mostly used in the UK, and Diversity, Equity and Inclusion (DEI) is mostly used in the US. They are interchangeable and mean the same thing. I tend to use EDI, but where someone I quote uses DEI, I have stuck with their preference.

CASE STUDIES

This book contains a range of case studies of specific instances and outcomes where policies, procedures and practices around inclusion have been used well. I make no judgement as to either, the ongoing use of these, or the overall inclusive culture of the organisation quoted, well aware that my own award-winning work may not be maintained where I have delivered it. The case studies are illustrations and opportunities to learn what can be replicated and when it can work well.

Any errors or mistakes are mine alone, for which I am wholly willing to take responsibility.

Foreword

In view of rising disparities, increasing poverty levels and climate change impact, architects can no longer remain aloof from the social and eco-logical injustices that are on the rise. As social and eco champions, by adopting divergent pathways in the practice of architecture, architects are poised to play a lead role in enabling those living on the margins to achieve a better quality of life. No longer can we afford to continue to deplete the planet's resources, instead we need to adopt the principles of circular economy with its 5 Rs: Reducing, Reusing, Refurbishing, Repairing, Recycling along with adoption of the tenets of Barefoot Social Architecture (BASA) for humanistic humanitarianism: Low Cost, Zero Carbon and Zero Waste which leads to Zero Poverty.

For an architect such as myself, who prides herself in being addressed as 'Architect for the Poorest of the Poor', the Royal Gold Medal 2023 was of course a great honour. By taking this brave decision, the RIBA have sent a powerful message that architects no longer need to vie for the attention of the privileged and the wealthy, but equally be ready to serve humanity.

Marsha recognised this when she asked me about the responsibility of institutions to actively support the diverse pathways for the expanded role of architects in society.

Marsha's earlier career in broadcasting, 'Giving the Unheard Voice a Place to Speak', as she tends to say, mirrors the agency we need to give the people we serve through our work, for the long term. Providing skills, materials, space and support to fulfil their own needs and dignity, is a level of co-creation that we should encourage for a more equitable and fair society.

Marsha argues for inclusive, sustainable, ethical and safe building, starting with our behaviours. She asks us to consider who we are, and who we should be, as professionals with the power to shape a human experience. She helps us reflect on how coloniality and history has shaped our current thinking. In order to build a different future, the introspection we engage in here can be the difference between more of the same, or a more inclusive, sustainable, ethical and safe environment.

Picking up *Building Inclusion: A Practical Guide to Equity, Diversity and Inclusion in Architecture and the Built Environment* is an opportunity for the change that the architectural profession needs; architects and our professions using our skills for the greater good. Through our design ability, our architectural creations can empower people, and at the same time give agency to those who have no voice. We can no longer design only for the gratification of the privileged but ensure that our creations tread lightly on the planet to demonstrate the duty of care for next generations.

This book helps us to ensure that as designers we need to create a more humanistic world by providing social and ecological justice through architecture.

It gives me great pleasure to write this foreword. This work, and the advice within it, is hugely important, and the tools presented here are invaluable for those in the built environment.

Dr Yasmeen Lari
Pakistan, October 2023

Preface

I was eight. We were in the changing room after PE. Me, with my little Trinidadian body, next to my best friend with her little Jamaican one. Our skin tones, almost the same.

I don't know how we arrived at the conversation, but I remember what was said:

You're Indian, she stated.

No, I'm not. I'm West Indian. I'm from the Caribbean. I'm like you.

You'll never be like me, she said.

My little mind was whirring that night. Upset. How can I not be like her? We *were* the same! Same kinds of people, music, laughter, food. Culture.

Hang on. Maybe not.

Maybe, I remember thinking, I'm not like anyone. Maybe, I'm the only me. And she's the only her. And, if I'm the only me, and she's the only her, then, maybe, everyone is the only them.

From that day on, when faced with difference, I try to recall, 'everyone is the only them'.

* * * *

I'm calling this out right away – I am not an architect, nor do I have any training in a built environment profession. I've checked, and being brilliant at assembling Ikea furniture or using Lego doesn't count.

So, how the devil did I end up here, writing this book?

I had a 30-year career in broadcasting before I ended up in full-time inclusion work. (Despite my youthful looks I wasn't quite a baby. I broadcast my first radio show on FM when I was 15. My first national news bulletin at 16.) As my girls now take the mickey out of me for saying – with a sham mid-Atlantic drawl to boot – I believe that *radio is what I want to do, but inclusion is what I need to do.*

Throughout my journalism career I was focused on local communities, what are their stories? What do they want to say? How do they want those stories told? How can we facilitate their media literacy? How do we represent those communities amongst our staff? How do we amplify and progress those people?

It wasn't always straightforward to do this work. Far from it, at times. Despite my success in engaging communities, the organisational culture, some individual personalities, and at times, my own naivety, were barriers to overall progress. I set about trying to improve my theoretical understanding of organisational development, the people function, leadership, developing my praxis to deliver on diversity and create inclusive cultures.

I discovered a missing link – cultural intelligence, the key behavioural skill to demonstrate inclusiveness. I brought it into play with some pilot training and recruitment programmes I produced, but it became clear after feedback from others, I needed to deliver this work by creating my own consultancy. I started Unheard Voice and ran it as a 'side-hustle' for a few years.

I had made my decision and left my broadcasting career, throwing myself, like a trapeze artist, from one career towards another to focus on strategic inclusion, when I spotted the role at the Royal Institute of British Architects (RIBA) for their inaugural Director of Inclusion and Diversity. My full-time consultancy was off to a good start, but when I saw that advertisement, I thought, *I don't need that job, but I want it.*

Two memories flashed through my mind in an instant. The first was of Stephen Lawrence, who, of course, wanted to become an architect. It was a key fact I remembered about him and it had always stuck in my mind, so it surprises me when I learn how few people outside the sector know it too. I wondered if the RIBA were aware and if it was working with the Lawrence family (how little I knew!). The second was, I recalled, that many years ago, when the refurbishment work at the Palaces of Westminster (at the time of writing, still ongoing) was first being touted, there was a radio discussion about it that I heard. There were suggestions that the work of Parliament could move out of the Palaces and travel around the country. That policy could be made in circular rooms and spaces – and there was incredulous laughter in the radio studio. Guests scoffed at the idea that policy could be made by people sitting in a circle, or, God forbid, in Newcastle, let alone Conwy, Dunblane or Derry.

I remember thinking at the time, this is fundamental to our problems. We are governed by people who face-off at the dispatch box. The very nature of the space encourages combat, rather than collaboration. Maybe, if Parliament travelled around the country and explored different physical, as well as geographical, spaces we might have a more conciliatory and compassionate approach to policymaking. I fundamentally understood how space influenced how we thought, communicated and behaved.

So, when I saw the job, those memories sparked for me, and I realised, if I could influence the creation of inclusive spaces, I could influence the creation of an inclusive world.

No small task, but a rewarding and purposeful one. One I believed in. One, I hoped, I could encourage others to believe in too.

I found myself at the RIBA, and I got to work.

'The do good, to be good' principle is one of the most important lessons psychology has to offer.[1]

ENTERING THE BUILT ENVIRONMENT

The significance of our physical spaces is one that I understood inherently, but not academically or intricately.

Seeking answers as to *what is the purpose of architecture? How do we form our built environment? Who makes the decisions? Who decides what is aesthetically pleasing or functional? How are communities consulted? What processes need to be examined?* just led to more questions and debates, than answers.

What was clear, however, was that not everyone had access to be involved, and the inclusive outcomes of the professions were patchy at best.

Many people have asked me whether architecture/construction/ real estate is the worst profession for this. Funnily enough, when I've been in higher education rooms, finance companies or health leadership sessions, I get asked the same question, but for their professions.

I always answer to say the issues that affect the built environment are societal. No sector or profession exists outside of our society. And so, no, is the short answer. This book is the long one.

And so, the research and immersion to understand this sector went on.

It is said that in order to test whether you're fully absorbed into a culture you should be able to effectively tell a joke in it … so I came up with this one:

Why didn't the building designer finish their Part III?
Because BIM there, done that.[2]

Now you know, I'm not only not an architect, but I'm not particularly funny either. You can decide whether my research has got me

DOI: 10.4324/9781003435747-1

to a fully encultured state and resist the temptation to put down this book as I attempt to entertain, as well as inform, you throughout this journey.

The reflection I've had about this process to learn more and understand built environment professions, is that I found myself falling in love.

When the *Architects' Journal* did their write-up about my new role,[3] I admitted that previously I'd not really given architects much thought. A LinkedIn post[4] by Jason Boyle, Fellow of the Royal Institute of British Architects (RIBA), suggested that architects are smart, hard-working, stylish, engaged artists who love nature and Paris – what is there not to fall in love with?! And indeed, given I started my role during the COVID-19 lockdown, where every interaction was by appointment and those that engaged with me were the ones who *wanted* to, rather than, perhaps, those that *should* have, you might see how I formed this attraction from the bubble I found myself in. And, perhaps, it's the only explanation for the madness that keeps me here!

The challenge and irony, of course, is that it is those that don't engage with the inclusion conversation who are the ones that most need to, and the reality is that the culture of the wider built environment professions can be one more that 'only a mother could love' or, given the demographic, maybe it should be 'father'; as I discuss elsewhere, the culture can be quite ugly. It is really only the overrepresented population in the professions who think they're doing well on inclusion efforts or that enough progress is being made. I'll come back to this.

The punchline of Jason's post: the problem is, architects tend to be broke! And, in all seriousness, this is also part of the issue around access for that profession; others in the sector seem to have less of a problem in terms of time invested studying and return on that investment. So, when my younger daughter recently dropped the bombshell that she wants to do an architecture undergraduate degree, I went quite pale.

I have been reflecting on recent Royal Gold Medal winners as potential sources of people who, arguably, shape the best environments, and David Adjaye's words when receiving the accolade in 2021:

> Architecture, when it's great, speaks about the things that are very difficult to put language to sometimes, and very difficult to quantify beyond the function. Great architecture silences you to make you think about other things.[5]

He went on to describe an approach which I summarised as Function. Beauty. Community.[6]

Like some others who have been recognised in the profession, controversy now surrounds Adjaye too. I encourage you, then, to handle the existence of multiple truths. A discredited individual[7] doesn't necessarily make something they said less relevant. We can fall foul of Halo or Horns biases[8] otherwise. This is a particular challenge I explore within these pages.

Speaking to Professor Flora Samuel, Head of the Department of Architecture at the University of Cambridge, she suggested that in theory being a chartered architect is to be working for the public good. They are professionals who should be able to balance up different things to make sure that we get a built environment that's fit for purpose. The decisions that architects make can have enormous impacts on the lived experience for people in the places that they design, and on the buildings that they create. In practice, the profession has lost control of the financial and the planning side of the project delivery journey, with fees plummeting down to minute levels, and there are a lot of architects that are just clinging on. Samuel believes that architects' lack of diversity has contributed to the plunging status of the profession (see Figure 4.9).

She added that architects love to talk to each other. However, having a more diverse gene pool of ideas can appeal to a more diverse group. So, quite apart from the moral and ethical imperatives of being diverse, there is a huge business case for being diverse and inclusive, because the profession would have better ideas, be able to appeal to a wider range of clients and be able to devise new and more resilient funding streams.

I found it fascinating that on a recent tour of 66 Portland Place, the headquarters of the RIBA, literally written into the fabric of the building and the images of the profession, is a small acknowledgement of women's place in it (see Figure 0.1). On the imposing bronze doors that adorn the front of the institute, there is a woman student carrying her portfolio. The institute was forward-thinking about the role of women in the profession in the 1930s, when those doors were commissioned, not long after all British women received the right to vote on the same terms as men. Despite this, and the fact that the institute had – unusually for the time – a Women's Lounge, the acceptance of women in the institute and the wider profession doesn't appear to have translated into any development of equality decades later. What happened?

Figure 0.1 Image of woman and a non-gendered student from RIBA's bronze doors, 66 Portland Place. Photograph by the author.

When we add together those who engage in the inclusion conversation, the wider cultural issues, the absence of women in leadership, the outcomes – literally – on the streets, the costs of training and the impact of poor wages, who gets to have a say as to what is functional, what is beautiful, and who in the community is heard, the equation results are lopsided.

Maybe, in the 'silence' that 'great architecture' seemingly inspires, what we need to do is listen.

WHY YOU NEED THIS GUIDE

This book is divided into seven chapters, subdivided into bitesize sections to help you get started and moving through your inclusion journey, in order to place a fresh lens over the issues you face in doing your role. It's peppered with good practice case studies from across the sector to help you create an inclusive built environment, and testimonials of professionals' experiences of discrimination, and their advice to remind you why it's important to keep reading.

'The "do good, to be good" principle is one of the most important lessons psychology has to offer' says Professor Timothy Wilson, in his book *Stranger to Ourselves, Discovering the Adaptive Unconscious*. He adds that 'behaviour change often precedes changes in attitudes and feelings … it can be helpful to alter your behaviour in a more positive way … to establish a desirable pattern of habitual responses, the best advice is to practice, practice, practice'.

But practice which positive behaviours exactly?

The RIBA Inclusion Charter[9] was shared with members in November 2020. It listed some useful start points and commitments regarding being inclusive, but didn't describe how to fulfil those commitments. The Chartered Institute of Building (CIOB) Charter[10] mentions five actions, which are described as 'not difficult in and of themselves but making all five work together over time to produce results will take thought and commitment'. The Royal Town Planning Institute (RTPI) Inclusive Framework[11] is more structured, with tangible support offered on how to deliver on policies, procedures and practices. However, there is a still a significant gap in helping people identify how they deliver inclusive behaviours and cultures.

Sometimes, we're clear about *why* we need to have inclusion efforts, we might even know *what* we want those outcomes to look like, but the *how* is missing. This book addresses the *why* and the *what*, but crucially the *how*, too.

In November 2021, whilst I was at the RIBA, a team of us created RIBA Radio,[12] a live online radio station which ran for seven days, four hours each day. Alongside the music, features and laughter, it supported the Inclusion Charter by supplying insight, actions, measures and potential outcomes to help members and the wider profession with effective guidance on inclusion matters; provision for how to fulfil the Charter commitments. It now exists as 29 podcast episodes on architecture.com and on various podcast platforms, and they can usefully be consumed alongside this book for all in the built environment professions. At specific points I signpost particular episodes. I'm using QR codes to help you access such free resources there and then on a page, as having them alongside whilst you read can be helpful.

A quote attributed to Einstein is 'the definition of madness is doing the same thing over and over again, and expecting a different result'. I believe that is what has been happening to date in the Equity, Diversity and Inclusion (EDI) space. We know this, because we're not seeing different results despite all the initiatives, schemes and promises. So, I think in addition to this, his actual words are more useful:

a new type of thinking is essential if [hu]mankind is to survive and move toward higher levels.[13]

When we ask ourselves why are we not making greater progress in improving EDI in the built environment, and we continue to peel back the layers to the answers we give ourselves, if we're honest, inevitably, we will land on the issue of bias.

Not all bias is unconscious. Not all unconscious bias is unhelpful.

Be clear, though, that to be human is to be biased. The shortcutting of information is a human biological cerebral need. We wouldn't be able to function effectively if our brain didn't have the capacity to make assumptions and create heuristics due to the sheer amount of information it has to process. However, due to repeated inputs, socialisation, cultural messaging, and so on, stereotypes and biased information work their way into our psyche, and they then play out in our behaviours.

Bias is our biggest enemy when it comes to sustained and sustainable change, so how we move forward must always be cognisant of this. That's why it's so important to surround ourselves with a diversity of lived experiences, and listen, and act, recognising those voices that are very different from our own.

Knowing that we are all biased is not an excuse to absolve yourself of responsibility for it. On the contrary, it's an opportunity to break the cycle of our unhelpful biases, which then support our systems, which perpetuate in society, which then reinforce our bias, and we get stuck in a vicious circle and very little changes (see Figure 0.2). This in turn leads to diversity fatigue and I'd wager, even as you read this, that there may be a prickle of discomfort. Recognise these prickles as you read this book. Challenge yourself and how you're feeling. Ask yourself, why am I feeling this way?

Can we afford to tire of facing, and dealing with, these matters? Should we give up with the signs of discomfort, because it's all just too hard? If we're to create a built environment for public benefit and inclusive spaces for all, should we fatigue of these issues?

If we value life, in all its richness, we place *value* on *all* life. 'Great architecture' should never look at value purely in terms of pounds and

The Unhelpful Bias Cycle

Personal unhelpful bias supports the systems, which embed in our organisations, which perpetuate in society, which inform our personal bias.

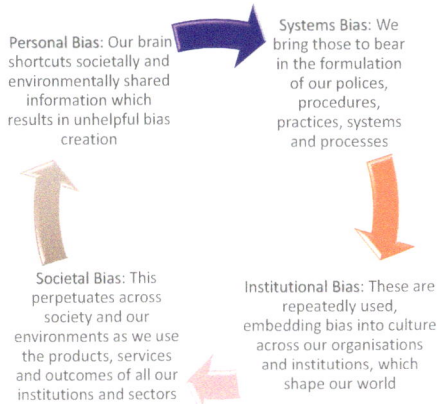

Personal Bias: Our brain shortcuts societally and environmentally shared information which results in unhelpful bias creation

Systems Bias: We bring those to bear in the formulation of our polices, procedures, practices, systems and processes

Societal Bias: This perpetuates across society and our environments as we use the products, services and outcomes of all our institutions and sectors

Institutional Bias: These are repeatedly used, embedding bias into culture across our organisations and institutions, which shape our world

Creating a Helpful Bias Cycle

Personal *unhelpful* bias can be challenged through conscious CQ framework mitigation; then, we can create procedural changes to our systems; this informs inclusive cultures in our organisations; which perpetuate in society; which can lead to more *helpful* personal bias creation.

Consciously slowing down to think about what we're thinking about, may, in time, become more unconscious processing.

This may take decades to filter through and embed, but it starts with personal conscious behaviours, for which we can take responsibility. This can start now.

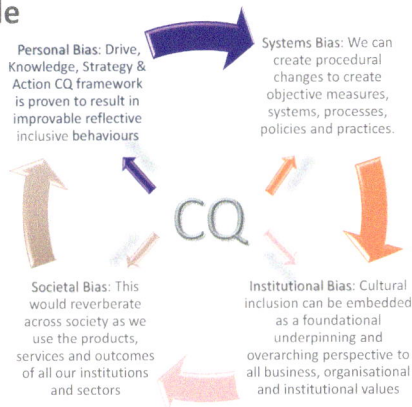

Personal Bias: Drive, Knowledge, Strategy & Action CQ framework is proven to result in improvable reflective inclusive **behaviours**

Systems Bias: We can create procedural changes to create objective measures, systems, processes, policies and practices.

CQ

Societal Bias: This would reverberate across society as we use the products, services and outcomes of all our institutions and sectors

Institutional Bias: Cultural inclusion can be embedded as a foundational underpinning and overarching perspective to all business, organisational and institutional values

Figure 0.2 The unhelpful bias cycle (a) and creating a helpful bias cycle (b).

pence – when we've done so, we've lost many valuable gifts in our history, as well as our humanity.

Shouldn't our built environment brim with humanity?

Thinking about the challenge of EDI, and creating an inclusive culture in the built environment, is very much about these issues.

The built environment achieves so much in how it can serve people, place and planet – but all the data shows that it could be so much more, if we persevere with an inclusive path.

HOW TO USE THIS GUIDE

Reports have been circulating for at least 30 years[14] about the impact of diverse teams, and whilst some of this has been correct, it has since evolved to show how you need both diverse teams and inclusive cultures for eight times better overall business outcomes and six times more

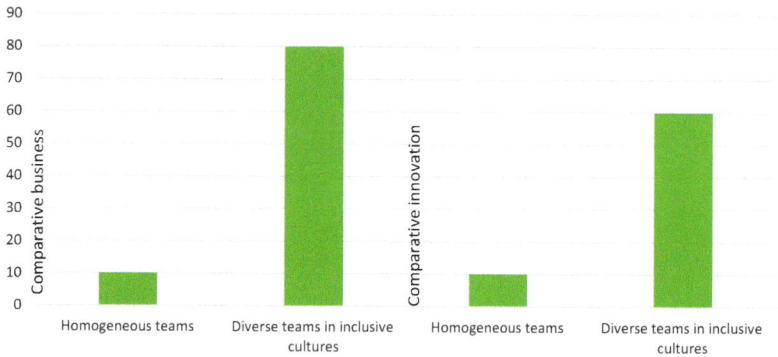

Figure 0.3 The benefits of an inclusive culture.

innovative organisations[15] than those with homogeneous teams (see Figure 0.3).

When it comes to *a new type of thinking* in EDI in architecture and the built environment this is where my paradigm – underpinned with cultural intelligence – comes in. It's crucial that you understand the introspective piece of work required in order to be effective at delivering the actions, measures and outcomes described in later chapters. The basic building blocks are covered in Chapter One.

As I have travelled through these professions, I have discovered that there is a belief system, especially in architecture, that it is made up of truly innovative, radical and 'out-of-the-box thinking', yet the demographics of the profession remain dominated by the same people, of similar backgrounds, and EDI polices remain a tick box – at best – when winning awards and competitions.

Throughout this book I do make some radical, even outlandish, suggestions as they might be traditionally perceived. How you approach these ideas may well be a mark of how open you are to pushing ideas of originality and invention.

The myths that perpetuate about architecture's capacity for creativity and innovation must be challenged whilst those that run the profession's education and practice continue to be overrepresented by a similar demographic.

According to the Office for National Statistics (ONS) quoted in Henry and Ryder (2021),[16] white, not-disabled, heterosexual men based in the South-East of the UK make up only 3.1 per cent of the UK population.

The Architects' Registration Board (ARB) updates the profession's demographic statistics every month. At time of writing, nearly 78 per cent of all registered architects provided their demographic details. Statistics show, of all architects registered, this is the demographic breakdown as compared with the ONS UK population data (see Table 0.1).

Table 0.1 A comparative table of the demography of architects versus the overall UK population.

Demographic characteristic	ARB statistics[17]	ONS UK population
White	80%	81.7%
Not (declared as) disabled	99%	82.5%
Man	69%	49%
Declared as heterosexual	96%	89.4%
Based in South-East England[18]	50%	27%

Even though this information is not aggregated to give a figure for the percentage that intersect all five characteristics, and given the profession is heavily weighted in the London area, where racial diversity is far greater than the wider population, it could be surmised that the statistical likelihood is that architecture's demographic is very much overrepresented by the white, not-disabled, heterosexual man in the South-East.

We can't be willing to sit back and simply rename it *patriarch*itecture.

As of November 2023, we have four men and one woman 'in charge' of the profession, in terms of the CEO, President and Chair of RIBA, and the CEO and Chair of ARB. Two of the group are not white, from having five white men in 2021. Whilst this is progress in representation, as this book will describe, individual appointments do not a system-wide change make. Given the well-documented challenges the profession has been facing, we also have to be aware of the phenomenon of the glass-cliff,[19] where those from underrepresented groups are more likely to be given leadership roles during times of crisis.

In her book *Thrive: A Field Guide for Women in Architecture*, Sumita Singha usefully pulled together a list of countries throughout the world from where she could gather data on the gender of architects.[20] In Ghana, there is a 50/50 split, and, for example, in Croatia, Latvia and Greece, there are more women than men in the profession, but she admits that these disparities are not easily explained without a proper look at data trends.

In other built environment professions, less than 19 per cent of the Royal Institution of Chartered Surveyors (RICS) membership in 2022 identified as women. Of those who declared, 93 per cent of Institution of Civil Engineers' membership didn't have a disability[21] and 92 per cent of their Fellows (Fellow CEng) are men.[22] In a 2022 demographic study of the profession, landscape architecture registered a statistical zero percentage of Black people in the profession.[23] There is also a statistical zero percentage of women in landscape management, so the fact that there's now a call for women to be involved in park design, because we can feel unsafe in them, is now more clearly explained.[24]

It is structural discrimination that results in these kinds of statistical outcomes, and should have us all asking, 'How do we tackle this?'. If you believe that one privileged demographic of the UK population deserves to be overrepresented in the overwhelming majority of power positions, running our institutions, professions and politics, if your view is that this is meritocracy in action, the next question has to be, why do you think that? This book will seek to help you understand your answer to this question too.

It's clear from anecdotal evidence, as well as reports like Howlett Brown's into the culture at the UCL School of Architecture – The Bartlett – and the Levitt and Bichard Reviews for RICS, that psychological safety is missing in large parts of the profession, from education into practice, and this sorely needs to be addressed, and not just by this book.[25] I take a look at how to hold yourself accountable for supporting meaningful change in Chapters Two and Three.

It is essential that we make the profession accessible for all, for all voices to be heard, for all to be represented. There are people who could bring much-needed innovation, diversity and progress to these professions but we're not letting them in.

The underrepresented who do get in aren't always given a strong enough voice. Chapter Four addresses how we attract, retain and progress people in the built environment professions. Underrepresented groups are further marginalised, and drop off at alarming rates, despite starting out and wanting to follow these vocations. The testimonials you'll read throughout this book will remind you of the impact of poor behaviour and poor culture.

Chapter Five helps with some frameworks and best practice in how you can generate and embed inclusion in all you create. I ask challenging questions around some of the preconceptions that exist about permanence in design. I lobby for rethinking fundamental practices in order to be inclusive and bring together the value placed in both people and planet through inclusion and sustainability. Ego, Euro-centricity and decolonisation are all areas we need to think about across the professions. I signpost inclusive design guidance and advice that exists in the sector, in particular the RIBA Inclusive Design Overlay to the Plan of Work.[26]

Chapters Six and Seven are about being inclusive with those you work with. There is increasing demand in public sector procurement to address issues of EDI in better detail, not just as a tick-box exercise, but as a meaningful part of design and planning. No one in the built environment professions works completely on their own, and asking those who you work with, as well as who you work for, to consider their own inclusivity is vital, and will benefit everyone impacted by your design. The co-authorship work and co-design is a necessary part of all engagement, and I argue should occur before pen ever meets paper in terms of design. The Towards Spatial Justice overlay[27] will also be discussed here. RIBA is also rolling out a Community Engagement overlay, referenced here, and I explore how to have inclusion conversations with your client.

As a creative, proactive as well as reactive professional, I'm hopeful that you can be effective at inclusion in your role, by engaging in the rethinking required about how you approach your job. A cognitive evolution must befall all humanity for progress, peace and prosperity, and we can start in the built environment by delivering on that unlearning and relearning to create inclusive outcomes.

As you travel through this book, I will pose some philosophical – existential even – questions to prompt that cognitive (r)evolution in how we approach our spaces. Serving as a devil's advocate and friendly nudge, we cannot expect to create a different future if we approach things in the way we always have done.

Certainly, we cannot do so comfortably. As with physical exercise, when we feel the discomfort, we know good change is occurring.

Sound Advice, 2021

Although COVID-19 touched us all, its impact was disproportionately felt by people of colour, who have suffered and died in greater numbers than white people, often as a result of urban planning issues such as overcrowded housing, lack of public space and poor air quality.

COVID-19 brought these inequalities into sharp relief, and things such as household density, proximity to neighbours, access to open spaces and essential services, and transport to work became indices of vulnerability. For people of colour, it has become clear that powers that create the urban frameworks in which we live have rigged the game.

The murder of George Floyd sparked demonstrations across the world, with people of colour taking to public spaces just to ask the system not to kill them. It also sparked trends such as #BlackoutTuesday, when millions posted black squares on Instagram in supposed solidarity with the Black Lives Matter movement. For Sound Advice, however, such gestures rang hollow – a performance of allyship that fell far short of driving genuine change.

> We got angry, hurt and frustrated and realised that we weren't the only ones. Totally fed up with how the built environment sector tackles (or doesn't tackle) race, we wanted to hear from people who are already fighting to make the changes. What was their response to this moment? Where do they think we can go from here? How can we disrupt the inertia of the profession?
>
> (Pooja Agrawal, Sound Advice)

Determined to incite meaningful action, Pooja Agrawal and Joseph Henry reached out to their network, their friends, family and colleagues of colour and asked them what should change, and how. Over the next few months, they received a stream of considered personal and practical responses – which today form the book *Now You Know*, an insightful exploration of how architecture, design, urbanism and technology could give us the tools to develop a more just built environment.

> Through *Now You Know* we wanted to explore a compelling alternative and more plural vision of the future in our voice and within our own space. The contributors have created an incredible manifesto so we really hope that people engage with the content in the book and don't just leave it collecting dust on a coffee table or to decorate a Zoom background.
>
> (Joseph Henry, Sound Advice)

Although this book is currently sold out, the team may be convinced to do another print run in future with enough demand.

USING THIS GUIDE TO TAKE RESPONSIBILITY

The Stephen Lawrence Prize, set up in memory of the man who was at the beginning of the road to becoming an architect when he was murdered in 1993, is intended to encourage fresh talent and inspire others in the first few years of their architectural career.

There are many outside the profession that do not realise who Stephen wanted to become, and only think of his name in relation to his death, so I hope my coming into the built environment to work on equity and inclusion having been inspired by his potential, is gratifying for his family.

In the years that Baroness Lawrence has been alongside the built environment I have seen her push for the sector to be one that he would have thrived in (see Figure 0.4); the RIBA adjusting the criteria and supporting the Prize[28] is one way of doing that, but there is clearly much more to be done.

This book offers some practical advice and solutions, so anyone who wants to support young people from across our society to come into the sector can be skilled, supported and developed. This is something that's advocated for at the Stephen Lawrence Day Foundation – Stephen's name as a force for good, to help all marginalised young people to have access to opportunities so they can contribute to society and live fulfilling and meaningful lives.

If we are to encourage fresh talent and inspire those in their built environment careers, we need to ensure the profession and sector is one

Figure 0.4 The author with Baroness Doreen Lawrence at RIBA HQ, 66 Portland Place. Photograph by Morley Von Sternberg, used with kind permission of Baroness Lawrence.

in which they can flourish, and the guidance offered in this book is the opportunity to do that, thoughtfully, so we can reach and maintain the equitable outcomes we'd all like to see.

I ask that, as a reader of this book, you take responsibility for what you need to do to make that happen, and fight for justice – spatial, racial and otherwise – that we need to see in the world.

So, who am I to be asking you to take this journey? Not an architect or surveyor or builder or planner, but I do have the insight to provide you with a new lens and an extra set of skills to help you do what you do more inclusively. And I deeply care that you do.

And, in the end, isn't that all it takes to change the world? A bunch of people who care to do so?

Let's begin.

NOTES

1   Timothy D. Wilson, *Stranger to Ourselves: Discovering the Adaptive Unconscious*, Harvard University Press, 2002.

2   For the non-architects reading, architecture education in the UK is broken down in three parts; after Part III people can register with ARB and officially call themselves an architect – it's a protected title. BIM stands for Building Information Modelling. It is part of the planning, design and construction of structures and buildings. Yeah, I know – it's a rubbish joke.

3 Ella Jessel, 'Profile: Marsha Ramroop, RIBA's first-ever head of diversity', *Architects' Journal*, 21 May 2021. See www.architectsjournal.co.uk/news/profile-marsha-ramroop-ribas-first-ever-head-of-diversity [Accessed 29 November 2023].

4 Jason Boyle FRIBA, LinkedIn, 2023. See www.linkedin.com/feed/update/urn:li:activity:7073276203880587264/ [Accessed 23 November 2023].

5 Lucy Tilley in Conversation with Sir David Adjaye OBE, 2021 RIBA Royal Gold Medallist, see https://www.youtube.com/watch?v=qhhbSwZi9bM timestamp 5:11 [Accessed 30 April 2024].

6 Marsha Ramroop, Twitter, 2021. See https://twitter.com/MarshaRamroop/status/1397625816608088070?s=20&t=W6QfBpW2Vol9XFI8Vkmiww [Accessed 23 November 2023].

7 Richard Waite, '"Ashamed" Adjaye denied allegations of sexual misconduct', *Architects Journal*, 4 July 2023. See www.architectsjournal.co.uk/news/ashamed-adjaye-denies-allegations-of-sexual-misconduct [Accessed 4 November 2023].

8 Simply put, the Halo effect is the cognitive effect where we think that someone who possess one or more wonderful attributes is wonderful in all respects. Horns is when we focus on negative aspects of a person and assume that everything about them is negative (the opposite of the Halo effect).

9 RIBA, *Inclusion Charter*, 2020. See www.architecture.com/about/equality-diversity-and-inclusion/inclusion-charter [Accessed 23 November 2023].

10 CIOB, *EDI Report and Charter*. See www.ciob.org/specialreport/charter/diversityandinclusion [Accessed 23 November 2023].

11 *RTPI Inclusive Framework*. See www.rtpi.org.uk/new/our-strategic-priorities/equality-diversity-and-inclusion/rtpi-inclusive-framework/ [Accessed 23 November 2023].

12 RIBA, RIBA Radio, 2021. See www.architecture.com/about/equality-diversity-and-inclusion/RIBA-Radio [Accessed 23 November 2023].

13 'Atomic education urged by Einstein, scientist in plea for $200,000 to promote new type of essential thinking', *New York Times*, 25 May 1946. See www.nytimes.com/1946/05/25/archives/atomic-education-urged-by-einstein-scientist-in-plea-for-200000-to.html [Accessed 29 November 2023].

14 R. Roosevelt Thomas, Jr., 'From affirmative action to affirming diversity', *Harvard Business Review*, March–April 1990. See https://hbr.org/1990/03/from-affirmative-action-to-affirming-diversity [Accessed 29 November 2023].

15 Stacia Sherman Garr, Candace Atamanik and Bersin by Deloitte, *High-Impact Diversity and Inclusion: Maturity Model and Top Findings*, Deloitte Consulting LLP, 2017.

16 Lenny Henry and Marcus Ryder, *Access all Areas*, Faber & Faber, 2021.

17 ARB, *Equality & Diversity Data*, 2023. See https://arb.org.uk/about-arb/equality-diversity/data/ [Accessed 4 November 2023].

18 ARB, *Architects Today: Analysis of the Architects' Profession*, 2022. See https://arb.org.uk/wp-content/uploads/ARB-EDI-Report-April-2023.pdf [Accessed 4 November 2023].

19 Michelle K. Ryan and S. Alexander Haslam, 'The glass cliff: evidence that women are over-represented in precarious leadership positions', *The British Journal of Management*, 2005, 16(2): 81–90. See https://onlinelibrary.wiley.com/doi/10.1111/j.1467-8551.2005.00433.x [Accessed 29 November 2023].

20 Sumita Singha, *Thrive: A Field Guide for Women in Architecture*, RIBA Publishing, 2024, pp. 16–17.

21 *ICE Membership Diversity 2020–2021*, p. 53. See www.ice.org.uk/media/ogwlhrvs/ice-diversity-member-data-december-2020–2021-full-report.pdf [Accessed 4 November 2023].

22 Ibid., p. 60.

23 *Skills for Greener Spaces*, Landscape Institute. See https://landscapewpstorage01.blob.core.windows.net/www-landscapeinstitute-org/2022/12/773450-Landscape-Institute_INTERACTIVE.pdf [Accessed 4 November 2023].

24 'Women should be involved in park design to combat safety fears, say study', *BBC News*. See www.bbc.co.uk/news/uk-england-leeds-65544868 [Accessed 11 May 2023].

25 UCL Howlett Brown Environmental Investigation report. See www.ucl.ac.uk/bartlett/sites/bartlett/files/the_bartlett_school_of_architecture_environmental_investigation_report_june_2022p_6.pdf [Accessed 29 November 2023]; RICS Levitt Review. See www.rics.org/news-insights/rics-governing-council-publishes-independent-review-and-accepts-all-recommendations [Accessed 29 November 2023]; RICS Bichard Review. See www.rics.org/about-rics/corporate-governance/the-bichard-rics-review [Accessed 29 November 2023].

26 RIBA Inclusive Design Overlay. See www.architecture.com/knowledge-and-resources/resources-landing-page/inclusive-design-overlay-to-riba-plan-of-work [Accessed 29 November 2023].

27 Towards Spatial Justice overlay. See www.dsdha.co.uk/research/645503b69b0f42000c91b41e/Towards-Spatial-Justice [Accessed 29 November 2023].

28 'RIBA announces new-look Stephen Lawrence Prize and student mentoring', Architecture.com. See www.architecture.com/knowledge-and-resources/knowledge-landing-page/riba-announces-new-look-stephen-lawrence-prize-and-student-mentoring [Accessed 29 November 2023].

BEHAVIOURS

Chapter One

Power properly understood is nothing but the ability to achieve purpose ... Power at its best is love implementing the demands of justice, and justice at its best is power correcting everything that stands against love.[1]

TERMS AND DEFINITIONS

Language has the capacity to ebb and flow, and over time we may find that these terms don't quite suit their uses. What I ask is that you fixate less on the language and terms and more on the spirit and essence of the definition as changes occur in future.

There are some terms you'll come across frequently in this book, so it is useful to understand how I use them:

Diversity is simply the fact of visible and invisible difference. Everyone is part of 'diversity'. Diverse is not something an individual is, but something a group might be.[2] Aspects of diversity include, but are not limited to, age, race, gender, marital status, physical ability, neurodivergence, and so on. It also encompasses concepts like geographical location, access to technology, experience of abuse, body shape, and so on. Anything that could result in discrimination, and elements that don't. You can't hire a 'diverse candidate', that's a nonsense. You might hire to create a more diverse workforce, but really, when people talk about diversity, they're usually trying to do something about addressing the **underrepresentation** of certain demographic 'protected characteristics' as usually defined by the Equality Act of 2010 (UK).[3]

Underrepresentation is when the demographics of your organisation/process doesn't reflect its societal context. This could be any group, but to take a brief look at race: I tend to use the phrase **underrepresented racialised groups** to describe what was previously termed 'BAME'. Others use **global majority**, people who experience racism, or non-white.

DOI: 10.4324/9781003435747-3

Inclusion is the act of creating an environment where people feel that their identities, values and lifestyles are acknowledged, understood and respected. Understanding doesn't have to mean agreeing with someone else's choices, but inclusion is more than mere tolerance, it's conscious work to recognise that perspectives and decisions are for individuals to have, not for any of us to judge. Inclusive behaviours help us proactively tackle bias.

Equity is equality of access to life/society/opportunities based on individual need and making up for historic imbalance. Equality is about everyone getting the same, which is fine if we're all at the same starting point, but we know that is not the case. This is the outcome when a diverse group enjoys inclusive environments.

Cultural intelligence is the capability to function and relate effectively across difference. It is described using a behavioural framework which allows you to navigate the bias activated when faced with difference (Diversity), so you can behave with acceptance and understanding (Inclusion), to create outcomes which are accessible to all (Equity). CQ stands for cultural intelligence quotient, because it is a measure, as well as an improvable skill.

I like to summarise this as 'Diversity is a fact; inclusion is an act; equity is the impact, when CQ is unpacked'.

BAME

The purpose of the term **BAME** is to group together all people who are not white. There are various reasons for needing to do this, the roots of which all trace back to racism and the othering of those without white privilege, and to identify the systemic nature of racial discrimination and underrepresentation. The use of the term BAME is part of the systemic problem and so we need to stop using it. Changing our language is one of the tools of inclusion. Race is a made up idea – it's cultural, not biological – so trying to pin down definitions around it is difficult.

To superficially look at these things, using BAME hides racial diversity when disaggregation is important. Also, when we use Black, Asian and Minority Ethnic as a group term, without the acronym, the issues still exist within these terms as in BAME, and diversity within racial diversity is hidden.

What is Asian? South Asian? Indian? Do we mean Black African, Black Caribbean? And who are minority ethnic people when, in fact, these groups comprise a global majority.

Black people, that is to say all those with deeper melanated skin and with historic and recent African heritage, is an acceptable term for most Black people. We should always disaggregate where we can, and use Black Caribbean or Black African, if that's what we mean. If it's not, think carefully about what you're trying to say and adjust accordingly.

Asian doesn't refer to skin colour but refers to a continent – that comprises of 48 countries, according to the United Nations (UN) – from China, to India, to the Maldives and Yemen. All very different people. So, again be specific, who do you mean? If you mean Chinese/Japanese/Korean, East Asian heritage would be sufficient, but also ask yourself why are you grouping these people together? If you mean Brown people, you may choose to use 'South Asian heritage'. Although, for a Brown person like me, you have to go back several generations to get to my indentured servitude from India.

Some Brown people feel comfortable calling themselves Brown, however, I would recommend, if you are not Black or Brown, you are specific as to why you're referring to race.

Minority ethnic or ethnic minority is supposed to encompass pretty much anyone else, which is a complete misnomer because this mass of population forms part of the global majority who are not white. Everyone has an ethnicity, including white people, so to say 'ethnic' when we mean not-white is also erroneous. So, once again, be specific. Who do you mean and why.

Invariably, we group these people together because they experience systemic and, sometimes, individual racism. There is a clear distinction as to the treatment of these groups and those, that is, white people, who are not in these groups.

So, if we need to group what is known as 'BAME' people together, we need to consider the context before choosing an alternative.

If we're talking about the built environment professionals, then underrepresented racialised groups, or discriminated-against racialised groups, draws attention to the underrepresentation/discrimination and the racialisation of the people, and the fact we're grouping them together. 'Global majority' groups is another term.

Whiteness isn't a racialised identity. Whiteness is not an 'identity' so much as a 'standpoint' rooted in structural power.

If we're talking about multi-generational housing, these groups are not 'underrepresented' here, so you may wish to talk about cultural norms of communities who may choose to live in a particular way together.

If you're talking about COVID-19, it would depend on the context, and it may be better to talk about the impact of systemic racism and racial inequality on certain populations.

The #BAMEOver campaign[4] suggested the term 'people who experience racism', and it may be that that's the point you're trying to make, so be explicit. Marcus Ryder came up with this term in a tweet a couple years ago. He talked about making the acronym PoWER,[5] but that was a joke. Don't ever make acronyms from these phrases.

When others self-identify as BAME, this may happen partly because using the term 'BAME' for majority white organisations opens their doors, especially those organisations with a declared interest in trying to be more racially diverse. It's not that most people self-identify in this way, it's that they're using the language they think we want to hear. Sometimes it's due to historic branding, and emphasis on language is less important to the organisations than the work being done to improve racial access.

My suggestion is to revert, asking the individuals in question to be more specific as to how they'd like to identify, explaining that 'we no longer use the term BAME in an effort to recognise and see race as the power structure that it is'.

If in doubt, ask.[6]

TESTIMONIAL

When I started training as an architect, all I wanted to do was to train as an architect. It was my experience that forced me to realise that actually I'm being treated differently. It was something that was imposed on me by my education and, kind of frustratingly, in a way, I've had to kind of develop into a professional ethnic minority and activist when all I wanted to do was be an architect. This is the kind of shit that you have to deal with – I'm not trying to be a Black Panther, I'm just trying to be an architect.

Culture: A shared pattern of beliefs, values, assumptions, and behaviours that distinguishes one group from another. What is acceptable and familiar to a group.

Explicit/conscious bias: These are attitudes and beliefs we have about a person or group at a conscious level.

Implicit/unconscious bias: These are subtle and non-conscious thoughts that happen to all of us, all the time. Difference can activate bias, so it's important to acknowledge difference. Phrases like 'I don't see colour' aren't helpful when needing to tackle bias (see QR Code 1.1).

Intersectionality is a term coined by Kimberlé Crenshaw in 1989.[7] It speaks to the multiple social forces, social identities and ideological instruments through which power and disadvantage are expressed and legitimised. Essentially, the layers of discrimination that a person, or group, can face due to the complex nature of the politicisation of identity.

QR Code 1.1:
READ: A handy guide to cognitive bias.

Privilege may be considered as the opposite of intersectionality; it is certainly the lens through which intersectional identity can be understood more wholly. It's the layers of characteristics which mean someone won't be exposed to discrimination. It's not necessarily anything to do with being 'posh' or 'elite', but simply being white, rather than black, means not likely to face racism, or, being a man rather than a woman, means not likely to face sexism – where sexism and racism are societal and structural power outcomes, not just individual cases of discriminatory treatment. Access to private education is a layer of privilege. I have found that I am able to use mine to hold white spaces. At the time of writing (2023) all the Brown and Black people in the UK Conservative Cabinet are privately educated or educated abroad. There is something in the ease with which privately educated racialised people can integrate into white space, and make whiteness more comfortable with tolerating individual instances of race.

Whilst I reference this a little more throughout this book, I would suggest specific reading around race and whiteness to understand this more fully. The Allyship Bookclub[8] is a good place to start. This book's purpose is to focus on individual and organisational behaviours, not people's identities, or to discuss characteristics per se.

Allyship is a combination of behaviours when we acknowledge our own identities and take action to break down barriers, without taking up space, and listening to lived experiences. Writing a blog for Stephen Lawrence Day whilst at RIBA, I suggested that in order to be a good ally, we need to pick up our CAMERA:[9] Courage – be prepared for pushback that is aligned with the discrimination that groups can face; Acknowledge privilege – (see above) recognise that you have it and how it can be used to others' advantage; Manage mistakes well – Chapter 3 has a guide on how to do this; Educate yourself – this book and a range of associated and aligned resources will help; Recognise and believe – discrimination of all kinds is endemic in our society, and therefore, in our organisations there are structural biases, so if someone says they're facing discrimination they probably are; Advocate for others – amplifying the voices and needs of others, especially when they're not in the room, and before sharing your own, is a powerful tool of the ally (see QR Code 1.2).

Amelié Lamont has produced *A Guide to Allyship*[10] that she's made available as an open-source starter guide to help you become a more thoughtful and effective ally. If you find yourself using it, please support the work – which in itself is an act of allyship.

QR Code 1.2:
READ: RIBA blog, 'How to Be a Better Ally'.

INCLUSION FITNESS

I liken inclusion fitness to physical fitness.

Imagine you are not particularly fit, but everyone is telling you being fit is the thing to do and you decide, OK, I'll give it a go. So, you decide that you're going to start with a 'Couch to 5K'.

Firstly, you have to want to get up off that couch. Are you motivated to get out that door? But, do you want to? Being driven to make the change starts with your motivations. And if you're not motivated, how do you motivate yourself?

Next, what do you need to know? About your body, about any equipment – can you run in your Converse shoes? What about in a bikini? A combination of the two perhaps? (This is a book on inclusion, I'm not judging.) Who are you asking about what you should do? Where are you getting your information? That twinge in your left hip, is it OK to run with that? What stretches do you need to do?

When you have the information you need, you then might look at your diary; darn, coffee with neighbours on Thursday and doing shopping for mum on Saturday, Friday – yep, you can step out the door then. You're feeling OK in yourself and you've checked off all your prep.

Friday rolls round and you do it, you go for your first jog at a pace that suits you. Constantly thinking about what might make it better. Maybe a soundtrack? Or, not when it's raining. Or, actually, you've prepared perfectly. Or, it's all gone horribly wrong, you need to start again.

Inclusion fitness is like this. What I've described here is similar to the first steps to developing your **cultural intelligence** – or CQ – which is the framework to being inclusive, which allows you to work well with a diverse group of people. It's made up of four capabilities:

- **CQ Drive** is your level of interest, persistence and confidence working and relating with others (Do you want to get up off the couch?).
- **CQ Knowledge** is your understanding about how cultures are similar and different (What do you need to know?).
- **CQ Strategy** is your awareness and ability to plan for working and relating with others (Have you checked your diary and are you feeling OK?).
- **CQ Action** is your ability to adapt when relating and working with others (Going for the run).

The Q in CQ stands for quotient, because you can measure cultural intelligence as well as improve it as a skill. It is defined as the capability to work and relate effectively across difference. It is academically proven, if you are high in CQ, you will think, communicate and act inclusively.[11]

Whilst helpful, it's not necessary to do an assessment and get a score to improve your cultural intelligence. Simply using the principles of this tool allows us to work on the behaviours required, and to improve them, when you want to be inclusive.

Research into CQ has been conducted in nearly 170 countries around the world,[12] and surveys to assess it have been taken by more than 250,000 people, responding to 'what's the difference between those that succeed in today's multi-cultural globalised world, and those that fail'. Essentially, what's the difference between those that are great, and those that are not, when working with those different to you.

The research led them to conclude that you need the four capabilities, CQ Drive, CQ Knowledge, CQ Strategy and CQ Action (see Figure 1.1).

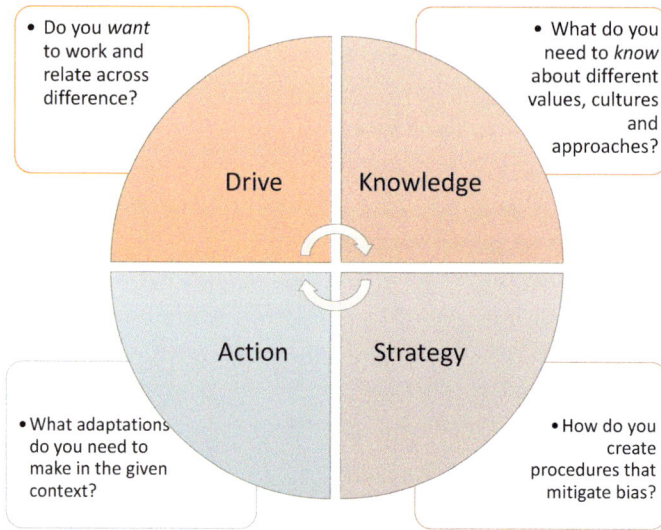

Figure 1.1 The CQ capabilities.

CQ Drive

Do you want to work with those different to you? You may well *say* yes, but do you mean it? This is when the discomfort of the introspection begins. When you look around you, are you really working and relating with those different from you? There's a level of honesty required with CQ Drive which can then activate your fear and defensiveness. This is a problem, because this can stop you 'getting off the couch'. CQ Drive necessitates that you push through that fear and discomfort, and look in that mirror to be clear about what needs to change about you so you can be more inclusive.

Change isn't easy. Just like physical fitness, when you push yourself, the discomfort means you're creating change. Confronting the issues and relationships, which you may not have done in the past, will help you grow.

You must turn to that which motivates you. Are you intrinsically motivated by the thought of trying new things? Or, does the fear of missing out propel you to do something? Tap into those.

The cultural intelligence model breaks down each capability into further sub-categories. For CQ Drive, those are intrinsic motivation, extrinsic motivation and self-efficacy. When you are not motivated how do you use your motivations to push you through the awkwardness. And self-efficacy is being able to pick yourself up, dust yourself off and start again with confidence, with learning along the way when things don't go quite the way you planned. In Chapter Three I delve into this a bit more.

CQ Knowledge

What do you know? What do you need to understand, not just about different lived experiences, but belief systems, languages, operational systems, leadership styles? These are the sub-categories of this capability.

Considering aspects of diversity here should include things very broadly, Do you have access to technology? Where in the world do you live? What kind of economic background do you come from? Have you had cancer? Do you walk to work or do you take the train? Do you have access to public transport? It can be, what's your business' cultural background, for example, a sole trader trying to do work with a massive corporation, these are different cultures. Or, the different language that you might use. It could be anything. The considerations are wide and context is important.

Language is not just about that which is your first tongue, but, for instance, the lexicon of architecture versus the lexicon of graphic design, or the nomenclature of 'RICS matrics' – essentially early career surveyors – and 'landscape not landscaping' – where one is the professional discipline and the other is more the physical construction of a space.

Cultural difference across operational systems could be how the RIBA might work with the ARB; or a small practice with a larger one.

It's important to note here the difference between cultural norms and stereotypes. I tend to say that **stereotypes** are oversimplified, judgmental and frequently pejorative; **cultural norms** are researched, observed and descriptive.

Culture is, in part, informed by a range of **cultural values**. Hofstede,[13] Trompenaars[14] and Meyer[15] are all people who have researched and tracked cultural norms across the world and landed on lists of varying lengths, six or seven cultural dimensions. The Cultural Intelligence Center built on this work and their own research to identify ten cultural values,[16] which describe preferences, at an individual level, based on early childhood socialisation. There's no judgement in these preferences, they are purely descriptive, however people imply judgement based on their own preference and bias. For example, one of the most powerful cultural differences in how we think and behave is whether we're individualistic or a collectivist. Others include are we direct or indirect communicators. Also, whether we are expressive with our emotions or neutral. As we like to be with people like us, our biases can lead to people of similar preferences grouping together and when those are prevalent in leadership, this bias can cascade into organisational behaviours, structures and processes.

Understanding the difference between personality issues and culture issues tends to come with time and investment in a relationship, but there are some key ways to determine which might be at play. For example, bearing in mind that culture is about norms, not stereotypes, does someone's approach seem very different to those around them? Are the behaviours specific to interactions with you? What organisational dynamics might be influencing individual behaviours? What about interpersonal power dynamics? It's in these circumstances, where culture isn't the issue, that emotional intelligence may play a greater role in helping with the situation. It's also worth reflecting on whether your own bias might be playing a part in how you perceive someone else's behaviour.

Where culture is more likely to be the issue, it's worth noting that gorging on the books, articles and blogs is useful in gaining knowledge about how to work effectively with others – understanding issues about race, for example – but doesn't make you actively inclusive; to use the running analogy, just because you know how to place one foot in front of the other doesn't make you fitter.

I tend to emphasise here that CQ Knowledge is the biggest piece of the inclusion puzzle; as you can never know everything about everything, and everything about everyone, it's important to surround yourself with a diversity of backgrounds and listen to those voices, especially if they're very different to your own.

This understanding is, of course, crucial, but it's what you then do with it that really matters.

TESTIMONIAL

It's [in this practice] that I started to pick up on all the issues related to how offices treat you as a contractor; how people treat you as a junior member of staff; and also the challenges of being the only Black person wearing religious dress, and not being a part of the usual drinks and socials because of this.

CQ Strategy

This is the most important piece of the inclusion puzzle, because if you're motivated and you have some knowledge and you move straight into action without stopping to think about what you're thinking about, then you're likely act, lead and communicate in a stereotypical and tokenistic way. Stopping to plan properly, be self-aware and check your knowledge is a crucial part of the process. Slowing down to make conscious, thoughtful decisions will set you up for more sustainable success. For example, how you might shortlist candidates for a role at your firm or practice might be based on 'gut' instinct and where they trained, rather than deciding on objective determined measures which are assessed by a range of people. You might say you're motivated to hire differently and gather some knowledge about different backgrounds, but unless you plan for a different process the decision would be the same.

The sub-categories in the CQ model are planning, awareness and checking.

The quote attributed to Eisenhower is, 'Plans are nothing, planning is everything'. Strategising for multiple outcomes based on your motivation and understanding helps you to be consummately prepared for working and relating across difference, but when it comes to action, being prepared to throw it out the window and adapt according to what's happening in front of you is part of being culturally intelligent.

Awareness is about understanding personal power and authority, how you're feeling and presenting. This is important here. If you come from a big practice, even if you feel you're an insignificant cog in the wheel, and you're meeting with a site manager, recognising any power dynamics that might be at play is important. Are there gender dynamics? What about race? Or physical stature or accent?

Checking your assumptions about any norms you may have learned about is also vital, because you could be in danger of stereotyping. What could also be true about the situation/relationship/circumstances you're facing? Remember, whatever you believe to be true, the opposite may also be true.

It's in CQ Strategy that we create procedural changes to mitigate the impact of unhelpful bias.

CQ Action

CQ Action is when you're adaptable and adjust, *because you choose to*, in order to be effective at working and relating with others. You are motivated, have the knowledge and strategy to behave in a way that understands what's acceptable and familiar to people who are not necessarily like you, and embark on a relationship/interaction/policy that is effectively and consciously inclusive.

The sub-categories here are speech acts, verbal and non-verbal.

Speech acts is about the mode and method that we communicate, so email, phone call, face-to-face, and also being aware of different cultural values at play, so whether someone is a more direct or indirect communicator, or physically expressive or not. From an organisational perspective, having clear guidelines about, for example, giving feedback, being contemporaneous and what method could be expected, is this element in use.

Verbal is to do with actually speaking; so, tone, pitch, speed, volume, whether to pause and leave silence or not. All of these things are cultural preferences, and when the preference may be different to ours, we can get frustrated and make judgements, which aren't helpful.

I, for one, know that I have a tendency to try to finish other people's sentences or fill silences, when others might just be thinking of the right word. On one occasion, a friend was thinking whilst she was speaking, drawing out her words, saying to me 'I'm not you …' and I jumped in to say, 'I know you're not me', but she was saying 'I'm not used to having someone …' – guess who looked like an idiot?

Non-verbal is, as you'd expect, more to do with body language, for example, proximity, eye contact, tactility, and so on. In an organisational perspective this may be understood rather than prescribed, but in order for clarity around what is and isn't acceptable, it is useful to have guidelines about hugging, handshaking and other physical contact, to avoid issues, especially in a post-COVID world where people have different opinions from a health perspective, not just a gender one, as to what level of physical contact might be acceptable.

Another example could be deciding to speak to someone over the phone, rather than use Teams, despite the latter being your preference, because they have good reasons for not finding Teams easy to use.

There's a really interesting theoretical approach to likeability in communication, which was put together by Albert Mehrabian, in which he claimed that in communication, likeability is 55 per cent in your body language, 38 per cent in the tone that you use, and only 7 per cent in the actual message. Email, for example, is actually only 7 per cent because you infer tone. Unless someone's using bold, underlining, exclamation marks, caps lock, then in everything that you read in an email, you are inferring the tone based on a relationship with that person. Mehrabian would argue you cannot make a judgement about likeability from an email. And yet, ask yourself if you don't do this all the time.

When you pick up the phone, suddenly you get that extra 38 per cent, where you can gauge more likeability due to if it's a harsh tone, or it's something softer where you're trying to get across your message. And you would have thought that with Zoom and with video calling that you would get that extra 55 per cent. What I've discovered, and I'm sure Mehrabian would have picked up on it, had he had video calling at the time he came up with the theory in the 1970s, is that there's something about energy. I'm not sure what percentage it should be, but there is a particular energy you get from being in a physical space with another person that you can really engage with them in a way that you don't when you're just flat on screen. It's not everyone's comfort zone, either, spending time in a virtual environment. Quite often people either look at themselves and the screen, not down the 'barrel of the lens' to address the people they're talking to, anyway.

Of course, there are further considerations of culture here, looking someone in the eye is a mark of trust in some cultures and symbolic of disrespect in certain contexts in others, so always gathering CQ Knowledge and Strategy are crucial to deliver effective CQ Action.

CQ Action Is a Choice

I make the point that CQ Action is a reflective decision, rather than an obligation, because to hide who you are is not the purpose of CQ. When you hide who you are in order to make others feel comfortable, that's is not CQ Action, that is code-switching/covering. Many underrepresented groups have to do this simply to navigate away from discrimination. Consider the biases and tropes regularly shared about how Black women communicate when excited, passionate or rightfully peeved. Having to consciously tone that down for fear of being seen as 'The Angry Black Woman' is not for them to do, but for us to navigate our unfairness.

Stereotype threat refers to the risk of confirming negative stereotypes about an individual's racial, ethnic, gender or cultural group, which can create high cognitive load and reduce academic focus and performance. The term was coined by the researchers Claude Steele and Joshua Aronson,[17] and it's been seen as one of the attributes to the attainment gap in education. Labi Siffre described his experience:

> I am an atheist, homosexual, Black artist. Virtually every day of my life,
> I've been told that as a homosexual, I'm a bad person, and that as a

Black person, that I'm worthless. And that's every day. It's constant. In sheer self-defence, I have to pay attention to things that lots of people don't have to bother with.[18]

There are many discriminated-against groups who constantly modify their behaviours – in 'self-defence' – so as not to be seen through the frames of a stereotype or set of stereotypes.

When a racialised person fears they may be perceived as a stereotype, they can then overcompensate with certain behaviours. The example I tend to give is that I was once told that 'Asian people always leave their hair all over the showers [in the gym]', and so I assume now that whenever anyone follows me into a public cubicle that even though I might have found it in a state, the people who follow are going to assume I'm responsible for the mess. Therefore, I always clean up a cubicle if necessary.

In the LeanIn.Org and McKinsey Report 'Women in the Workplace 2023', there are a number of other examples after 27,000 women were surveyed. They called this type of behaviour **'self-shielding'**.[19] A few years ago I determined that it is a **stereotype threat adjustment behaviour**, or STAB. When reflecting on this with me, Roianne Nedd, author of the *Trusted Black Girl*,[20] a book about the stereotypes foisted on Black women, agreed this was a good acronym because every time we do it, it causes us pain.

TESTIMONIAL: A Letter to My Younger Self

Tara Gbolade, Architect, Gbolade Studios

You, with the midnight skin; from the ingenuity of the Igbo (Nigerians) you embody, to the wealth of the Ashanti (Ghana) you adopted, from the wit of the Maasai (Kenya) you personify, to the strength of Mursi (Ethiopia) you exemplify, from the fiscal astuteness of the Yoruba (Nigeria) you married into, to the leadership of the Zulu (South Africa) you represent; your rich tapestry of cultures, religions, communities surround you, yes you with the midnight skin; your healing diviners and tribal origins directed from your African narratives; do not forget from where you came. Do not forget your power.

When you arrive in the room, do not let them push you out, for you bring with you this inherent power. Your cultural diversity exemplified by your myriad of creative ideas because you are always piecing the worlds around you together. This not only qualifies you to be in the room, it propels you to SIT AT THAT TABLE! You, with the midnight skin, who has to navigate the space between, and still belong to, both ancestral heritage and the world you are born into; a world where you are not seen as equal or heard as loudly; a space where your pain is ignored and your words disbelieved. Do not forget your power.

Yes, their knee is on your neck when you are assumed as not smart because you have a different accent, an African accent, the promotions overlooked, the favouritism not afforded to you, the leadership withheld from you for so long that you no longer aspire for it. Yes, their knee is on your neck when you are assumed to be the assistant and not the associate, when you are asked to get the drinks, because surely you are the waiting staff? When you walk into a room and they turn their backs to you – yes, I noticed that too. Each time you force a smile for fear of being branded as 'angry' or 'threatening' or 'aggressive'.

Yet you are brought in under the pretence of 'community engagement' so they can parade pictures of you when presenting to clients saying 'look, I engage with the one with the midnight skin'; but withhold design work – because surely you are incapable. Sweet one, DO NOT FORGET YOUR POWER.

You think of the stark disconnection between your actual job and your lived experience; the fact that you passionately create places and spaces for communities to thrive, all communities it seems, except yours. The constant state of relentless and super-heightened awareness you must confront daily, knowing that someone who smiles at you could be plotting to attack you. THE DISTRUST IN THEM THAT THIS BREEDS IN YOU. The divide it creates when there is a potential for deep connection. Dear one, do not let this frustration take away your power.

'Well' they say, 'if you don't like it go back to your country'; we should therefore ask them to please return the 13 million Black slaves they stole, because prior to their arrival, we thrived for millennia without their input. Ask them to return to London and Liverpool and Bristol. To return the production that formed the foundation of world trade, return their industrial revolution,

Also, they should not forget to return your rich cultural art that they stole, Ah yes, they forget that we are inextricably linked, Do not let the hate that runs in the very structures that hold up the institutions you worked to thrive in stop you; for remember this; YOUR NAME CARRIES MEANING, a deep meaning that carries with it a destiny every time it is spoken, Do not forget your power.

The San (South Africa) from which you originate believe that through death, life evolves; death has the power to catalyse the creative process, A process they must now be aware is needed. So, my dear one with the midnight skin, take up space. Laugh as loud as the Lozi (Zambia) from which you descended, dance as joyfully as the Nandi (Kenya) whose blood runs beneath your skin, live as fearlessly as the Chewa (Mozambique), and be as carefree as the Ihanzi (Tanzania). Do not waste your time on the ones who do not understand, instead seek to walk alongside the giants who look to bring change. DO NOT FORGET YOUR POWER.

(First published in *Now You Know: A Collection of Sound Advice to Challenge Spatial and Racial Inequality from 60 Architects and Urbanists*, Sound Advice, 2021)

Cultural Intelligence Is an Ongoing Process

I will keep coming back to these four capabilities, because it has been objectively proven, if you are high in cultural intelligence you will think, communicate and act inclusively, and it's your behaviours and discipline that drive your actions and outcomes (see QR Code 1.3).

That said, it has been noted that there is a potential 'dark side' to cultural intelligence, that those very practised in it might use it to manipulate others or be opportunistic in taking advantage of those who are low in the capability.[21] Those who have done the initial research into this suggest that understanding how it can be detrimental can serve as an

QR Code 1.3:
LISTEN: RIBA Radio episode one: 'What is Cultural Intelligence with David Livermore'.

opportunity to be proactive in mitigating any such outcomes. Like any skill, how we use it is up to us. It is important to ensure one's own integrity, morality and ethics, as well as see CQ as a core, but adaptive, tool in the EDI work.

Being culturally intelligent is also about listening and welcoming those challenges where someone says to me that they're not entirely sure I've got it right. I have to stop, think and reflect, and work through. I make mistakes all the time. I am, certainly, often inappropriate, especially in an attempt to be funny. I have to embrace my own anti-racism. Of course, I must recognise any internalised misogyny and homophobia that I would have grown up with, simply because I live in British society and was brought up as a Christian. My biggest learning is acknowledging my own fallibility, my own understanding, my own bias, and constantly trying to be conscious about tackling it.

A NOTE ABOUT REPRESENTATION

Representation matters. People ought to see and experience a mix of humans across all manner of characteristics as reflective of our wider society, in all professions.

You may have heard the phrase 'You can't be what you can't see', meaning that it's easier to consider yourself in a profession or situation, especially leadership, if you can see people like you in it, be that a woman, socio-economically disadvantaged, from a racialised background, and so on. This is why representation matters; however, I didn't grow up with that idea. It's only recently I've realised it's because of the privilege of my upbringing that I have always said 'If you can't see it – be it'.

My father, Andrew, with the support of my mother, Omatee, was the first person from a racialised background to own a tailoring business on Savile Row (Maurice Sedwell Ltd) in its 200-year history. To get there was a long journey, facing much prejudice,[22] and when he opened the Savile Row Academy to help salvage the dying art of bespoke tailoring (for which he earned an OBE), he didn't always get the support he needed from the profession for that either. My mother – a woman of significant achievement in her own right, serving others for 41 years in the National Health Service (NHS) – has always been the driving force behind my own achievements. Nothing was ever a barrier with her encouragement. With these two strong Trinidadians as my heritage, and the tiny nation of Trinidad being home to many (a disproportionate number) great philosophers, historians, politicians, artists and activists, notably, the first

Black Dame, Jocelyn Barrow, and the likes of C.L.R. James, Darcus Howe and V.S. Naipaul, Floella Benjamin through to Nicki Minaj, it's pure luck of birth that I have been able to have role-modelled for me how to forge forward, sometimes brushing aside discrimination with comparative ease, maybe having been, even, naively blind to it in the past. In all cases, despite the initial hardship it caused, facing and fighting discrimination just made us stronger.

Most people don't have the benefit of this kind of upbringing, and underrepresentation is a symptom of not having an inclusive culture in your organisation and professional pipelines. Being able to see people who are visibly from otherwise unrepresented groups – or look like you – in leadership positions is, therefore, hugely important.

I have seen a lot of organisations that can get hung up on targets in order to manage underrepresentation and a diverse workforce, and in doing so may be under an illusion about what this means for inclusion.

Representation matters around having these different demographics in your organisation, but crucially,

just because someone comes from an underrepresented group doesn't mean they represent all of that group, or that they themselves have inclusive behaviours.

It's at this point that I tend to be very upfront and say that the former UK Home Secretary (sacked in November 2023), Suella Braverman, and I went to the same school (see Figure 1.2). Suella is about four years younger than me. I was the first Head Girl who was Brown or Black, in that school, indeed, I was one of her Head Girls. She, then, held that position a few years later. We had the same teachers; we had the same head teacher. We had the same sorts of people around us – my peers had siblings in her year, both our respective parents were immigrants to the UK, both worked in order to put us through education (just to state too, we were both privately educated) – and, yet, you cannot have a person whose values and approach to life appear to be more different than my own.

If you were to just put us side-by-side, see we are both Brown women, we both have shoulder-length black hair, similar age, we both went to the same school, and became Head Girl, with similar backgrounds, and

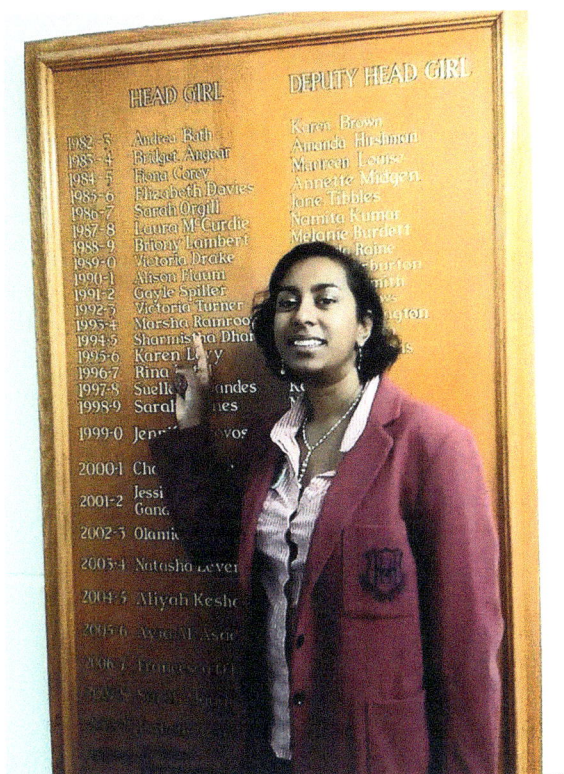

Figure 1.2 Heathfield Head Girl board showing Marsha Ramroop (1993–1994) and Suella Fernandes (now Braverman; 1997–1998). Photo taken at the Heathfield closing reunion event in 2014. Photograph by the author.

you might look at us, and say 'clearly, these two people would be very alike'. This is not how I see us at all.

It has been reported that Suella Braverman's policies are divisive and xenophobic,[23] and she has repeatedly[24] been called racist.[25] She was sacked on the grounds that she accused the Metropolitan Police of bias over protests in London campaigning for a humanitarian ceasefire in Gaza – demonstrations she called 'Hate Marches'.[26] For the record, I don't subscribe to the validity of her policies or approach in dealing with other humans or human rights issues.

So, it's very important that you realise, when you're thinking about inclusivity and you're thinking about how you manage underrepresentation, remember, just because you're bringing in people who address that underrepresentation, that doesn't mean they themselves are inclusive, or that they have inclusive behaviours.

It matters that people are not discriminated against because of a particular characteristic, and we must have methods which seek to undermine discrimination and bring about better demographic mixes across our society and provide access to opportunities. It's also worth remembering that one person from a particular group doesn't represent all of that group, even where different elements or characteristics and identities may seem aligned as well.

Building People CIC, amongst other things, is a network of more than 60 networks that amplify the voices of underrepresented groups in the built environment. Partnering with organisations like this is an opportunity to access those who can help with targeted approaches when that is your purpose.

Meanwhile, it is beholden upon all of us, whatever our own identities, to act with inclusion, as just because someone looks a particular way or subscribes to a particular identity, doesn't mean they themselves are inclusive or not inclusive. We should never make assumptions about these things.

Identities

Generally, in this book, I am not singling out specific characteristics. This is deliberate.

You need to take personal responsibility for who you are and who you want to be when it comes to wanting to, thinking, communicating and acting inclusively, and the values you want your organisation and practice to espouse.

Inclusion isn't about other people and their characteristics – it's about us and our behaviours.

We're all made up of multiple layers, characteristics and identity. It's far more effective to look at what we do, not who other people are.

Being confronted with a cultural idea around identity and considering whether an identity is wrong or right can be a philosophical journey. What makes something wrong, rather than simply a matter of culture or practised norm?

This comes down to intent and impact.

If the intent is to harm, then it's wrong. If the impact harmful, then it's wrong.

If the impact is not harmful, it may be a cultural choice or preference, which we may disagree with, but that doesn't make it wrong, it's just a different perspective.

We may think someone identifying in a particular way is crazy/outlandish/ridiculous/outrageous/nonsensical, and so on, but that doesn't necessarily make it wrong. We have to learn to understand and build a bridge between our perspective and theirs, so we can communicate and be effective humans, together.

The issues arise when rather than having respectful conversation and debate, we try to force views on others. This can lead to conflict and the entrenching of attitudes. Bridge-building becomes less possible and perspective-taking more difficult.

My point is, it is how we behave when faced with ideas and constructs of identity or alternative preferences, which shape us as inclusive humans, not our opinion of the identities themselves.

Inclusion isn't necessarily about agreement, and everyone thinking and feeling the same; it's about acknowledging, understanding and respecting that difference exists and navigating it well. Holding multiple truths, whether you believe in all of them or not.

As notorious slaver, racist and anti-Semite, Voltaire, said: 'I disapprove of what you say but I will defend to the death your right to say it.' His controversial background doesn't make these sentiments less pertinent, if human rights are not becoming human wrongs in the process, by advocating for something harmful.

We have to cognitively evolve to embrace the two, or more, truths, of personal disapproval and respectful acknowledgement, simultaneously. Inclusion isn't a zero-sum game. To make it one is to uphold the status quo. It's almost always 'this/and' and hardly ever 'either/or'.

THE INCLUSIVE CULTURE PYRAMID

I've just briefly outlined the conscious behavioural framework of cultural intelligence that I'd recommend in order to be more inclusive as an individual. How does this translate into an organisational culture shift which can permeate everything you and your practice can do?

If I may extend the fitness analogy, organisational and sector-wide inclusion effectiveness only works if we're not all running off in different directions.

Creating a comprehensive, cohesive approach to inclusion, and being strategic about it, is straightforward to describe, but harder to do.

I break it down like this: there are four cultural intelligence capabilities, four cornerstones of change, four levels of action, and four areas for implementation – together they create my overall approach to inclusion strategy, which I call the Inclusive Culture Pyramid (see Figure 1.4).

The foundation of organisational behaviour may well be summarised by Peter Drucker who mentioned in his book *Management:Tasks, Responsibilities, Practices*[27] that 'The spirit of an organisation is created from the top', or Steve Gruenert and Todd Whittaker in their book *School Culture Rewired*:

> The culture of any organisation is shaped by the worst behaviour the leader is willing to tolerate.[28]

I reframe this as:

> The culture of any organisation can be shaped by the best behaviours leaders are willing to demonstrate.

What are the best behaviours? How do we demonstrate them? Who are the leaders? What is culture?

By every measure, inclusive behaviours are the best ones. Research shows that organisations with diverse teams and inclusive cultures are twice as likely to exceed or meet financial targets; three times as likely to be high-performing; six times as likely to be innovate and agile; eight times more likely to achieve better business outcomes;[29] nearly three-quarters of people value working with an organisation with inclusive leaders;[30] increased employee engagement drives growth,[31] and so on. To be clear, it is not true that only diverse teams get this outcome (see Figure 1.3).

> Long before the current interest in virtual global and far-flung teams, researchers have been interested in assessing whether culturally homogeneous teams are more or less effective than heterogeneous teams.[32] The results indicate that diverse teams that are well managed perform better than homogeneous teams, but poorly managed diverse teams do not perform with the same effectiveness as homogeneous teams. The reason for the increased performance of well-managed heterogeneous teams is due to the synergy that comes from their diversity. The reason for their ineffectiveness when poorly managed comes from their problems overcoming the complexity of their teams.[33]

When heterogeneous teams can overcome the difficulties of managing their diversity, they are able to capture the benefits of their synergy and be more effective than is the case with homogeneous teams.

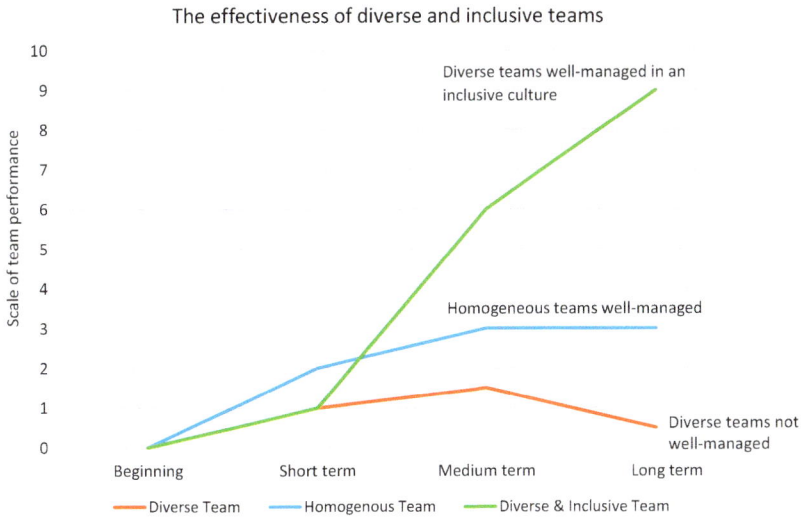

Figure 1.3 Graph depicting the effectiveness of homogeneous and heterogeneous teams.[34]

Again, the research shows that using the cultural intelligence framework of behaviours helps with managing that diversity to result in inclusive outcomes,[35] so individually understanding and demonstrating Drive, Knowledge, Strategy and Action is an excellent start.

As I described, each capability is broken down into sub-categories which help pinpoint and improve the skill, and these can be considered when working on developing your cultural intelligence.

On an organisational level, building a more diverse and inclusive organisation requires a change management process. This also involves an investment, both with direct and indirect costs like use of supplies, consultants and outside professionals, and the significant time involved in company employees providing and receiving training and participating in other aspects of analysing and implementing diversity management.

To deliver inclusive organisations we need to weave together individual culturally intelligent behaviours with organisational behaviour, and introduce a change model.

The Culturally Intelligent Foundation: Four Levels

We build a solid foundation of cultural intelligence, which paves the way to an intersectional approach to leading inclusion and effectively managing diversity. The four capabilities of Drive, Knowledge, Strategy and

Inclusive Culture Pyramid.
4 Levels; 4 Sides; 4 CQ. Cornerstones; 4 Areas

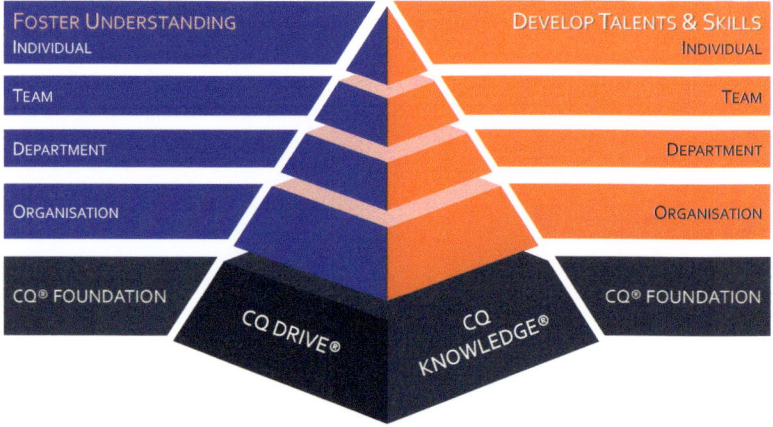

FOSTER UNDERSTANDING
INDIVIDUAL

DEVELOP TALENTS & SKILLS
INDIVIDUAL

TEAM

TEAM

DEPARTMENT

DEPARTMENT

ORGANISATION

ORGANISATION

CQ® FOUNDATION

CQ® FOUNDATION

CQ DRIVE®

CQ KNOWLEDGE®

Organisational Areas of Implementation
Attract ⚶ Retain ⚶ Create ⚶ Engage

Inclusive Culture Pyramid.
4 Levels; 4 Sides; 4 CQ. Cornerstones; 4 Areas

ROLE MODEL
INDIVIDUAL

SUPPORTIVE FORMAL MECHANISMS
INDIVIDUAL

TEAM

TEAM

DEPARTMENT

DEPARTMENT

ORGANISATION

ORGANISATION

CQ® FOUNDATION

CQ® FOUNDATION

CQ STRATEGY®

CQ ACTION®

Organisational Areas of Implementation
Attract ⚶ Retain ⚶ Create ⚶ Engage

Figure 1.4 Side one of the Inclusive Culture Pyramid (a) and side two of the Inclusive Culture Pyramid (b).

Action can be honed and improved continuously at an individual level. Organisations are made up of individuals who then do the work, write the policies, create the services, and so on, and it becomes consciously part of the organisation's behaviours.

When an **individual** – especially leadership – practices cultural intelligence, and the senior **team** develop cohesive effectiveness across difference, this cascades through **departments** in behaviours and policies, ultimately embedding change across a whole **organisation**.

The Change Cornerstones: Four Sides

To create equitable outcomes, the inclusive approach needs to be embedded as a change strategy into the organisation. McKinsey identifies four cornerstones as the basis of change: fostering understanding and conviction; reinforcing changes through formal mechanisms; developing talent and skills; and role-modelling.[36] McKinsey research suggests that you're eight times more likely to implement change successfully with all four cornerstones in use than if you try just one.

The model states that 'I will change my mindset and behaviour if …'

Role-modelling: 'I see my leaders, colleagues, and staff behaving differently.'

Why it works: People mimic individuals and groups who surround them – sometimes consciously, and sometimes unconsciously.

Fostering understanding and conviction: 'I understand what is being asked of me and it makes sense.'

Why it works: People seek congruence between their beliefs and actions – believing in the 'why' inspires them to behave in support of a change.

Reinforcing with formal mechanisms: 'I see that our structures, processes and systems support the changes I'm being asked to make.'

Why it works: Associations and consequences shape behaviours – though all too often organisations reinforce the wrong things.

Developing talent and skills: 'I have the skills and opportunities to behave in the new way.'

Why it works: You can teach an old dog new tricks – our brains remain plastic into adulthood.

To bring about sustained and sustainable inclusive change, I suggest you need to implement this new way of thinking and working across the four areas of the business I've identified:

How you **ATTRACT** people into your business.

How you treat, progress and **RETAIN** your staff.

How you **CREATE** the services and products of your business.

How you **ENGAGE** with your external stakeholders, for example, users/customers/clients/communities/supply chain.

So, there are four inclusive behavioural capabilities – Drive, Knowledge, Strategy, and Action; for four layers of the business – Individual, Team, Department, and Organisation; using four cornerstones of change – Role-Modelling, Understanding, Mechanisms, and Development; across the four areas of the business – Attract, Retain, Create, Engage.

Straightforward to describe. But, harder to do.

While the pyramid describes an overarching strategy and underpinning philosophy about how to embed inclusion into architecture and the built environment, there are very detailed pieces of work to do to get to this point. From Chapter 4 onwards, I describe an array of the policies, procedures and processes that start to delve into the detail of attract, retain, create, engage.

They will only be successful, however, if you have committed to changing behaviours to see though the actions, measures and outcomes, otherwise all you will have are well-meaning bits of paper and policy.

Taking personal responsibility for your role in creating inclusive change comes first, as I further describe in the following chapter.

The demonstration of taking of personal responsibility is exemplified in the Martin Luther King quote about how we use our power towards meaningful change and self-fulfilment:

Power properly understood is nothing but the ability to achieve purpose ... Power at its best is love implementing the demands of justice, and justice at its best is power correcting everything that stands against love.[37]

We don't tend to talk about love in business – to our detriment, I might add. If we did, we would feel more purposeful in our goals towards a betterment of society and how we treated people, place and planet. Creating cultures of inclusion is rooted in the aim to ensure harmonious purpose and allow all we work with to feel purposeful too.

There are no quick fixes, no magic wands, no silver bullets – just conscious inclusive actions, informed by specifically researched behaviours, practised over time.

TESTIMONIAL

… and she did treat the other person on the project completely different to how she treated me. Consequently I left because I felt it wasn't a place which was nurturing. It was actually the opposite – it traumatised me.

YOUR JOURNEY

I'm in danger of mixing my metaphors, but I'm going to say this anyway: If Diversity is the richness of the landscape, and Inclusion is the road through it to our destination of Equitable outcomes, then cultural intelligence is the best, most robust vehicle to get us there. There may be other lands, but they're not Diverse, there may be other roads, but they're not necessarily Inclusive, there may be other destinations, but equity is the aim of EDI work, and there may be other vehicles, but they're not as tried and tested.

This book serves as a map, and other expertise as Sat-Navs. But you are the driver. Only you can lead your own journey; I can't even hand you the keys, you must pick them up yourself, and that's why the introspective behavioural piece always comes first.

RELEVANCE FOR MICRO FIRMS TO LISTED BUSINESSES

EDI is relevant for all sizes of practice, and all practitioners across the built environment, because the issues that need to be solved are societal and not specific to any one profession or sector. In addition, within the opportunity of diversity and inclusion is the prospect to truly innovate design, engage communities and context more holistically, as well as consider who you work with and how to do that well.

'Did you know the neurotransmitter for curiosity is dopamine? Our brains are instinctively wired so that if we stay curious, we will keep learning and growing' write Nathan and Susannah Furr.[38] And, learning from difference is the most rewarding aspect of pushing through the fear that can face us when dealing with these issues.

Recognising that the global diversity of the built environment profession and practice is almost as wide as that of the population, it may be perplexing to consider that there may be an approach to inclusion that would work for all.

The core of EDI work, as I describe it, with the Pyramid, starts with the behaviours of an individual, so whether you're a single person studio, or amongst a team of hundreds in an infrastructure project, there is an extra skill you can develop here.

If you're a sole practitioner, you are unlikely to do a project from beginning to end on your own. If you are in an interdepartmental council team, you are likely to be called on to work with different disciplines. Whatever your context there is an opportunity for you to put this learning to work.

If you're part of a bigger organisation and can embed the behaviours across policy too, or you can influence the structures and processes, this will help the bigger picture and help you and support you with your behaviours.

An inclusive Workforce Lifecycle – which covers the nine stages of employment from the workforce planning to the cessation of roles, and polices to formally structure support for inclusion for staff – might feel less relevant for sole traders and smaller practices, however, understanding this, if you choose to grow, will set you up well as you employ others, and form the foundations of your developing business, as well as help you hold to account the larger firms you work with. You can grow confident by creating a culture with the 'best behaviours'. When you do this, the impact on your design and service delivery, as well as how you treat your users, customers and clients, will feel positive and rewarding.

Inclusive approaches should be an underpinning principle and an overarching perspective on all elements of organisational behaviour which can be listed as: the behaviours of people, the process of management, the organisational context in which the process of management takes place, the organisational processes and the execution of work, and the interactions with the external environment in which the organisation takes part.[39] Sometimes these are dependent on size, most of the time they are not.

Setting and/or embodying the values and culture of your practice as inclusive values and culture, communicating it well, especially with a growing emphasis on participation and empowerment of workers, is, therefore, quite fundamental to how you consume this advice.

A holistic view of approaching design, relationships with clients and communities, and EDI success, is all tied up in who you are, what thoughts you have, what actions you demonstrate and what communication you deliver. Being able to relate and work effectively with the broadest possible range of people within and without your organisation is relevant to you.

This is an opportunity to embrace a new type of thinking, as you unfold multiple levels of possibility in innovating the built environment professions, no matter what size your practice, or how wide or narrow you believe your influence to be.

KEY TAKEAWAYS

- Understand the definitions of Diversity, Inclusion, Equity, Intersectionality, Privilege and Cultural Intelligence.
- Get to grips with how each of the cultural intelligence capabilities, Drive, Knowledge, Strategy and Action, can be broken down and improved to work on your behaviours.
- Using your circle of influence how can you cascade these behaviours across your team, departments and organisation depending on your size – or how might you do so with a wider project team?
- There are many elements to identity. Don't get hung up on it, focus on your behaviours.
- Consider how you can embed culturally intelligent behaviours through the four change cornerstones, Role-Modelling, Developing Talents and Skills, Formal Mechanisms, and Fostering Understanding and Conviction.
- Believe that you can take personal responsibility for inclusive change, no matter how large or small your involvement in an organisation or firm.

NOTES

1   *The Essential Martin Luther King, Jr.: 'I Have a Dream' and Other Great Writings*, Beacon Press, 2013.

2   If you struggle with this idea, think about a single flower – you wouldn't describe the biodiversity of a singular flower, more in terms of the genus. Furthermore, the Human Genome project identified that despite all efforts to ascribe meaning to any biological differences we may have – that we are overwhelmingly, categorically, one, very homogeneous species. Humans are the most homogeneous species on the planet – that is to say, we are so similar to each other, any alien coming to Earth and systematically cataloguing its life forms would find us singularly boring. There are many, many species and subspecies of birds, bees, bacteria, even cats, but humans are almost identical. The variations between people occur in only 0.1 per cent of our genomes. And within that 0.1 per cent, there is, in fact, greater variation within a described group, than there is between groups.

3   The Equality Act 2010. See www.legislation.gov.uk/ukpga/2010/15/contents [Accessed 23 November 2023].

4   *What Next? #BAMEOver – A Statement for the UK*, 2021. See www.whatnextculture.co.uk/bameover-a-statement-for-the-uk/ [Accessed 29 November 2023].

5   Marcus Ryder, Twitter, 2020. See https://twitter.com/marcusryder/status/1276697929495937024 [Accessed 29 November 2023].

6   This toe dip into the term hardly scratches the surface of the problem of 'race' and why it's difficult to define. I recommend Angela Saini's *Superior* (Fourth Estate, 2019), as a first look, for an in-depth analysis of the problematic nature of the ideology of race.

7   Kimberle Crenshaw, 'Demarginalizing the intersection of race and sex: a black feminist critique of antidiscrimination doctrine, feminist theory and antiracist politics', *University of Chicago Legal Forum*, 1989, 1: Article 8. See http://chicagounbound.uchicago.edu/uclf/vol1989/iss1/8 [Accessed 29 November 2023].

8   The Allyship Bookclub. See https://uk.bookshop.org/shop/Allyship [Accessed 23 November 2023].

9   RIBA, 'How to be a better ally', 2022. See www.architecture.com/knowledge-and-resources/knowledge-landing-page/how-to-be-a-better-ally [Accessed 29 November 2023].

10   Amelie Lamont, *A Guide to Allyship*, 2016. See https://guidetoallyship.com/ [Accessed 23 November 2023].

11   List of CQ Research, CQ Center, 2019. See https://culturalq.com/wp-content/uploads/2017/04/Van-Dyne-et-al-CQ-Bibliography-Oxford.pdf [Accessed 29 November 2023].

12   Data from internal briefing with the Cultural Intelligence Centre, 2022.

13   Geert H. Hofstede, *Cultures and Organisations: Software of the Mind*, 3rd edition, McGraw Hill, 2010.

14   F. Trompenaars and C. Hampden-Turner, *Riding the Waves of Culture*, Nicholas Brealey Publishing, 1997.

15   E. Meyer, *The Culture Map, Breaking through Invisible Boundaries of Global Business*, PublicAffairs, 2014.

16   FAQs on CQ and the Cultural Values. See https://culturalq.co.uk/about-cultural-intelligence/faqs/ [Accessed 29 November 2023].

17 C.M. Steele and J. Aronson, 'Stereotype threat and the intellectual test performance of African Americans', *Journal of Personality and Social Psychology*, 1995, 69(5): 797–811. doi: 10.1037//0022–3514.69.5.797. PMID: 7473032.

18 BBC, *Imagine … This is My Song, Labi Siffre*, 2022. See www.bbc.co.uk/iplayer/episode/ m0014jmn/imagine-2022-labi-siffre-this-is-my-song [Accessed 23 November 2023].

19 *Women in the Workplace 2023 Study*, LeanIn.Org and McKinsey & Co. See https:// sgff-media.s3.amazonaws.com/sgff_r1eHetbDYb/Women+in+the+Workplace+20 23_+Designed+Report.pdf [Accessed 23 November 2023].

20 Roianne Nedd, *The Trusted Black Girl: Challenging Perceptions and Maximising the Potential of Black Women in the UK Workplace*, True Voice, 2018.

21 M. Brand, C. Schlaegel and G.K. Stahl, 'Addressing the dark side of cultural intelligence: a conceptual model and research agenda', in *The Handbook of Cultural Intelligence*, Edward Elgar 2023.

22 BBC Radio 4, *Desert Island Discs*, 2022. See https://www.bbc.co.uk/programmes/ m00193r6 [Accessed 23 November 2023].

23 'Suella Braverman won't say Rwanda deportation flights will start by summer', *The Guardian*, 2 April 2023. See www.theguardian.com/politics/2023/apr/02/suella-braverman-wont-say-rwanda-deportation-flights-will-start-by-summer [Accessed 23 November 2023].

24 'Suella Braverman blasted over response to golliwog dolls seizure', https://www. thenational.scot/news/23446344.suella-braverman-blasted-response-golliwog-dolls-seizure/ [Accessed 29 November 2023]; Dr Shola Mos-Shogbamimu, Twitter, 2023. See https://twitter.com/SholaMos1/status/1645418823179284480?ref_ src=twsrc%5Etfw [Accessed 29 November 2023].

25 'UK Home Secretary faces backlash over "racist" comments about British Pakistani men', *Middle East Eye*. See https://www.youtube.com/watch?v=Pd0EkWURmFg [Accessed 29 November 2023].

26 'Rishi Sunak sacks Suella Braverman as home secretary', *BBC News*, 13 November 2023. See https://www.bbc.co.uk/news/uk-politics-67401753 [Accessed 13 November 2023].

27 Peter Drucker, *Management: Tasks, Responsibilities, Practices*, Harper Business, 1993.

28 Steve Gruenert and Todd Whittaker, *School Culture Rewired: How to Define, Assess and Transform It*, ASCD, 2015.

29 Juliet Bourke, *Which Two-Heads Are Better Than One? How Diverse Teams Create Breakthrough Ideas and Make Smarter Decisions*, Australian Institute of Company Directors, 2016.

30 See https://www.cnbc.com/2017/07/26/75-percent-of-execs-would-leave-their-company-for-one-that-values-diversity.html [Accessed 30 April 2024].

31 Deloitte, *Unleashing the Power of Inclusion*, 2017. See www2.deloitte.com/content/dam/ Deloitte/us/Documents/about-deloitte/us-about-deloitte-unleashing-power-of-inclusion.pdf [Accessed 29 November 2023].

32 J.J. DiStefano and M.L. Maznevski, 'Creating value with diverse teams in global management', *Organizational Dynamics*, 2000, 29(1): 45–63.

33 Ibraiz Tarique, Dennis R. Briscoe and Randall S. Schuler, *International Human Resource Management: Policies and Practices for Multinational Enterprises*, 6th edition, Routledge, 2022, p. 289.

34 Adapted from J.J. DiStefano and M.L. Maznevski, 'Creating value with diverse teams in global management', *Organizational Dynamics*, 2000, 29(1): 45–63; Audra I. Mockaitis, Lena Zander and Helen De Cieri, 'The benefits of global teams for international organizations: HR implications', *The International Journal of Human Resource Management*, 2018, 29(14): 2137–2158; David Rock and Heidi Grant, 'Why diverse teams are smarter', *Harvard Business Review*, 4 November 2016.

35 Gallup, *The Benefits of Employee Engagement*, 2013. See www.gallup.com/workplace/236927/employee-engagement-drives-growth.aspx [Accessed 29 November 2023].

36 Tessa Basford and Bill Schaninger, 'The four building blocks of change', *McKinsey Quarterly*, April 2016. See www.mckinsey.com/business-functions/people-and-organizational-performance/our-insights/the-four-building-blocks--of-change [Accessed 14 March 2023].

37 *The Essential Martin Luther King, Jr.: 'I Have a Dream' and Other Great Writings*, Beacon Press, 2013.

38 Nathan Furr and Susannah Harmon-Furr, *The Upside of Uncertainty*, HBR Press, 2022.

39 L.J. Mullins, *Management and Organisational Behaviour*, 7th edition, Pearson Education, 2005; McKinsey & Co, *Enduring Ideas: The 7S Framework*, 2008. See www.mckinsey.com/business-functions/strategy-and-corporate-finance/our-insights/enduring-ideas-the-7-s-framework [Accessed 29 November 2023]; T.J. Peters and R.H. Waterman, *In Search of Excellence*, Profile Books, 2015.

Chapter Two

> There are no more worlds to conquer, except, at least one, our inclination to conquer each other.[1]

'STREAMing your EDI' is all about the necessary factors required to make EDI efforts successful and sustainable (see Figure 2.1). It's not a one-off thing; just like I mentioned in the previous chapter, about fitness, in order to stay fit, success is rooted in consistency.

To make it work, you have to continually address the inequalities in your organisational systems, policies and practices. That means tackling not only the obvious biases but also those unhelpful biases. You know how skipping the gym or stopping practising your hobby for a while can set you back? Well, the same goes for EDI if you don't keep up the effort.

Effective leadership is key to driving your EDI strategy forward. Clearly defining your vision, mission, and strategy for EDI is crucial for its success.

Think: what do we want to achieve as a result of our inclusion work?

And it's not just about top-level management; everyone in the organisation needs to be on board. Embracing EDI should be evident in how people treat and interact with one another.

An inclusive built environment sector ensures equitable access to jobs, learning and development opportunities for everyone involved. It fosters a sense of connectedness and mutual respect among all stakeholders. It's not enough to just talk about inclusivity; you must also walk the talk by aligning your policies and practices with these principles as you move forward. Integrity is key.

DOI: 10.4324/9781003435747-4

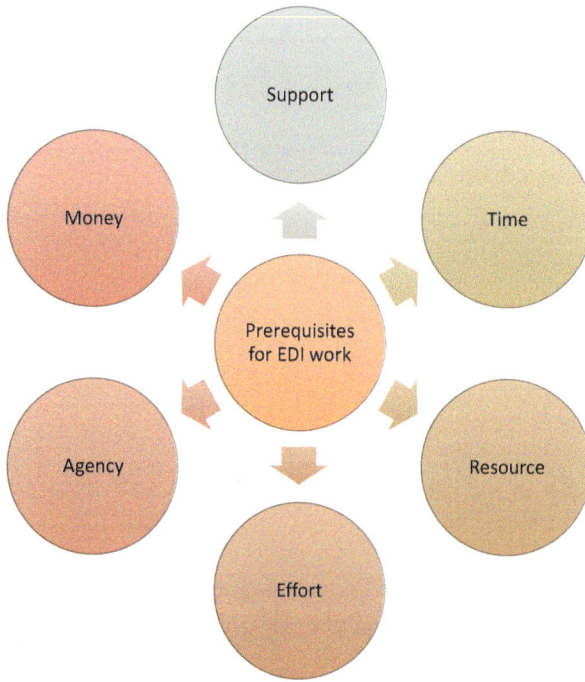

Figure 2.1 STREAM: The prerequisites for EDI work.

'STREAMing your EDI' is an ongoing commitment. It requires embracing diversity, challenging biases and promoting fairness consistently. By making EDI an integral part of your organisational culture, you can achieve lasting positive change and create an inclusive environment for everyone.

QR Code 2.1:
READ: 45-point EDI Joint Institutes action plan.

In 2022 the six built environment institutes, the Royal Institution of Chartered Surveyors (RICS), the Royal Town Planning Institute (RTPI),the Chartered Institute of Building (CIOB), the Royal Institute of British Architects (RIBA), the Institute of Civil Engineering (ICE) and the Landscape Institute (LI), representing 350,000 built environment professionals, committed to a 45-point action plan (see QR Code 2.1) which detailed how the sector can move forward and reiterating the STREAM approach.[2] The EDI leads who put together the plan recognised that it could only be effective if the behaviours to implement and enforce the work were publicly supported by the leaders of the professions, and this commitment was signed off by the organisation's CEOs and chairs, having been approved by their boards. This is a public document which they can be held accountable for delivering against.

It is vitally important, that, in addition to each organisation driving change in its profession, that the professions work together, rowing in the same direction regarding what good looks like, so we can achieve systemic change.

The Greater London Authority (GLA), which convened the institutes, was clear that mobilising as a singular unit around EDI, with a consistent approach to behaviours, resources and initiatives, was crucial to achieve inclusive outcomes for the built environment. Speaking to Louise Duggan, Head of Regeneration, and Sarah Considine, Good Growth by Design programme manager at the GLA, who were vital in bringing the group together, they impressed the importance of gathering the influencers, maintaining momentum to get an agreement around what those outcomes should be, and supporting the delivery in a coordinated way.

Particularly relevant to their convening role was their position as representatives with the credibility of the Mayor of London behind the initiative. They were able to provide enough practical support that they could do simple things, like physically host the secretariat sessions, try to make sense of the sessions and push for clear actions from them. Although that sounds quite simple and practical, having that little bit of resource that was dedicated to keeping things moving along was quite impactful in terms of contracting, a clear aspect of the job from their side, that wouldn't be an aspect of the job from the professional institute side.

That kind of demonstration of Support, Time, Resource, Effort and Agency, was a crucial part of enabling the agreement, and one that others can learn from.

The below approach supports that work and the overall actions in that Plan. **STREAM** stands for:

Support: Leadership demonstrative and vocal about EDI in thought, behaviour and practice.

Time: People given the opportunity to change and EDI team/leads given the time to reflect and support comprehensively.

Resource: Facilities made available to allow for the full implementation of inclusive changes.

Effort: EDI expertise and enough people to manage the workload effectively.

Agency: The EDI lead (the expert) to have visible support from leadership and, if applicable, regular opportunities to gain formal approval from the board.

Money: Budget implications met as EDI work requires delivery.

Especially in larger organisations, all the elements of STREAM need to be observed, otherwise the success of any policy or proposed action, measure or outcome, detailed later in this book, will be limited.

Effective EDI doesn't exist in a vacuum. The relationships, the management, the structures and the environment have to work together to embed the right culture.

SUPPORT

Leadership demonstrative and vocal about EDI in thought, behaviour and practice.

What does this mean?

Essentially, if you're the leader of your business, having the right behaviours is foundational to progress. Leadership is accountable for developing EDI principles and objectives, which, when delivered through a framework like the Inclusive Culture Pyramid described in the previous chapter, can permeate all elements of the business.

Role-modelling behaviours include:

- valuing all people inherently, as individuals as well as recognising they can identify as part of a group with a specific culture;
- having an understanding and appreciation of intersectionality, this is how different layers of identity can create multiple levels of discrimination.

Leaders also should be aware that legislation and regulation can play a role in someone's identity, and so it's not useful to be 'blind' to those characteristics. For example, some people tend to say 'I don't see colour', as in racial identity, or 'It doesn't matter if you're a man or a woman, I just want the best person for the job'. Given that the demographics of our professions don't reflect that of society, however, we need to see people and their identity – it doesn't mean we're judging them on it – but recognising that people can be, and are, discriminated-against because of these characteristics means we can be more effective at targeting more inclusive outcomes.

Also, as we'll come onto in Chapter Three, it's a fallacy that a belief in our own personal objectivity, or a belief that we are not sexist, makes us less objective and more likely to behave in a sexist way.

Caroline Criado Perez, in the feminist bible *Invisible Women*,[3] says:

> Men (women were not found to exhibit this bias) who believe that they are objective in hiring decisions are more likely to hire a male applicant than an identically described female applicant. And in organisations which are explicitly presented as meritocratic, managers favour male employees over equally qualified female employees.

As the formal mechanisms are developed, inclusive supportive leaders promote the use of new systems and processes, as well as supporting policy changes and operational adjustments. Leadership support needs to exemplify the commitment to these approaches, rather than leave it to others to do. All leadership models are very clear on this point, it can't be a case of do as I say, not as I do.

What is ethical and socially acceptable can be a matter of perspective, however for leadership to be supportive of EDI measures, they need to act accountably, mindful of perception as well as action. Working relationships should be fairly framed and employment rights upheld.

Leadership support also role-models the fact that there is not just one way of communicating messages. Realising there are a variety of options for modern communication and accessing as many of those as possible in order to demonstrate inclusivity is a necessary role for a leader. Sometimes that means face-to-face meetings, other times it would be with blogs, on other occasions it's all-staff meetings. It's said in marketing that you need to communicate a message at least seven times before it might be acted on, and effective inclusive role-modelling is about ensuring you'll hit the audience at least seven times with each single message reiterating that 'inclusion is the culture here'.

Excellent inclusive leadership includes the willingness to be held accountable when evaluating your EDI opportunities and risks. Integrity shouldn't be the underrated leadership value that it seems to be, and consistency in behaviours, communications and actions should drive the reviewing of performance and progress in achieving objectives and the impact of their outcomes.

When colleagues and staff see these imperatives being lived by leadership, underrepresented groups, in particular, are more engaged with their work.

TESTIMONIAL

I didn't know why I was not getting interviews, even though I had had so many applications to so many different practices. At some point I suspected it may have something to do with my name. I got married and my husband has got a very English sounding name – I joked with him that the minute I changed my name, I would get a job. Lo, and behold! I got a job interview after changing my name, after six months of not getting a single response.

Employee Resource Groups/Staff Networks

Many organisations have Employee Resource Groups (ERGs). It is the leaders' responsibility to advocate and champion EDI by actively influencing and promoting these groups, however it is not the responsibility of staff networks to fix the issues of discrimination in an organisation. That is the job of leadership supported by all staff. ERGs are there to raise issues, provide insight and celebrate their identities. We cannot, and should not, expect the discriminated against to mitigate our bias. Showing support for these groups is to listen to them and develop the practices and behaviours suggested in this book to tackle the fundamental issues which require the group to exist in the first place.

Often these groups are run by volunteers, trying to create support for themselves whilst doing the day job. If you do have volunteers doing this work, they should be given time off the day job to convene and time allowed to attend meetings within the working day, not within their breaks. The groups should be funded and proper terms of reference applied. I advocate the use of Cherron Inko Tariah's *The Power of Staff Networks*[4] for excellent guidance and templates for this.

Support does take time; investing this time is the difference between excellent support for EDI and mere lip-service.

Belonging

When we speak of support and leaders being responsible for role-modelling inclusive behaviours, often we can also hear organisations start to encourage that people should 'bring their whole selves to work' and 'have a sense of belonging'. I wish to sound a note of caution here.

> True belonging requires us to believe in and belong to ourselves so fully that we can find sacredness both in being a part of something and in standing alone when necessary … But true belonging is not something we negotiate or accomplish with others; it's a daily practice that demands integrity and authenticity. It's a personal commitment that we carry in our hearts.[5]

Brene Brown is suggesting that we need to be our whole selves for ourselves. We ought to believe we belong in the world and have a right to exist.

It's not clear when or where the term *belonging* started to be used in the context of organisational EDI, though my feeling is that at some point, relatively recently, someone misinterpreted Brown's definition. Using the term 'belonging' in the EDI sphere – across job titles, department names, and most importantly, our thinking is problematic.

My primary concern is that the term 'belonging' is about how an individual feels. By using this term, we place the onus on them and their interaction with their workplace. 'Inclusion', however, places the responsibility on the organisation to address and change systemic and structural issues.

Many people are quite happy to go to their workplace and be productive in a space where they feel included but don't feel the need to *belong*. Indeed, many people may prefer to *belong* at home with family, friends or even in a solitary space. Whatever a person's preference, everyone should feel their values, differences and perspectives are respected in an inclusive environment – **a responsibility that lies with an organisation's leadership**.

In his book *Reinventing Organisations*, Frederic Laloux raises a caution that an emphasis on *belonging* to an organisation can suggest that a whole person's life should revolve around work – socially, financially, environmentally – meaning an individual is psychologically trapped within the workplace; lose your job, lose your life.[6]

There are some organisations that have made *belonging* so essential that they've been designed so people needn't go home; there are play spaces, kitchens and even massages at the desk. Whilst on the face of it, this may seem wonderful, expecting staff to expend all their emotional and social energy at work results in burnout. If organisations are framing their EDI policies around belonging, they're thinking about how they want their staff to feel in the organisation. However, that isn't up to the organisation to decide. What they should be doing is working towards creating a diverse and inclusive space so that if people choose to belong at work, they can.

The word belonging can come with a sense of ownership too: possessions – 'this pen belongs to me'; relationships – 'we belong together'; systems – 'they belong in jail'. Also disturbing in an organisational context is the historical connection to slavery – the enslaved individuals belonged to their masters.

Belonging is a personal choice, not an organisational or business imperative, unlike inclusion. Inclusion, as a reminder, is the act of creating an environment where people feel that their identities, values and lifestyles are acknowledged, respected and accepted. So, leaders should foster an environment of inclusion, of welcome, where a sense of belonging is possible for those who wish to belong at work. Belonging should not be a factor driving outcomes.

Fostering a sense of belonging can inadvertently lead to bias, known as affinity bias, where we tend to gravitate towards individuals who are similar to us. While organisations may strive to promote belonging, this can result in the segregation of employees into small, like-minded groups, hindering efforts for inclusivity. Moreover, when an organisation emphasises a 'belonging' culture, it risks falling into the trap of prioritising 'culture fit', where individuals are hired based on their alignment with the existing organisational culture. Instead, organisations should focus on creating a 'culture add' environment, where diverse perspectives and backgrounds are welcomed, and individuals can contribute their unique strengths, leading to a more inclusive and conducive atmosphere.

In trying to force a culture of belonging you're in danger of doing EDI work simply because you have a fixed idea of what workplace culture should be, rather than iterating it based on the people you have working with you at any given time – which is an inclusive culture.

If you have been running with the term belonging, there is no shame in dropping it. The work of the EDI champion is constantly evolving, and as you learn more about what this work means, it's an opportunity for you to refine your thinking.

As Maya Angelou suggested, forgive yourself for not knowing something before you learned it.[7]

Part of demonstrating a truly supportive environment is for there to be a genuine open environment to raising, challenging and addressing behaviours that would be inconsistent with the EDI principles you are setting for yourself and your organisation.

This should involve some kind of whistleblowing function, for example a Speak Up app. Of course, better would be, before it gets to that stage, that there is an openness to supporting, believing and protecting those who experience and raise these issues.

Processes needn't be about public flagellation, but senior leaders should be accountable, and procedures should be transparent and timely, with next steps clearly communicated.

TIME

People given the opportunity to change and EDI team/leads given the time to reflect and support comprehensively.

When an organisation has a long history of inclusion *faux pas* there's an element of needing to 'turn a tanker'. Anyone coming in to deliver on this work may be limited in their effectiveness immediately.

Establishing relationships, allies, converts to the cause, takes time.

Understanding, unpicking and reshaping an inclusive culture is a conscious, effortful piece of work for which everyone has a role and responsibility. The realisation of EDI principles, and everyone maintaining and establishing an inclusive culture at work, doesn't happen simply because we will it to be that way; it happens because – returning to the running analogy – people take the time out to maintain their muscle, and be conscious about it. At no point do these conscious behaviours become unconscious; they may become habitual, which is the aim, but the effort is always there.

You may want to recruit a diverse team and crack on with a project in the way you always have done, but the differences in perspectives will take time to navigate. You cannot assume everyone has a shared set of assumptions, and you shouldn't proceed believing those educated in the same place will have the same shorthand.

Everyone will need to take the time to establish new ways of working.

A culturally intelligent organisation does not adapt to everyone and everything. It has its own culture that is shaped by a unique set of shared organisational norms and routines. Employees do not have to compromise their personal and cultural values to be part of a culturally intelligent organisation, but everyone will need to be flexible in their behaviour to work together to create a third culture that drives results (Ang et al., 2021). The organisation's shared norms and routines ensure staff are equipped to make sense of multicultural situations on the fly by flexing their thinking and behaviour to adjust to the unexpected.[8]

Of course, such an approach requires some patience and diligence, but the rewards are multiple, and the staff engagement, gratifying.

RESOURCE

Facilities made available to allow for the full implementation of inclusive changes.

Resource, beyond human effort, time and money, is necessary to fulfil EDI work. This could be access to spaces, collaborative efforts across departments, expertise from colleagues, the purchase of international standards information or templates of good practice, and so on.

Staff should be able to attend talks and webinars, conferences and networking, because all efforts help shape and round the growing area of expertise that is EDI.

Being able to aggregate and compile good data requires access to particular resources as you track and monitor change, but also in order to manage how you build trust and communicate priorities in the 'Fostering Understanding and Conviction' change cornerstone.

Data

Gathering data and using it effectively is a massive resource in EDI work.

KEY RESOURCE: Gathering Good Data

Sathya Bala of True Change

What is good DEI data?

Data is really vital in helping us be accountable. When we are looking at diversity, equity, inclusion (DEI), in an organisation or in a community group, in any space, data is really critical in understanding how we measure progress and to have an idea of what success looks like.

Often the issues aren't fully known or there are a lot of unknowns. The only way we can uncover unknowns and really know where to direct limited resources, data is really that laser focus to give us the confidence that we're focusing that effort in the right place so that we can then demonstrate credible progress – credible being really important.

That transparency is what ensures our reputation and that we are walking the walk and not just talking the talk.

Just like any business problem, DEI isn't unusual. You wouldn't try to improve something, drive change in an organisation without data; data is that critical tool.

It's not the answer, but it's the enabler, and it is no different with diversity, equity, inclusion.

It comes down to data governance, things like data ownership, like do we know who owns the data? So, if we are looking at supplier diversity, how are we engaging with procurement to make sure there is someone on the hook for that.

Data definition is important: have we defined whether it's diversity data of the demographics of our workforce, whether it's inclusion data about how people feel around belonging, maybe through surveys or maybe it's data around the employee life cycle of how we promote people and how that stacks up across different demographic groups.

We need to be really selective in terms of where we focus our energy. And then it's that quality of the data. And, once it's captured, it's accurate, it's maintained.

How do you gather it?

I would really remind people that if you are not clear on what your organisation's or your team's DEI priorities are, and there aren't measurable commitments that have been made yet, we need to pause on data, we need the clarity on the objective and then the data that we collect and we look at and we measure needs to be focused on that.

We should know how we're using it before we collect it. Building trust and making sure people feel confident sharing that data, it's really important at the time of collecting it that you are really clear with people how it'll be used. We shouldn't be changing that approach as we go.

Are there things we want to be measuring in terms of customer reach, like that our people represent the customers that we serve? All of those things we need to start with almost the purpose and the use first. When you start to engage with your privacy teams on making sure that we are doing this in a controlled way, that's one of the early questions that they will ask. If we know what we're using the data for, there's far fewer roadblocks in terms of getting through those approvals. The other thing I would say is look at it from an opportunity standpoint. How can some of this data help us with understanding some of the positive progress we're making? For example, a lot of organisations in this sector will be dealing with projects with different clients. We use the data to see if client satisfaction is higher in our more diverse client-facing teams. Is there a correlation there that more diverse teams mean better engagement with clients?

And then you're starting to have that data show not just we need to tick some boxes, but it's showing some of the benefits it's driving within the business, some of the additional value.

What are the limitations of gathering data?

I think it is around assuming that data is going to have all the answers. What data provides us with is a direction to then further dig. We collect data that we need to understand the root cause of, for example, there not many people of colour progressing past a certain grade in our organisation. While looking at the root cause of that, we probably need to do more fact finding to understand it. Perhaps asking, do we need to do listening groups?

And with DEI this is a long-term gain. We're trying to drive long-term change and that requires commitment, ongoing motivation, and making sure these things stay on the agenda irrespective of how the context might change. Even if there's an economic downturn, even when there's other priorities that come in, how do we make sure that this doesn't fall off the radar? The stories are really critical in making sure people feel personally motivated to make the changes that they need to do.

Data and storytelling is really linked, but I think often people look at data in isolation. I also think those stories provide a bridge to people that perhaps think that DEI is not for them. It's about helping those other people, those underrepresented people. But what if you are from a dominant group? What if you're a straight white male? Well, stories help us understand, as well as data, the fact that this is win-win.

Knowing how to gather the data you need is one thing, but getting people to share is another. This comes back to the transparency and accountability of the work you're doing and aligning what you say and do around EDI with integrity.

Individuals will want to know why, and for what purpose, the data is being collected.

For the statistics to have relevance and functionality, there needs to be a high self-declaration rate, a high proportion of those you're asking must be willing to share their personal information, so they need to understand the purpose of the collection activity and feel confident that the information they share will be used to help the organisation become more inclusive, across the employee work lifecycle, how you create your products and services and reach out to customers and clients and do your community engagement. Traditionally, underrepresented groups have felt that demographic data-gathering has been used to tick boxes and/or to discriminate against them.

A d/Deaf architect told me he removed the fact he was d/Deaf from job applications, was shortlisted, having not been when he had stated it explicitly previously, and then was told he was deceptive for then not revealing it, thus he was not progressed in the recruitment process. This was a recent incident.

This feeds into the other areas of STREAMing EDI.

> They need to hear the commitment and see the participation of leaders and other respected colleagues. Furthermore, they need evidence of positive change or they will not be willing to declare personal or sensitive data, or self-identify, causing even the most advanced data collection strategy to fail.[9]

The ARB has recently started collating and sharing anonymised demographic data on the profession. This has caused some backlash[10] from those who appear threatened by this simple task; however, the data provides much needed insight into the state of architecture and who is working in it.

The ARB states:

> It is important to note that Equality and Diversity (E&D) survey data may vary from Architects Register data. This is because every architect must provide certain, legally recognised information as part of the registration

process. In contrast the E&D survey is voluntary, reflects how architects self-identify and includes different categories.

We recognise the importance of being as transparent as possible with information we hold. We hope this data is useful to policy makers and those that are able to effect social change. It also enables us to ensure our ways of working are in line with the Equality Act and as free from discrimination as possible.[11]

This approach aligns with the recommendations on how to gather this data and the reasons for doing so. At the time of writing, 77.1 per cent of the register replied, but there is still a high proportion of 'prefer not to say' responses for some questions.

Skidmore, Owings & Merrill (SOM) the multi-disciplinary architectural firm, have an incredible approach to gathering data in order to build-in equity into their work. Julia Skeete, Senior Associate Principal at SOM, told me they started by looking at themselves (see Figure 2.2), their practices groups, and had discussions and hackathons, took the qualitative data and reinserted it back into the technical deliverables to ensure equity at every stage of design. The equity in design toolkit they produced looks at quite large scales, multiple neighbourhoods, and checks for a shift in the dial around outcomes which they display on a changing dashboard for the project. It's all rooted in gathering good data, so they can track and monitor the change.

Figure 2.2 SOM staff at work with Julia Skeete. Photograph by Aaron Hargreaves.

All resources, access to talks and high-level insight are useful. However, the breadth and depth of resource required won't all be free, and this cross-references with the M of the STREAM prerequisites.

As I tend to say, it's rarely 'either/or'; it's usually 'this/and'.

Free resources are not without value, and if coming from expert sources, can be excellent starting points. RIBA Radio is a good example. Of course, it costs money to create them in the first instance, so it's worth noting, very rarely is anything actually free, and consider financially supporting the work of those who are creating them if such resource is needed, and you value it.

EFFORT AND EXPERTISE

EDI expertise and enough people to manage the workload effectively.

You need to have the right people directing your EDI efforts. I have to admit that it still bewilders and frustrates me that organisations in the built environment feel that because someone has some lived experience of a particular characteristic that's enough to qualify them as an EDI expert.

The equivalent would be hiring someone to lead on Fire and Life Safety because they've been evacuated from a building, or hiring a head of data governance because they installed Norton Antivirus (other malware protectors are available), or to be your director of finance simply because they enjoy using Excel (everyone knows Numbers isn't as good).

The point is, there is a growing number of EDI professionals who have spent many years developing their praxis even though there is no specific route to becoming a practitioner in this space. Many have a human resources (HR) background and have specialised in EDI through the obligation that the People function needs to address issues of discrimination. Others have developed through their other professions, like me, inclusive ways of working which have solidified though study and practice over decades. Many of these people also have intersectional identities with lived experience of discrimination, fighting discriminatory systems and understand the issues from the inside. This gives us, not only credibility, but real understanding and empathy beyond sympathy for those we're doing this work for.

Therefore, when looking for expertise, qualified people should be able to:

- Describe the theoretical bases and references for their praxis.
- Explain what EDI relevant qualifications they have and courses completed.

- Provide detailed examples of origination and development of supportive intersectional policies, procedures and practices.
- Describe the outcomes from those.
- Provide references from other recognised EDI experts.
- Interrogate their own experiences for useful learning and development.
- Detail a clear methodology for progress and some key priorities.
- Continue to track, deliver and guide vehicles for change.

I recognise that not all organisations can afford to have an employee or team of employees doing this work, hence me writing this book to encourage you to take personal responsibility to apply your inclusion lens and make the right changes; that said, there is plenty of expertise available in the forms of consultancy, plus courses and training to help guide you, and when run by people with credible professional experience in EDI, they can benefit your inclusion journey and your own success and credibility in this sphere.

Effort is tied in with Expertise as misdirected effort can send you off in the wrong direction (remember, this book is a map, and experts are Sat-Navs), but once properly focused, it is about constant, continuous, conscious action. It must also be recognised that it is not up to just one person to deliver, even if you have an EDI lead. Organisational and sector-wide change is about the charabanc all moving in the same direction. The Sat-Nav maybe fully loaded ready to take you off in the right direction, but you have to support that vehicle to move. The journey is continuous.

AGENCY

The EDI lead (the expert) to have visible support from leadership and, if applicable, regular opportunities to gain formal approval from the Board.

Teeth: The difference between effective accountability and ineffective work is the voice you give the person that's been hired to guide the delivery of your EDI. Tokenistic, tick-box appointments of EDI expertise will lead to a revolving door, and/or money flying out the window with little change to show for it. There is no point hiring someone to work with you on EDI unless you intend to listen to them, and give them the agency of having the ear of the highest paid people in the organisation.

A critical friend is still a friend, and, in fact, the very best kind, because they're honest and help you to be better, holding up a mirror and pointing out improvements. And who doesn't want to improve organisational efficacy?

EDI leads will ask for accountability, transparency and enthuse a message of change. They need to be given the authority, freedom and space to help deliver on those things, otherwise what is the point of them?

Such journeys for businesses aren't always comfortable, but there should be safety established for all parties, and integrity should be at the heart of these relationships.

A reminder too, that toothless tigers still have claws, which can result in reputational damage rather than help you attack the problem when there's a disconnect between the message they're advocating for and the action you're taking.

MONEY

Budget implications met as EDI work requires delivery.

Money is a transactional tool; we use it to buy goods and services, because we'd be here forever if we were still bartering. Spending money on EDI isn't about anyone with credibility and scruples profiteering from human rights, but it's about recognising that these things have value and the expense must be borne.

Just like you need software, technicians and the right equipment to help with your data governance, or health and safety, so it is with EDI.

People-power and the brains and expertise that comes with them may be the main expense, but in addition, access to the best resources and the depth and detail behind them, also may need to be paid for. Training, courses, e-learning, assessments, tools, books, all require budget. Support systems like whistleblowing apps, and sponsoring activities that amplify the underrepresented and their work, all cost money. Travel and subsistence for that expertise, and to avail of it, should also be budgeted for.

If you'd be willing to fork out for a celebrity to do a talk, then you should also be willing to pay the panellists at your International Women's Day event, at the very least, their travel expenses, as well as a fee if EDI is their bread and butter.

ERGs and staff networks must also have budget to prioritise how they will celebrate their identities, find speakers to support the wider agenda, and any other resource they think the business needs. The EDI lead holds this budget, but gives the groups, in turn, the agency to use it.

This work cannot be done without a healthy budget, which, as the work grows, may need to grow too, or it is absorbed across other areas of budget, for example, Inclusion CPD becomes automatically part of learning and development funds, or ERG spend is part of the wider HR support budget.

However, explicit ring-fencing is a necessity, as it is part of giving 'Agency' to the EDI lead, so that they don't have to go begging to other departments.

STREAMing the EDI work is about taking matters seriously, demonstrating a proper commitment to change and amplifying the underrepresented in the profession. This isn't the work of one person with a job title, but also requires leadership having sight of the reins and supporting the journey, asking everyone to take shared and personal responsibility and do what's required.

TESTIMONIAL: You Want to Be an Ally? Show Us Some Real Action My Friend

Ibrahim Buhari, Architect and Senior Urban Design Officer

As a profession we have the responsibility to reflect the society we serve. We purport to be critical and reflective thinkers but for years have failed to acknowledge the problem in our industry, let alone begin to look at how we tackle the barriers to entry, progression within practice and procurement of diverse practitioners.
There are three areas of focus that need your urgent attention:

Entry/access: statistics show that on average, to receive an interview, black professionals will need to apply for 80% more job applications than their white counterparts ... practices should be challenging recruiters who only send through white candidates as well as connecting with companies or communities who could help identify diverse talent. There are a wealth of black social enterprise groups that are doing amazing work. Partner with them to expand your reach, talking points and internal events. Don't fall back on the excuse that there are no black students applying. There are plenty.

Retention: to the practices that have black members of staff within your organisations— having one black member of staff in your company of 20, 30, 40... Does not make you diverse. Do not rely on one or two black people to represent the black experience and do not suddenly force your only black employee to be the face of your brand, further to this, practices need to ensure they are supporting their black employees to excel and providing genuine opportunities for progression as well as mentorship. Finally remember to be culturally aware. Being a black employee within a predominantly white space can be challenging. Be mindful of creating an inclusive environment where everybody can contribute to conversations and office culture without fear of 'othering'.

Progression: black talent disproportionately occupies entry and junior level roles ... While meritocracy is essential for a fair workplace, at present, progression opportunities are unequal. Equal access to progression requires everybody to have an understanding of how to progress. Those at the top need to signal, very clearly, what they want to see for people to do well and visible diversity leadership reinforces the message that it is possible for everybody. Practices need to transparently define the promotional pipeline for employees and continually review progress in 1:1 meetings.

In addition to this, black members of staff should be supported by management and encouraged to excel through internal mentorship.

These points are by no means an exhaustive list but represent areas of focus in which a number of further actions could be taken ... your allyship has to be on-going when no one is watching – even when it's not convenient, popular or easy. We can no longer be silent about these issues because they are uncomfortable to talk about, for in silence we allow the very systems that create barriers to continue.

(First published in *Now You Know: A Collection of Sound Advice to Challenge Spatial and Racial Inequality from 60 Architects and Urbanists*, Sound Advice, 2021)

KEY TAKEAWAYS

- STREAMing your EDI requires ongoing commitment.
- Support starts with leadership, and requires meaningful demonstration.
- Change won't be instantaneous.
- Free resources have some use as a starting point, but rarely provide the depth of intervention required to deliver wholesale structural and cultural change.

- Having lived experience isn't enough to qualify anyone to be an EDI lead, you need proper qualified expertise.
- Make sure properly qualified expertise has the ear of the key decision maker(s) in the organisation.
- Fund the work properly.

NOTES

1   Timothy R. Clark, *The 4 Stages of Psychological Safety*, Berrett-Koehler, 2020.

2   See www.architecture.com/knowledge-and-resources/knowledge-landing-page/built-environment-bodies-unite-to-improve-inclusion-and-diversity [Accessed 23 November 2023].

3   Caroline Criado Perez, *Invisible Women: Exposing the Data Bias in a World Designed for Men*, Chatto & Windus 2019.

4   Cherron Inko-Tariah, *The Incredible Power of Staff Networks*, Filament Publishing, 2015.

5   Brene Brown, *Braving the Wilderness: The Quest for True Belonging and the Courage to Stand Alone*, Vermillion, 2017.

6   Frederic Laloux, *Reinventing Organisations*, Nelson Parker, 2014.

7   Shane Parrish, 'Maya Angelou on haters, life, reading and love'. See https://fs.blog/maya-angelou-on-haters-life-reading-and-love/ [Accessed 29 November 2023].

8   Soon Ang, Linn Van Dyne and David Livermore, *Organizational CQ: Cultural Intelligence for 21st-century Organisations*, Elsevier, 2021.

9   *Workforce Data Equality Guide*, Greater London Authority, January 2021. See www.london.gov.uk/programmes-strategies/communities-and-social-justice/workforce-integration-network-win/workforce-data-equality-guide [Accessed 30 April 2024].

10 'LinkedIn backlash to ARB's statistical data work'. See www.linkedin.com/posts/marsharamroop_architecture-inclusive-behavioural-activity-7052554285808545793-wVe- [Accessed 29 November 2023].

11 *ARB Equality and Diversity Data*. See https://arb.org.uk/about-arb/equality-diversity/data/ [Accessed 29 November 2023].

Chapter Three

Years from now, our children and our grandchildren will look up and lock eyes with us. They will ask us where we were when the takes were so high. They will ask us what it was like. I don't want us to just tell them how it felt. I want us to tell them what we did.[1]

MOTIVATION

A much underrated and neglected area of change, motivation has to be the key attribute you can take responsibility for when moving forward with EDI in your work.

In Chapter One, when I described CQ and the inclusive behavioural framework, the first capability was CQ Drive – do you want to work and relate effectively across difference?

I hope, because you're reading this book, the answer may be 'Yes! Of course I want to!' But, it's easier to say and harder to do when the stuff hits the fan, you are under stress and the apprentice in the team – your so-called 'diverse hire' – has just challenged you on overworking. The conscious behaviours you'd been exhibiting up to that point may go out the window, and, unless there's a safe environment for them to raise it, any impact your behaviours may have had at that point, may go unchallenged, and you may well be none the wiser of what those impacts were.

So, how do you motivate yourself when faced with difference? How do you drive yourself to learn and adapt to those who can have approaches and values different to your own?

What drives us to do any of the things we do? What is it that pushes us to accomplish anything? A simple answer would be personal gain, but the question is much more complex than that. When it comes to working and relating across difference, the key ability of successful people is that they know how to motivate themselves effectively.

The skill of being able to push through rather than falling on your default behaviours is what increases your chances at being successful at being inclusive.

DOI: 10.4324/9781003435747-5

There are generally considered to be two types of motivation. That which arises from outside you – extrinsic – and motivation that arises from inside you – intrinsic.

When we put both to use, we're more likely to achieve our goal, and I believe that intrinsic motivators are the more sustainable, but there are benefits to both types of motivation.

Extrinsic motivation is the behaviour you use to perform tasks and learn new skills because of the promise of reward or to avoid punishment. You engage in behaviour not because you enjoy it or because you find it appealing or satisfying, but in order to obtain something of value in return, or evade something disagreeable.

Intrinsic motivation is doing something that does not have any obvious external rewards. You do it because it's enjoyable and interesting to you, or you're driven by purpose, not because of any outside incentive or pressures, like pay rises or the sack. Intrinsic motivators propel you because the activity is for its own sake. Essentially, the behaviour itself is its own reward.

I consider intrinsic motivation to be more sustainable especially when it comes to working and relating across difference, because it ties in with overall personal growth, a sense of duty and the recognition of purpose, while extrinsic motivation is often more about financial incentives, status and public recognition. That said, I do see helping influence the creation of an overall inclusive society as an extrinsic motivation.

In the mid-1990s, fresh out of university, one of my first jobs at the BBC was working at Television Centre (TVC) at BBC World News, in the Japanese Translation Unit. Every time I entered room 3147J (yes, the J was for Japanese), it was like culturally entering Japan.

The norms dictated that there was a very hierarchical environment. Elders were treated with significant respect. What we ate, how we did so, how we managed mistakes and accountability were very clearly defined – if you knew the rules.

My role as a News Production Assistant was to facilitate the live translation of BBC World News into Japanese. It required me to tell this group of people what to do. In a very direct manner. This suited me. Early 20s, full of my own self-confidence, with Trinidadian sass, plus I was probably up my own arse with my private education, and already six or seven years of broadcasting experience under my belt, it was going to be a jolly good laugh, and a breeze to get them on my side. And no, I didn't know any Japanese, I didn't need to – I gave all instruction in English.

Initially, things did not go well. I'd tell them what to do, and they'd ignore me, doing their own thing, glancing at the eldest member of the group, who they referred to as *Sensei*, who was usually covering the simultaneous translation of the news anchor. He'd give a little nod, and between them as a team, they'd decide when to swap who was translating. I was not in this team.

This led to some on-air problems and not least some frustration from me.

A few years later, towards the end of my time with them (a role I loved and chose to leave to, amongst other things, travel to Japan), I walked into 3147J, called out 'ohayo gozimasu' – good morning – to the room, and, because my pronunciation was so spot on, the editor turned round to check, who was that new Japanese person coming into the room?

What happened in-between?

I didn't know about cultural intelligence or CQ at the time; indeed, it had not been invented as a measure or scale yet, but I absolutely wanted to succeed at this role and, on reflection, I see I acted on each capability.

I loved the buzz of BBC Television Centre. The News Centre was brand new. I had literally bumped into the Spice Girls on the corridor only to get the dirtiest look off Scary, and getting stuck in the lift with Anna Ford once was a highlight. I recognised the amazing talent of the Japanese people I was working with and wanted them to do well. How they performed was a reflection on me. I was inherently curious, and the absolute alien nature of the culture fascinated me. Humility?! Who knew that was a thing?!

When things were going wrong, I consciously decided to win everyone over by understanding them better, why they did what they did, what it meant. The unsaid. The unwritten. What small words or phrases could I use?

I enrolled in Japanese evening classes where our tutor shared with us cultural cues as well as the language. I made a new friend in the class who was working for Hitachi at the time, and we spent a lot of time laughing, which encouraged me to continue to go too.

Winning over the Japanese team was about understanding each person as an individual too, as well as the overall norms at play. I found out what they wanted from their day's work and from the environment, and who were the exceptions to the 'rules'. I looked at the roster for roles each day and planned beforehand ways to make their lives easier. I created some papier mâché boxes to store the week's newspapers, which were otherwise just piled up. I labelled them in Japanese, for each paper and each day of the week. Small things that mattered to them, and because I wanted to do it.

Intrinsically, I wanted to succeed, I was curious and I was fascinated to learn more about the group who seemed so strange to me.

Extrinsically, there were millions of people listening in Japan, on my shift I didn't want any cock-ups, and I wanted to earn the respect of these incredible people.

So, by the time Bill Clinton was saying 'I did not have sexual relations with that woman', we were all over it – if you'll pardon the expression.

I'm telling this personal story because what motivation will look like when it comes to working and relating across difference will be individual to you. What intrinsically motivates you would be different to that which motivates me. Whether you are more extrinsically motivated, where promotion or awards for your work or not wanting to annoy someone would be your drivers, or you're driven intrinsically, and you can dig into your desire for self-improvement, you enjoy collaboration or simply because you believe in it – all of this is very individual.

From an organisational perspective, there will be key performance indicators for projects and strategic business plan objectives which can create shared motivators. Some of these might be about fulfilling organisational values, others might be about the bottom line, but in all cases, diverse teams with inclusive cultures are shown to be ones that thrive.

A live broadcast environment is a highly pressured one, and it's times like these, when you're up against a project deadline, when any motivation to act inclusively can disappear. So, practising regularly helps build a stronger inclusive reaction muscle.

It's important to note that working across difference is not just about racial or national difference. Remembering the **diversity** definition, this is the mix of all difference, visible and invisible, and so how builders might work with engineers, and how a small practice might work with a bigger one, all require a level of motivation to approach those relationships with openness and understanding in order to be effective at working and relating with each other.

Is Money or Profit a Reasonable Motivator?

When financial gain is the end, in and of itself, frequently this comes at the cost of people, place and planet. There are many published arguments, for example, Naomi Klein (2014),[2] Yanis Varoufakis (2017),[3] Eric Williams (1944),[4] Angela Y. Davis (1981),[5] Emma Dabiri (2021),[6] Paulo Freire (1970),[7] to name just a few, which state that capitalism as a system forces us to subjugate others, and unfettered, unregulated growth is incompatible with inclusion and sustainability.

In Peter Apps' *Show Me the Bodies, How We Let Grenfell Happen*,[8] he says this:

The world that gave us the Grenfell Tower fire looks irredeemably dishonest. It is a story of corporate structures that allowed human beings to abandon their own conscience and sense of agency and to think only about sales and profit margins.

Poignant. Devastating. Grenfell is what happens when the built environment puts profit before people.

To make this point is not to say that a comfortable living should be sacrificed, but the fundamental rethink about what drives us to do this work requires us to rethink our approaches to the economy. Thinking of people, place and planet as potential to unfold, not problems to solve, requires us to put purpose before profit. It's also worth noting that when we unfold this potential, profitable outcomes always ensue anyway (see 'International Case Study' in Chapter Four) just in a different timeframe. This is a rethink of how we consider economic systems. Being forced into dichotomies of capitalism and socialism isn't helpful. We need to be cleverer than that and rethink our short-term approaches and long-term outcomes.

Building in social value as a fundamental motivating force in projects has been growing in strength recently. The Public Services (Social Value) Act 2013 requires people who commission public services to think about how they can create positive social, economic and environmental ripples. Whatever the kind of project in the built environment, it has a social, economic and environmental impact, and so this legislation could be seen as a lever to consider value beyond just the monetary.

In addition, as I'm about to discuss, bias can play havoc with our decision-making. Daniel Kahneman, who I mention below, is known for his work around what influences our logic. His analysis finds that money can fundamentally skew our behaviours in illogical ways.[9]

* * * *

In her autobiography, *The Truths We Hold*, the US Vice President, Kamala Harris, concludes:

Years from now, our children and our grandchildren will look up and lock eyes with us. They will ask us where we were when the takes were so high. They will ask us what it was like. I don't want us to just tell them how it felt. I want us to tell them what we did.

When we couple this sentiment with Einstein, we need to rethink, and then *act*. Future generations can't afford for us not to. Finding the motivation in ourselves to do so is a demonstration of conscientiousness that starts the ball rolling.

UNHELPFUL BIAS

You would have heard the term 'unconscious bias', I'm sure, and maybe even used it yourself. What is it? What is its purpose? Can you overcome it, and what is its relevance to your work? A reminder:

Explicit/conscious bias: These are attitudes and beliefs we have about a person or group at a conscious level.

Implicit/unconscious bias: These are subtle and non-conscious thoughts that happen to us all the time.

The temptation to write 'we are all biased, you just have to get over it' for this totality of this section is very attractive, but I won't – I'll give you a bit more background than that! The bottom line is though, we are all biased, and we just have to get over it.

I am lucky enough to have had a number of great conversations with Dr Pragya Agarwal, author of *Sway, Unravelling Unconscious Bias*, one of which we recorded for RIBA Radio (see QR Code 3.2).[10]

Dr Agarwal says: 'We are all human and we are all biased. We need some of these templates, or stereotypes or biases to process information in the real world. When we are bombarded with information, more so with social media, and so on, our brains don't have the capacity to process it all in a rational manner, so we make quick hasty impulsive decisions.'

Why do we make these hasty decisions? In her book and in Prof Timothy Wilson's *Stranger to Ourselves, Discovering the Adaptive Unconscious*, the research is distilled which states that we have 11 million pieces of information going into our brain at any given moment, when we have access to all five senses. The most liberal estimate is that we have the conscious capacity to process only 40. The other 10,999,960 pieces are all being processed unconsciously. The shortcutting of information, therefore, is a human biological need, and is at the root of bias creation.

This image shows the more than 180 biases that have been researched[11] to date (see Figure 3.1 and QR Code 3.1).

It divides types of bias into four categories, from needing to act quickly, to thinking about what we should remember, to having too much information and not enough.

COGNITIVE BIAS CODEX

What Should We Remember?

We store memories differently based on how they were experienced

We reduce events and lists to their key elements

We discard specifics to form generalities

We edit and reinforce some memories after the fact

We favor simple looking options and complete information over complex, ambiguous options

To avoid mistakes, we aim to preserve autonomy and group status, and avoid irreversible decisions

To get things done, we tend to complete things we've invested time & energy in

To stay focused, we favor the immediate, relatable thing in front of us

Need To Act Fast

To act, we must be confident we can make an impact and feel what we do is important

We project our current mindset and assumptions onto the past and future

We think we know what other people are thinking

We simplify probabilities and numbers to make them easier to think about

We imagine things and people we're familiar with or fond of as better

We fill in characteristics from stereotypes, generalities and prior histories

We tend to find stories and patterns even when looking at sparse data

We notice flaws in others more easily than we notice flaws in ourselves

We are drawn to details that confirm our own existing beliefs

We notice when something has changed

Bizarre, funny, visually-striking, or anthropomorphic things stick out more than non-bizarre/unfunny things

We notice things already primed in memory or repeated often

Too Much Information

Not Enough Meaning

DESIGNHACKS.CO · CATEGORIZATION BY BUSTER BENSON · ALGORITHMIC DESIGN BY JOHN MANOOGIAN III (JM3) · DATA BY WIKIPEDIA — creative commons attribution · share-alike

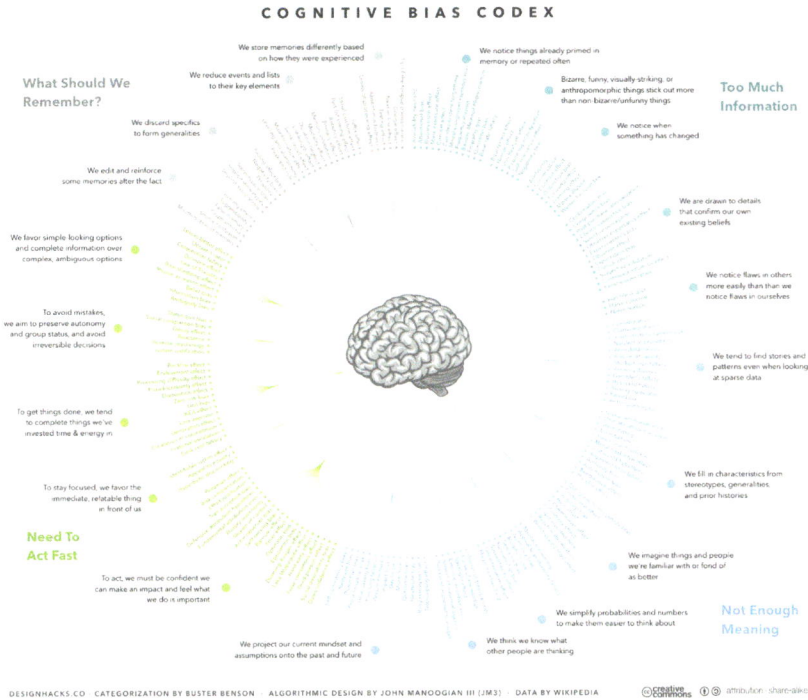

Figure 3.1 The Cognitive Bias Codex: 180+ biases. Designed by John Manoogian III.

QR Code 3.1: INTERACT: The Cognitive Bias Codex.

In amongst them is the Ikea Effect, in which people place a disproportionate value on things they create themselves. I have since wondered what this means in the built environment professions …

There is also the Google Effect, or digital amnesia. The first study into this effect shows the tendency to forget information which you think will be found readily online.

These are both types of bias that we can have, and they exist unconsciously. By way of demonstration, I like at this point to ask you to reflect on when was the last time you had to memorise a telephone number? The fact that we often pop numbers into our mobiles means that we may not even know the number of the person we're most frequently in touch with by heart. Twenty years ago or more, however, there's no doubt you knew your best friends' phone numbers. I just checked with my teenagers – one exclaimed 'It's not the 1960s!' They don't know their own numbers, let alone their friends'. So, technological changes impact our bias. Just like political, financial, economic, social, environmental impacts, all affect the creation of bias.

Bias isn't all bad, it is simply a term for the cognitive process that can shortcut information, and there are times, when faced with danger for example, when it is useful. Not enough education about the terms makes that clear.

Unconscious bias awareness workshops have been recommended quite extensively as a panacea to the diversity and inclusion concerns, but they are not one. We can look back to the McGregor-Smith review into race in the workplace. It was an independent review by Baroness McGregor-Smith considering the issues facing racialised groups in the workplace from 2017. In that report she said:

> We need to stop hiding behind the mantle of 'unconscious bias'.
>
> **Much of the bias is structural and a result of a system that benefits a certain group of people** [my emphasis]. This doesn't just affect those from a BME background, but women, those with disabilities or anyone who has experienced discrimination based upon preconceived notions of what makes a good employee. Fixing this will involve a critical examination of every stage of the process, from how individuals are recruited to how they are supported to progress and fulfil their potential. The importance of effective mentoring, sponsorship, role models and networks in delivering positive action needs to be understood at all levels of an organisation, with leaders taking responsibility for creating truly inclusive workplaces.[12]

As this report exploded into public life, unconscious bias awareness training sprang up, with online courses, face-to-face workshops and videos to watch. However, a lot of these interventions were one-off moments.

In December 2020, unconscious bias training was scrapped for civil servants in England because ministers said it does not work.[13]

The UK government followed the data which says there is no evidence that it changes attitudes. It also urged other public sector employers to end this type of training. Sadly, they didn't then replace it with more effective measures.

It is clear that realising unconscious bias exists, how it manifests itself and the impact is important, but expecting people to be made aware of their unconscious and mitigate themselves is not actually possible.

The academic paper, by Forscher et al., which aggregates 492 studies on one-off unconscious bias interventions, with nearly 90,000, participants concluded that the effects of one-off interventions are 'often relatively weak' and if there were behavioural changes produced, they were generally 'trivial changes in nature'.[14] Essentially, the intervention on its own didn't work.

The recommendation from the author of the report:

> Do not try to change implicit bias ... Instead focus on working around it. Target other inter group outcomes and teach folks to create procedural changes that prevent the influence of hidden biases.[15]

There is also research that bad training and one-off interventions not only don't work, but that they can be counterproductive, because people who have been through these interventions think 'OK, now I'm not biased', they then go on to make biased decisions. Research found that efforts to get people to suppress their stereotypes can actually work to reinforce them. Often, any positive change is weak and short term.

> One theory is that if training tells us we're all biased, we might no longer think we need to make an effort or that making an effort will make a difference. Afterwards, a participant might come away with a sense of relief: they've been shown that their bias isn't really their fault at all. **The eagerness to label all bias as unconscious could allow us to evade responsibility for the harm it causes** [my emphasis].
> Many businesses might see the UB training as a complete solution to their discrimination problems: a quick fix. But although unconscious bias training opens the door to fruitful conversations about bias, by itself it won't make you or your company any less biased than you were before.[16]

Face-to-face or online unconscious bias courses, whilst good at helping people realise unconscious bias exists and how it manifests itself, often don't focus enough on impact and still expect people to mitigate themselves, making no mention of the requirement of processes and structures that need changing in order to assist with mitigation.

In 2019, the *Journal of Social Psychology* published research: Psychologists showed people their own behaviours but pretended that they were the behaviours of some other person. When asked, the participants reliably said that they were less racist than that other person.[17] So, this amongst other research demonstrates there's a fallacy around our own personal objectivity, if we think we're not biased, really it doesn't mean that, in fact, we're not.

In January 2021, the *Journal of Forensic Sciences* produced a paper, 'Cognitive bias in forensic pathology decisions', which showed 'forensic pathologists were more likely to rule "homicide" rather than "accident" for deaths of Black children relative to white children' even when given identical medical information in Nevada.[18] So, those we believe to be basing their decisions on objective data still are shown to be interpreting that data in a biased way.

Daniel Kahneman, whom I like to call the Godfather of 'heuristics', the cerebral shortcutting of information, says it's extremely difficult to catch yourself doing something unconsciously. When asked why we made a decision, we'll convince ourselves of a valid reason, when in reality our unconscious forced us to come to a conclusion based on our bias and shortcutting of information, a cerebral process of which we're completely unaware. And yet the conscious decision-making process, which we do control, is 'who we think we are'.[19]

He talks about System 1 – your shortcutting, essentially unconscious processes (that 10,999,960 bits of info processing per second) and System 2 – your conscious, more effortful processes (40 bits per second).

> System 2 articulates judgements and make choices, but it often endorses or rationalises ideas and feelings that were generated by System 1. You may now know you are optimistic about a project because something about its leader reminds you of your beloved sister, or that you dislike a person who looks vaguely like your dentist. If asked for an explanation, however, you will search your memory for presentable reasons and will certainly find some. Moreover, you *will believe the story that you make up* [my emphasis].[20]

Report[21] after report[22] after report[23] shows the repeated suggestion that we can, only by being aware, mitigate our own bias is not correct. We must stop saying and teaching that. We need to put less store by one-off training interventions and more by the overall structures and processes we need to *create, implement* and *enforce* to mitigate it.

We must also put more effort into creating a culture of feedback where it's OK to call out others' bias and mistakes, because a diversity of people around us can see and feel it more clearly than we'd ever be able to in ourselves, and for the recipient of that feedback not to be defensive about it.

And, allow people who can see and feel them, to call out issues, and don't then vilify them for it.

A **microaggression** or microincivility is a 'low intensity act which violates the norms of respectful behaviours … whose intent to harm is ambiguous',[24] according to Dr Binna Kandola in *Racism at Work* (2018), they can be subtle slights and snubs that devalue people. The term 'micro' might suggest these things are small, and sometimes they might feel that way, the frequent mispronouncing of a name, or calling two people of similar heritage the other person's name, or only planning nights out in pubs, or being talked over in meetings. Some days those who have to deal with them can brush them off. Other times the same incident can feel like they've been hit across the face with a bag of bricks.

TESTIMONIAL

I had a colleague who once said to me that I looked like some-body who would work in the kitchen, even though he knew I was an architectural assistant and urban designer. There was another occasion where a consultant came in and shook everybody's hand in the meeting and skipped me.

Those who face microaggressions can and should develop a way of calling them out without being aggressive, when able. I was once producing a radio show speaking on the phone to a potential contributor who asked my name. When I told him, he scoffed and said: 'You'd want to be changing that then!' I simply responded: 'Oh yes? Why is that?' As he mumbled and bumbled his response, I chose to explain its history, that Ramroop actually meant 'God's image', and that I was proud of my Trinidadian heritage. I then chose not to use him on the radio.

Reflecting back the language that has been used towards you and asking a question about it forces the snubber to acknowledge what they've said and potentially their bias in doing so. I acknowledge this is an expending of emotional energy, and you can't always be bothered, but when you can, it serves as an educating moment, and hopefully would avoid it from them in future.

You may well be responsible for delivering behaviours like these, even if you've experienced them yourself. The important thing is to listen to the feedback, as suggested in the section below on Managing Discomfort. If you see something like this, you do have the power to act as an **ally** and respond with a **microaffirmation**. A microaffirmation is a small, subtle gesture to indicate you have respect for someone and value them as a person and colleague. These could take the form of pointing out when a colleague is speaking over someone else to say: 'I think they were making a point, which I'd like to hear before you share yours', or 'Caoimhe's name is pronounced Kwee-ver, so don't call her Carol, and it's spelt that way, because it is'.

It's at this point I'd like to share with you this powerful resource (see Figure 3.2).[25] Every single woman of colour I've shared it with has said it resonates with them. I've shared it a number of times on social media and so we're talking about hundreds of racialised women across the world.

What does it say about the insidious and overwhelming nature of racial bias when so many women 'of colour' around the world who have entered an organisation with white leadership feel that this is their story? What does this mean when so much of leadership in the built environment professions look like those who could cause these outcomes too?

Imagine being responsible for such outcomes. This is why I urge you to read the testimonials within this book too, to remind yourself how important the behaviours work is.

Rather than just exiting the organisation, I am sorry to say that the other outcomes tend to take the form of pain – physical, emotional and psychological – as the woman strives to navigate the situation, entering a vicious circle where she's in no state to be able to successfully secure a new role, and is compelled to stay, simply to pay the bills. I know this because I've been there.

* * * *

When approaching who you are designing with, how you are designing or shaping a design for a client, society, the public, consider that what you believe to be true, the opposite may also be true, and put in place the procedures and processes to help you see and understand that more clearly.

Known initially for her brutalist concrete designs, and a 'Starchitect' as Pakistan's first woman architect, 2023 Royal Gold Medal recipient

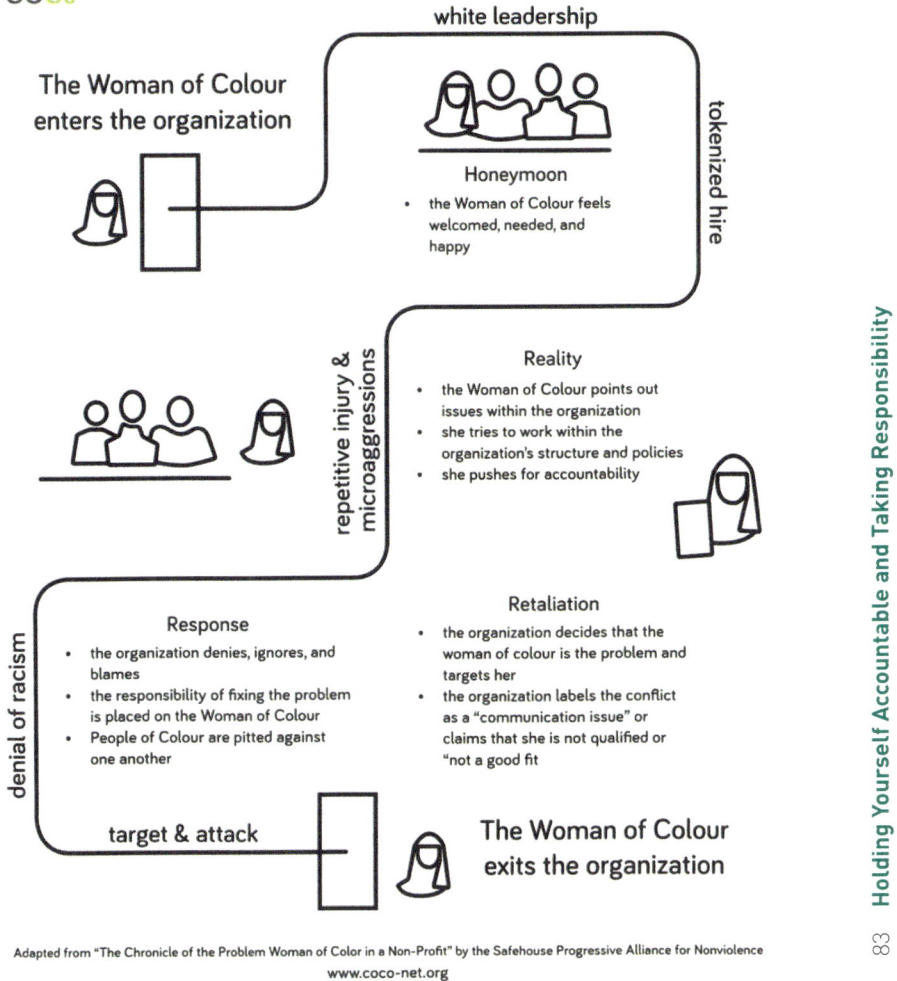

The "Problem" Woman of Colour in the Workplace

COCo

white leadership

The Woman of Colour enters the organization

tokenized hire

Honeymoon
- the Woman of Colour feels welcomed, needed, and happy

repetitive injury & microaggressions

Reality
- the Woman of Colour points out issues within the organization
- she tries to work within the organization's structure and policies
- she pushes for accountability

Response
- the organization denies, ignores, and blames
- the responsibility of fixing the problem is placed on the Woman of Colour
- People of Colour are pitted against one another

Retaliation
- the organization decides that the woman of colour is the problem and targets her
- the organization labels the conflict as a "communication issue" or claims that she is not qualified or "not a good fit"

denial of racism

target & attack

The Woman of Colour exits the organization

Adapted from "The Chronicle of the Problem Woman of Color in a Non-Profit" by the Safehouse Progressive Alliance for Nonviolence
www.coco-net.org

Figure 3.2 'The "Problem" Woman of Color in the Workplace'. Reproduced with kind permission of the Centre for Community Organizations.

Yasmeen Lari evolved her practice and approach by listening to users and prioritising their needs over the clients, eventually becoming 'Architect for the Poorest of the Poor'. In the Angoori Bagh housing provision, for displaced people, she heard the need for people to have a place for their chickens, stacking the design to give everyone terraces, without compromising structural integrity.

In 2005, when the earthquake in Pakistan happened, she went to the region affected and she'd never seen devastation like it. She realised they needed a rethink and argued against using industrialised systems to rebuild, but using what was available. In a country she describes as 'the fifth most vulnerable to climate change … there's nothing you can throw away or waste'.[26]

This isn't about second-guessing yourself, what you know about structure and form is of course valid, but your ideas of how you're treating people, aesthetics and the requirements of the space how it could, would and should be used, will vary with people, context and time. How you account for that may require you to challenge your thought processes in ways you've not yet imagined, and it's by keenly listening that you'll discover what these are.

Institutional Bias/Discrimination/Racism

I have faced the trauma that is institutional racism on more than one occasion, and certainly I have in the built environment.

When decision upon decision is made, and process and procedural excuses are used to support discriminatory outcomes, that is institutional discrimination. When the individuals and groups affected are from racialised groups, this is institutional racism. Racism is not just about race being an overt 'reason' for the prejudice. Racism is the outcome when people of racialised backgrounds are affected by the discrimination, especially when you see similar processes affect non-racialised people differently.

Individuals are responsible for creating, implementing and enforcing these procedures, policies and practices, and therefore individuals can make the choice not to do so, challenge those structures, or interpret them differently, especially when these impacts are fed back and explicitly pointed out. So, individuals are as culpable as the systems they uphold. When the effects are being made clear, and the feedback is being provided, there really is no excuse for it.

When mass job losses are being made and disproportionately, for example, Black women are affected, that is institutional racism, even though all departments may be working in isolation on determining whose job is to go. This is why proactive use of Equality Impact Assessments can be a procedural methodology to cast light on these issues.

An Equality Impact Assessment (EIA or EqIA) is an evidence-gathering approach designed to help organisations ensure that their policies, practices, events and decision-making processes are fair and do not present barriers, to actively promote equality and avoid inadvertent discrimination for any protected group.

This is a data and evidence-based method to highlight and target institutional bias.

There are many online examples of them and they can seem onerous and time-consuming, but going back to the STREAM prerequisites of successful inclusive outcomes, it is a Time, Effort and Resource approach worth taking if there's a danger of inequitable outcomes from strategic decisions.

As we explore community engagement later in this book, I consider that there is a role for something like EqIAs as part of the process.

I've reframed Calvin Lai's words to suggest that:

We need the behaviours to create, implement and enforce, the procedures, policies and practices to mitigate the impact of unhelpful bias.

By doing this we can acknowledge we all have bias, some of it unhelpful, and work consciously to navigate it to create the inclusive outcomes we want to see in our practices, design and relationships.

QR Code 3.2:
LISTEN: RIBA Radio episode three: 'Unconscious Bias with Dr Pragya Agarwal'.

MANAGING DISCOMFORT

If being a woman denies you the right to vote, you, ipso facto cannot grant it to yourself. And you certainly can't vote for your right to vote. If men control all the mechanisms that exclude women from voting as well as the mechanisms that can reverse that exclusion, women must call on men for justice.[27]

Women must call on men for justice. Racialised people must call on white people for justice. Younger people must call on elders for justice. Disabled people must call on enabled people for justice.

The introspective piece of work required to recognise one's agency in delivering justice and one's complicity in injustice is a tough mirror to hold.

And yet hold it up to ourselves, we must.

If you recognise your privilege, I call on you to help achieve justice. If you don't yet recognise your privilege, then read on; I am not surprised.

The mechanics, systems and ideologies that create and embed discrimination, when welded so firmly into our behaviours through bias, require us to face that bias if we're going to overcome it.

However, as Paulo Freire and others have suggested:

When all you have ever known is privilege, equality feels like oppression.

This can cause all manner of defensiveness and backlash.

Already, as you've been reading, you may have felt this prickle of discomfort. You may have thought I'm specifically talking about you and things you have done, or behaviours you've exhibited. This discomfort is not something you can afford to shy away from if you want to STREAM your EDI and be effective in this work.

I have described motivation and bias first, because I wanted you to understand if you benefit from multiple layers of privilege, you are as much a victim of the systems which cause discrimination as those who are weighed down by intersectionality, and it is entirely within your gift to manage your own cerebral processes to fashion narratives that support a more inclusive way of being.

You will be uncomfortable. You will feel defensiveness. You will feel fear. You will get things wrong.

How you deal with this is in your hands, and requires a good deal of emotional intelligence, calling on your self-awareness and listening acutely to feedback which won't be easy to hear.

I have developed a couple of frameworks which draw on the work of others in order to do this effectively.

Being prepared for managing discomfort requires practice, practice, practice.

Firstly, be aware of yourself and your body. You know what defensiveness feels like. Think about those times when you've snapped to justify yourself or your organisation. The prickle on the back of the neck, the knot in the stomach, the clench of the jaw, the tightness across the shoulders.

Secondly, listen out for the verbal identifiers, 'No, you're wrong', 'I'm sure it wasn't meant that way', 'I think you've misunderstood the situation', being some of the more polite rejoinders you might use. Or, maybe you just thought the above. This is also an indicator.

Thirdly, take a moment. It's said 90 seconds is the difference between a reaction and a response.

It's in those intervening seconds that you have a choice. You can choose to give into your defensiveness, to believe you are right and they are wrong. You could choose to walk away, and indeed, that would be entirely your right. However, if you do so, you will walk away from that interaction no better than you joined it. If, on the other hand, you acknowledge and lean into your defensiveness, you manage it and choose to listen to what you're being told, you will learn and you will grow from that interaction.

I ask that you choose to grow.

> Research shows that talking about racial issues with people of other races is particularly stressful for whites, who may feel they have to work harder to sidestep the minefields. Their physical signs of distress are measurable: Heart rates go up, blood vessels constrict, their bodies respond as if they were preparing for a threat. They demonstrate signs of cognitive depletion, struggling with simple things like word-recognition tasks.[28]

I'd argue that this is not just true of some white people, but people socialised in whiteness too.

What we all do about this requires deep thought, care and humanity. We are all victims of the system of racism, as recipients or upholders. This is why I don't think it's possible to be 'comfortable with being uncomfortable'; instead, we can only recognise, be self-aware and consciously lean into our discomfort to achieve the opportunities in learning and growth. That isn't a comfort process.

If we think we're comfortable, we're probably being complacent. I prefer to ask that we lean into our discomfort and remain conscious of it, so we can navigate it well.

Feedback

Both the giving and receiving of feedback can be discomforting.

If we need to give feedback to others about their behaviours, we need to do this contemporaneously. Ideally in person, face-to face. If that is not possible, it should be on camera. If, for whatever reason, it cannot be done contemporaneously, it needs to be properly noted at the time, so the feedback can be accurately given. Feedback should always be specific and targeted. When it's vague, it may be rooted in unhelpful bias.

You may have come across the COIN[29] or BIFF[30] method of having difficult conversations, and I subscribe to these when it comes to delivering feedback, focusing on the incident and specific example, rather than generics and not imbuing feelings with value judgements.

Context: the circumstances, event or issue that you want to discuss.
Observation: specific, factual descriptions of what has happened.
Impact: how the event or issue that you're discussing affects others in your team or organisation.
Next steps: a clear agreement on the changes or improvements in behaviour or performance that you expect going forward.

Or

Behaviour: Describe the behaviour that occurred.
Impact: Describe the impact of that behaviour on you, others, wider circumstances, short/medium/long term effects.
Feeling: take ownership of the feelings the impact had on you and share those.
Future: How would you like things done differently in future?

For example, 'During the project meeting just now, I was trying to share my idea, and you cut me off and spoke over me. When you did that, I wasn't able to contribute and I had something very important to say to the group. It made me feel devalued and that my opinion wasn't wanted. Next time, I would like to be allowed to finish my point before you begin yours. I'd like it if you would agree to that?'

When you are receiving feedback, embrace the learning opportunity and lean into the discomfort. Timothy R. Clark, who I reference below about psychological safety, suggests seven ways to handle tough feedback,[31] saying you need to let go of your pride of authorship so you can see the value of what's being offered.

1. Evaluate the source and intent. If the source is credible and the intent is helpful, remind yourself that negative feedback isn't an attack on your identity or dignity. In fact, you take a massive risk if you ignore or dismiss it.

2. Partially detach emotionally. You can't effectively process otherwise. Be proud of what you've brought to the table, then let others build on it (or even tear it down). There's value in learning to trade authorship for a better result.

3. Find the merit to the argument. Someone who takes the time to offer you specific, honest feedback wouldn't waste your time with comments of no value. Maybe they noticed something that you missed.

4. Ask questions to understand, not defend or deflect. Turn constructive criticism into a dialogue: identify the problems involved, ask for clarification, and brainstorm together so that you can find solutions.

5. Be your own loyal opposition. Tell yourself your argument, then deconstruct it. What are its weaknesses? What doesn't make sense? What could go wrong? This exercise will help feedback become a crucial part of your process.

6. Interpret your defensiveness. Is it emotional or intellectual? Is it built on feelings or strong evidence and logic? If your defensiveness is primarily emotional, take a step back and look at the whole picture.

7. Compare expectations. Do others expect something different than you? If so, this will be reflected in their feedback. A lack of clear expectations does not mean failure or incompetence, but it does provide an opportunity to try again.

TESTIMONIAL

It's not the hierarchy that makes talking about these issues difficult. It's the clear discomfort shown if the word race, or Black or Brown, is mentioned, the silence that ensues. If management is uncomfortable talking about these issues or saying these words, can you imagine how much harder that is for me?

Managing Your Discomfort With Their Discomfort

When giving feedback, about a microaggression or behaviour that has made you uncomfortable, this does require you to be vulnerable. I mention this in the section below on psychological safety, but I recognise this is not easy. Trust me, I know, it can be very uncomfortable and it doesn't get easier, especially if you have to speak to a close colleague or friend, but we have to give people the opportunity to learn and change.

You can prepare by talking it through with a supportive ally – not a person who will tell you 'Don't bother, they probably didn't mean it'. Have the ally to hand to practice the conversation and think through the different responses.

When you have the conversation, you may face tears from the recipient of the feedback,[32] especially if the situation is about race. In which case, you have to have some patience, but it doesn't mean you shouldn't continue with the conversation, or row back on the impact their behaviour has had.

I do know how tough having this kind of conversation about race can be; not just as the tearful recipient of uncomfortable feedback given to me, but when delivering this message, even to my darling husband. My hope for you is that it's used by you both as an opportunity to show how invested you are in the relationship, that you care, and want to be stronger and grow together, and you'll both leave the conversation(s) more robust than when you started, as – I'm pleased to say – we always do.

In the RIBA Radio episode about White Shame and Discomfort (see QR Code 3.3),[33] Jim Rooney also shared his journey when recognising the different experiences of how he navigates his life as opposed to how his partner does, who is a Black woman. So many of these experiences are shared in mixed heritage couples, even if we don't always talk about it.

QR Code 3.3:
LISTEN: RIBA Radio
episode seven: 'White
Shame and Discomfort'.

How to Listen

We can all do this better. There are different ways of listening which we all adopt at different times for different reasons. It can be useful to explicitly understand this in order to do it effectively when being told something we'd rather not hear.

Deb Barnard, of Relational Dynamics 1st, a brilliant coach and mentor, refers to the Five Levels of Active Listening,[34] which is useful to understand when coaching or supporting someone as an ally. She's kindly contributed to the below:

Level One: Me Now – Anticipating our moment to contribute: In this scenario, we're premeditating our responses, often off-topic, while the speaker addresses us, rather than truly engaging in active listening. Our focus lies in awaiting the speaker's pause to interject with our own thoughts.

For example:

'During the project meeting just now, I was trying to share my idea, and I was cut off. When that happened, I wasn't able to contribute, and I had something very important to say to the group.'

   'I wonder why we've been called to a meeting with the clients next week.'

Level Two: Just Like Me! – Relating our personal encounters: When we connect what the other person is saying to our own life and respond from that perspective, our replies tend to revolve around our personal experiences. This approach is commonly observed in typical conversations and is particularly fitting when seeking validation and fostering shared understanding. However, it can also undermine what has been said and the conversation usually closes down.

For example:

'During the project meeting just now ...'

   'Ugh, that happens to me all the time. Last week, I was with them and I was trying to talk about a thing. I think we should be using different materials to ...'

Level Three: Do It Like Me – Offering guidance: Actively hearing the speaker's words and providing them with unsolicited advice can still shift the focus to your own perspective rather than theirs, potentially leading to the same irritations as in Level One.

For example:

'During the project meeting just now ...'

   'If I were you, I'd ignore them. When I make my points ...'

Level Four: Encouraging – prompting deeper insights: In this approach, you pay close attention to the speaker's words and encourage them to delve further into their thoughts. This can lead to expanded thinking, as individuals often clarify their ideas as they speak. Interruptions that stray from encouragement may hinder this constructive process.

For example:

'During the project meeting just now ...'
'That sounds tough. What was going on there do you think?'

Level Five: Active Listening – Embracing the power of silence: This involves tuning into not only the words spoken but also the pauses and unspoken nuances. It's about harnessing your intuition to truly understand what's being conveyed.

For example:

'During the project meeting just now ...'
'So you felt unheard. What else was going on there for you?'
'I withdrew into myself and I didn't end up sharing my idea.'
'What are you thinking of doing about this?'
'Next time, I could try sharing again, but in a different way, or at a different time, making the point that I tried to do so earlier when I was interrupted.'
'Let me know if you'd like to practice that.'

If you are the recipient of feedback putting yourself at Level Five listening can be a stretch, especially as your first rection is likely to be defensive, but I urge you to practice this type of listening constantly, so that when feedback comes, you're able to adopt the right listening style. There may well be reasons for your behaviour, but by listening and understanding first, the other person feels heard and you can more effectively progress the conversation when you reflect on the impact – not intention – of your behaviour. Be self-aware, how your body is reacting and if you are being defensive, and force yourself to listen to what is being said to you.

For example:

'During the project meeting just now, I was trying to share my idea, and you cut me off and spoke over me. When you did that, I wasn't able to contribute, and I had something very important to say to the group. It made me feel devalued and that my opinion wasn't wanted. Next time, I would like to be allowed to finish my point before you begin yours. Would you agree to that?'

'I understand. You're saying when I spoke over you, you felt quite unheard. You do have valuable contributions to make. It's very good of you to let me know this. I need to go away to learn from this how I can support you to share your ideas in future. Your idea is a fair one and I need to consider how to curb my enthusiasm.'

As a person who delivers the feedback, thank the recipient for listening, and be willing to listen to them on their reflections about their intentions **at a later time**, with Level Four and Five, so you can effectively work and relate with your colleagues, and develop the conversation. You can react with understanding, and they can be cognisant of their learning, making the process two-way.

Mistakes

Sometimes we know we've made a mistake, and the moment can eat us up inside, haunting us later at unexpected moments; again, remember Maya Angelou – *forgive yourself for not knowing something before you learned it*, and laugh at yourself, 'How silly I was to do such a thing! Thank goodness I now know to do better!' Repeat this to yourself, and the anxiety will pass.

My framework for managing mistakes, again, helps achieve its goals if delivered contemporaneously. If you realise the mistake before it has been fed back to you, say sorry, straightaway, and show you mean it by describing the mistake and what you'd be doing differently to avoid it in the future.

I developed this framework after considering what it means to be cancelled and the difference between being cancelled and not.

If mistakes are raised with you, I recommend the following:

Acknowledge – when being told things have gone wrong, try not to be defensive. Instead, recognise the impact as having been different from the intention and acknowledge a mistake has been made and apologise with meaning.

Listen – really hear what is being said to you about the issue and what that impact has been. Listen to understand, not to respond.

Learn – thank them and tell them you're going away to learn from the experience. Take away that feedback and go away to learn more about the context and any wider issues at play.

Reflect – reflecting on what has been learned makes experience more productive. Reflection builds one's confidence in the ability to achieve a goal (that is, self-efficacy), which in turn translates into higher rates of learning.

Resolve – move forward differently using this new insight and consciously strive to behave differently in similar situations in future.

Return – go back to the person who gave you the feedback and tell them what you've learned and thank them for providing you with the valuable opportunity.

Growing from such a journey is powerful and you can feel the agency of personal change when you do so. The more you accept when you are wrong, the easier it gets to deal with the discomfort and defensiveness.

If you find yourself making the same mistake again, you have to go through the cycle again. But it becomes more difficult each time if you keep on making the same mistake. To be taken seriously if you apologise you have to find the procedural change that will stop you from repeating the mistake in future.

Reputational Mistakes

Organisationally, if the mistake is a public or an internal one, keep acknowledging the mistake for as many times as necessary, as promptly as you can. Make sure the acknowledgement is on all appropriate platforms. Reiterate your acknowledgement even when people come to your defence. Remember, being inclusive isn't about the loudest voices or just the ones we agree with. You can apologise for the impact of your mistake when you have a good intention that needs to be reframed or better communicated in future.

State your process for reviewing what happened and give a timeline for reverting with learnings and clear next steps. Invite a working party to review with you, especially if your internal processes involve the same people who created the issue in the first place.

This places your organisation in a far stronger reputational position than repeatedly making the same mistakes and hunkering down when you do. It also helps with your attracting a diversity of talent to your organisation, as underrepresented groups in particular appreciate transparency, learning, and seeing evidence and demonstration of an inclusive culture.

Leaders with high [CQ Strategy] are likely to be more deliberate when creating new norms. They tend to take the perspective of diverse others and draw on their cultural knowledge to anticipate their actions and reactions in planning for norm-interventions. Instead of merely adhering to their plans, leaders with high [CQ Strategy] monitor outcomes and pay attention to meaningful cultural cues. They suspend judgments until sufficient information is available for accurate sense-making, and adjust their assumptions when their experience disconfirms their expectations (Triandis, 2006). For example, Morris et al. (2019) showed that those with high [CQ Strategy] monitor judgment errors in intercultural contexts and revise their mental models accordingly.[35]

Whilst the echoes of Thatcher, 'U-turn if you want to …', might reverberate across the corridors of your mind, it's a fallacy that admitting to mistakes, proving you're learning from them, absorbing the new information and changing your mind is a sign of weakness.

Quite the opposite.

PSYCHOLOGICAL SAFETY

Psychological safety is particularly important within the built environment professions because not feeling you can speak up about issues, say, on a construction site, or worries with a design, can lead to outcomes of real physical injury, even death.

There are a couple of different definitions of psychological safety, and I use the work of Amy Edmondson, Timothy R. Clark and Gina Battye to introduce the ideas around it and urge you to follow up with their work for a more detailed look at the concepts.

Not enough research has been done to date by the Institution of Occupational Safety and Health (IOSH) and others into this and its relevance in construction and engineering. Articles written to date don't take into account cultural difference and the impact of that on creating cultures of psychological safety, so there's still much to be explored and done on this point.

Dr Chris Turner has done some incredible work pulling together evidence in the medical profession, on how 'Civility Saves Lives',[36] and this is definitely work the sector can build upon.

All of that said, it's clear that feeling safe to raise issues, learn, make mistakes and innovate can only benefit the built environment professions rather than stifle them. In turn this can benefit the creation of safe spaces in which we live.

The biggest issue I've found across many of the built environment professions has been fear around raising issues, especially of calling-out bullying, harassment and discrimination.

My own experience is that when accountability is asked for, the response can be intimidation and withdrawal of support, and it is no longer safe to continue in that environment.

I have heard that vulnerability is when I give you the benefit of the doubt, psychological safety is when you give me the benefit of the doubt. And, whilst that may seem simplistic, when vulnerability is met with psychological safety, we have the opportunity to learn about the impact and intention around behaviours, and try to make any gaps between the two smaller.

This is particularly important for women and people of racialised background as leaders. The room for vulnerability here is negligible. There is less room for failure as any such admission is often put down to an identity, not other factors; and so psychological safety and acts of vulnerability should always be viewed with a cultural and inclusive lens.

Amy Edmondson states that psychological safety isn't just about being nice, personality or just trustworthiness, it's an environment where workers

> feel comfortable sharing concerns and mistakes without fear of embarrassment or retribution. They are confident they can speak up and won't be humiliated, ignored, or blamed. They know they can ask questions when they're unsure about something. They tend to trust and respect their colleagues ... mistakes are reported quickly so that prompt corrective action can be taken ... potentially game-changing ideas for innovation are shared.[37]

Timothy R. Clark describes the four stages of psychological safety as being inclusion safety, learner safety, contributor safety and challenger safety.[38]

Timothy's approach to inclusion safety is to suggest that the basic decision to include or exclude is not about skill or personality:

> It's an act of will that flows from the empire of the heart.

I can't say I don't love this — it is beautifully poetic; however, I think this speaks more to intrinsic interest than recognising the extrinsic, and as much as I would wish it to be true, the cultural intelligence framework objectively shows us that we need to embed ourselves with a set of skills and capabilities which helps us to function and relate effectively with others, to create cultures of inclusion, with CQ Drive.

After that, his ladder to safety is on firmer footing. The foundational piece we both would agree is that individuals are granted the respect of their humanity, before they're able to go on to do anything else.

'There are no more worlds to conquer, except, at least one, our inclination to conquer each other', he says, and in here is a key component, especially for leaders, of being able to take humble steps backwards from our own focus, and invite teams to participate in meaningful ways towards better outcomes.

Learner safety is the absence of the hostility, as Edmondson also suggests, to fail and supporting the opportunity to develop from it.

Contributor safety is also absent from some built environment cultures, where speaking up to share an idea can be shut down. When we think of planning situations, who gets to have a say and who doesn't, it is very important to develop this safety with those communities who inherently distrust a process which may not have listened to them before.

Challenger safety introduces the comfort with which a team or other stakeholders can raise issues, ask questions, and for leaders to be prepared to be wrong and listen to the various opinions.

The case study we feature below, the Mamou-Mani architecture practice (see Figure 3.3), has all four of these aspects of psychological safety in their culture which are exemplified in their values.

> What I witnessed is once [the values] were set, they were a means for me to say, when something doesn't work, it's often because it mismatched with these values, as opposed to blame, or finger-point a problem.
>
> (Arthur Mamou-Mani)

Mamou-Mani Shared Values

We believe in radical self-reliance: we are the system and the change we want to see.

We believe in active listening and constant iterations. We do not hold on to preciously to our ideas, we evolve, adapt, share and most importantly, we listen. Do not stay stuck, move on, be quick!

We are curious without boundaries. We believe in wabi-sabi,[39] in the imperfect and letting go. Let your research drive you and in expressing what the materials have to say.

We let our designs shape themselves on the parameters that define them. We study, learn scientific facts and metrics to measure our statements.

Everything is design and everyone is creative. Let the world shape us as much as we shape it.

Figure 3.3 Altostrata by Mamou-Mani. Image courtesy of Mamou-Mani.

Gina Battye describes Five Pillars of Psychological Safety:[40] self, social, collaboration, curiosity and creativity. Where:

The first pillar centres around self-awareness. In Pillar 1, individuals ask three questions: 1. What affects my performance and behaviour at work? 2. How can I take back control of the things that affect my performance and behaviour at work? 3. What can I do to achieve my personal and professional goals at work?

The second pillar centres around communication. Individuals ask three questions: 1. How can I make sure I communicate my message clearly and in the way I intend it to be received? 2. How can I make sure I receive messages from other people in the way they were intended? 3. How can I get the most out of my exchange of communication with colleagues?

The third pillar centres around creating an environment where everyone in the team can thrive. Teams ask five questions: 1. What are our goals? 2. How can we create a safe space for everyone? 3. What is the work we need to do? 4. How can we get the most out of ourselves and the team? 5. How do we keep moving things forward?

The fourth pillar centres around Curiosity sessions, in which learning and development, reflective practice and experimentation are integral. The team asks one question: 1. How can we improve what we do and how we work together?

The fifth pillar centres around Creativity workshops, where you create an environment for creativity. The team asks one question: 1. How do we problem solve?

In all three models of psychological safety, learning, innovation, growth and a sense of self-worth are impacted by the levels of inclusion in the environment created.

Being Able to Say 'No'

Saying 'no' can be very difficult, and it takes acts of vulnerability, and the safety of your environment, in order to do so.

If you don't feel safe, I ask you to consider what's the alternative to it? I was once advised, when you say 'no' to something, you're normally saying 'yes' to something else, for example, your health or doing other jobs well. The setting of boundaries might feel too late if you've already set expectations about how you work, but it's never too late to say, 'I'm going to do things differently from today, which will ensure I'm happier and more productive overall at work'.

Sarah Cartwright, a leadership coach, says it can feel unhelpful and confrontational to say 'no', but in order to get comfortable she suggests trying the below:[41]

- Say the name of the person making the request.
- Acknowledge the request they're making, repeating it, and follow it with '**and** I'm going to say no'.
- Give one reason as to why.
- And, offer an alternative.

For example, 'Marsha, I understand you want me to stay for that meeting and I'm going to say no because I have another commitment this evening. I'm happy to help you tomorrow.' Note the use of 'and', not 'but'.

It's clear and it's assertive and it sounds less like an excuse that's up for negotiation.

If they push back, you can ask, 'What alternatives can we look at to address this situation? Who else have you asked?' and adopt a coaching style, to reiterate you're sticking to your 'no'. If it's someone else's poor planning which has landed the issue at your desk, it is worth also calling that out: 'I understand that this wasn't planned/ expectations weren't set differently, so we could have managed this situation better. Like I say, I have capacity to help you with this issue tomorrow.'

Of course, none of us want to overdo saying 'no', but if you over-commit to 'yes' you can burn out. People who say 'no' tend to be more productive, are less stressed and have happier lives.

John Amaechi, the renowned psychologist, suggests you can say 'yes' to extra work, if you make clear what you'll be sacrificing in order to do the new work,[42] for example, 'I can do this but I will put aside the task you asked me to do earlier'. He reiterates that organisations that are asking one person to do the job of three are exploitative, and they don't deserve you. He adds that not everyone has the privilege of simply walking away from a place that's doing that to you.

There is some cultural framing here, because if you have a cultural value which suggests you don't challenge hierarchy (known as High Power Distance) or you tend to be context focused in your communication style (known as Indirect) then this would be harder for you. So, if you're a leader, know your team and if they're trying to say 'no' to you, allow them to do so, and role-model that it's OK to do so with other team members who would be more assertive, so they can see this is acceptable behaviour.

If you are the one trying to say 'no', acknowledge your discomfort and practice with an ally. If on delivering the response you are met with derision, you will have a clear example of the culture you're in, and I refer you back to BIFF and COIN.

Facilitating Others' Challenging Conversations

If asked to mediate between others when a challenging situation needs to be faced, this is a particular skill, and only do so if you feel able to facilitate it well, otherwise you could end up in the tricky situation of being part-blamed if things escalate, or for taking sides.

- Bear in mind the frameworks described and encourage the parties to stick to them.
- Ensure each party has their say without being interrupted.
- Encourage each party to listen, to understand and process, not to respond.
- Allow thoughtful, not intimidating, silence.
- Encourage each party to reflect verbally what they think they've heard.
- Help the parties focus on the outcomes and changes needed to work well in future.

Start, then, with your own behaviours, self-reflecting and delivering them across all areas of your life and work, then, role-model, impacting strategic policies, procedures and practice. Take responsibility for what you can do and hold yourself accountable for delivering it.

CASE STUDY: A Psychologically Safe Practice

Arthur Mamou-Mani, Mamou-Mani

What compelled you to set your organisational values?

Architecture often starts with an individual. Obviously, it's in the name of companies, we may have too much that impression that it's extremely pyramidal, but the design process is extremely iterative. So, what I've noticed is that we needed to set a horizontal axis or transversal axis that would mean that people know why they're here and what matters to the company.

From my previous experience in different offices what unites a company might be the look of a building or a specific feature that might be the signature of the main architect of that office.

But I noticed that beyond the look of things, what mattered was the values behind these things. Not just the values, that these had a direct reflection on why what we're designing, let's say, looks natural or looks relatable to people. I think it's because a lot of our sincerity or authenticity was what made these pieces relatable.

I noticed that, and I felt pushed to write it down. I felt pushed to write them because I could see discrepancies in the team, and I could see why a project wouldn't work or why they would be driven by the wrong things in relation to the overall successful bits of our office (see Figure 3.4).

So, I was just trying to identify what's been successful and, and what were the values behind what was successful as opposed to just the project itself abstracted from the individuals that did it. It was like, what were the overarching values that led to the success of this or that? And then try to put it on paper because I needed to explain it to others. And I think anything that's written, systematised, external from us, can therefore be used as a means to refer back people to it and helps scale without losing your core.

When you implemented those values, what did you see happen?

What I witnessed is once they were set, they were a means for me to say, when something doesn't work, it's often because it mismatched with these values, as opposed to blame, or finger-point a problem. It will just be a little bit deeper than that, is that it just misaligns with what makes us who we are. And also, it's not a, a top-down commandment thing. It was really like, this is what I think makes our office work, and that's what people have been saying about us, and therefore this is it. But if you have a comment on them or if you want to add something, for example, a colleague added another one, and then it's in there, I can see that it's a dynamic thing. People can comment, but it has to somehow be coherent, and people have to buy into it, to stay with us or to be with us. And, if they disagree, then it might evolve, but it's a common core.

So far there's been very little change because I believe we grew how we are because people were naturally inclined towards those values.

We developed design-like systems. That means that they need to be documented. I would say our designs are like DNAs that have a common core geometrically, but they have an infinite diversity of possibility. And that's, in a way, parametric design. That's what it does. It's like you think of your systems, and then other people can adapt them to different conditions.

This prompts you to active listening: active listening to your colleagues, to the engineers, to the machine, active listening to the non-human elements around this. Let it grow means like by doing this process of careful active listening and iteration, things will slowly shape themselves as opposed to you trying to shape them. And so, it makes you humble because you accept the sort of forces of life as opposed to try and push them. Therefore, you don't assume anything and, therefore you can create the change.

Can you describe your approach to challenge?

I tend to give trust by default. If anything, what can happen is maybe more an abuse of that trust or disappointment, than withholding trust and therefore preventing from even the ability to make a mistake. So, it's risky on my side, but I think it's precious on their side, to the point that they don't want to compromise that trust.

I've seen this in action, and when it has happened, when trust was compromised, and I also expressed it, but the default of trusting hasn't changed. And, so, people have that ability to rise. To have their voice, even if that voice then leads to something that we don't implement, that voice has existed and has the ability to even be presented to a client.

We do something very, very, often, which is we put – if there is a debate on two options – then we put the two options on our Slack channel (our Slack channel is where everyone can voice themselves) and we vote. And, you know, the vote can go towards something I prefer or can go towards something else. But I'm really curious, if something goes towards something I didn't expect, instead of being like, 'Oh, damn, this was my design' or whatever, which would be the normal reaction, I genuinely want to understand. I'll speak to the people that would say why they prefer it, then I would learn.

It's deeply democratic in a way, because it has to be pleasing people. People have to be happy. It's very intuitive. Why do you prefer this versus that? I'm very curious why someone would prefer something that intuitively I thought was less good than something else.

So rather than shut down the other option, I take it as a mission to learn why that preference. And of course, the majority wins. There was never a case where majority preferred something else, and I said, it's the other one, simply because by the time we reach the vote, we know that both options are viable. So, there's no reason the vote shouldn't win. That also brings safety because there's no arbitrariness of choice, and so therefore people never feel resentment that something's been ignored or not done based on arbitrariness.

It's the scientific approach.

Figure 3.4 Portraits of the Mamou-Mani team. Photographs by naaro.

How you develop that sense of safety for people to fail?

This goes with 'iterate quickly and share the process'.

Let's say you're designing something on your own and you spend a lot of time on it, you will have built a certain bubble of stuff that you will be especially protective of because you spend lots of time on it. So, the idea of iterate quickly and sharing means that you don't even have time to build that layer of ego around something, because it was quite immediate, and therefore it's already out there in the world. That means that you might be less inclined to see a mistake or a success as something that you need to protect or feel bad about, because, it's so fresh and new and it's like, here's an idea, or here's a thought, and then people will be immediately like, yes or no. But then you're learning to let go of the preciousness of one single idea versus another one.

You could see this like in the analogy of natural evolution, where for the most beautiful things to happen as in nature, when you see an incredibly intricate flower, knowing that it's happened through billions of tiny decisions. Some worked, some did not. It mutates and then that didn't work out. It mutates again. That didn't work out, but it didn't dwell on that! It just kept going, until the mutation hits the ecosystem and creates this diversity. We know about how it fits within different ecosystems, but it's billions of years of micro decisions, so probably billions of micro decisions. It is not necessarily sudden. So, this is how we design.

How do you maintain integrity and profitability when challenged by clients?

I don't shy away from showing our values to the clients. In our proposal, I often say if something is aligned with our values, and I put the link to our values. I think this is a very public document and it's almost like a caveat; what we believe in. It's a lot deeper than a financial transaction.

There's a lot of cases where the people I worked with became deep friends because of this value element. I tend to find to just say 'it's just business' or 'it's just money' or that puts this moral separation somehow between what's acceptable or not.

We spend about a third of our life at work?! So isn't it a bit odd and impossible to say that a third of our life, somehow our moral standards or our values don't apply to that third, knowing that the final third is probably sleeping. Or to say that 'work is not personal'. You have to believe in what you're doing.

When I say everything is design and iterate quickly, it's also based on business decision because iterate quickly and do things quickly and test ideas, is the opposite of the stereotypical architect that will do a whole competition pack and it leads to nothing. Like I tend to say, let's do a concept and then send it to a client the same day. Let's not waste time because we might be in a completely different path than what is needed.

I want to apply this with the clients too. We produce something, we know it's beautiful, we all agree it's beautiful. Why do we need to spend even more time? I see this a lot in other practices when I worked there, it was like being almost more demanding with yourself than, you know, than the client requires.

It's a pattern we see in offices and probably what brings a lot of the profit down, because you just spend time on unnecessary stuff that no one really cares about. The general public doesn't care about it, the client wouldn't care about it.

We spend time on active listening to be right on the brief. We don't reinvent the wheel every time, which is also a problem of architects, they tend to try to reinvent things. They have this creation syndrome where they want to create an idea from scratch somehow, to have full authorship, rather than build a portfolio of DNAs that can speak to one another.

What reflections have you had on the way that you run your studio?

I wish I had these values a bit sooner. I wish I could have found that space for others sooner. I wish I could have formulated these core elements for the people that forced me to write them! I'm thankful for my mistakes.

I think there was never a lack of respect, it's just when someone mismatched your values, I remember sometimes sitting with them for three, four hours, to try and figure out like if we can still work together. It's those discussions, those frictions that helped me formulate better what we're about and what our office stands for.
All our values fit into a circular method that doesn't necessarily have a beginning and an end.

BEHAVIOURAL ANALYSIS

Intuitively, as individuals and as a practice, Mamou-Mani display all four CQ capabilities. They interact, overlap and feed into each other, as the framework does when inherently understood and demonstrated.

DRIVE: Curiosity is a fundamental part of who they are and how they act. They are OK with leaning into the discomfort of mistakes and learning from them.

KNOWLEDGE: They are completely open to learning, and iterating, and absorbing, and reflecting, about each other, process, and design. They listen intently.

STRATEGY: They have systems to plan and check their behaviours, process and design when they find one that works they document and reiterate it. There are explicit guidelines to decision-making which everyone understands to mitigate bias.

ACTION: They're adaptable and innovative, changing, listening, learning, reflecting.

I have said that the pillars on which we should build any organisation is that it should be inclusive, sustainable, ethical, innovative and safe. I feel quite lucky to have found Mamou-Mani to share with you in this book, as my observations are that they support all five of these ideals.

KEY TAKEAWAYS

- Discover motivations to work across difference and practice doing so, so when you're under pressure you're able to do better, rather than default to original behaviours.
- To be human is to be biased, we're all biased.
- We need to create, implement and enforce procedural changes to mitigate the impact of unhelpful bias.
- Develop the emotional maturity to accept constructive feedback about your behaviours, well.
- Acknowledge the discomfort around these issues and lean into it.
- Practice the framework for managing mistakes.
- Understand what it means to have a psychologically safe environment and put in place the pillars to construct it.
- It's OK to say 'no' sometimes.
- If working with others around feedback, help them to help each other and don't get stuck in the middle.

NOTES

1 Kamala Harris, *The Truths We Hold: An American Journey*, Vintage, 2020.
2 Naomi Klein, *This Changes Everything*, Penguin, 2014.
3 Yanis Varoufakis, *Talking to My Daughter About the Economy: A Brief History of Capitalism*, Vintage, 2017.

4 Eric Williams, *Capitalism and Slavery*, Penguin Classics, 1944.

5 Angela Y. Davis, *Women, Race & Class*, Penguin Classics, 1981.

6 Emma Dabiri, *What White People Can Do Next*, Penguin, 2021.

7 Paulo Freire, *Pedagogy of the Oppressed*, Penguin Classics, 1970.

8 Peter Apps, *Show Me the Bodies: How We Let Grenfell Happen*, Oneworld, 2022.

9 BBC Horizon, *How You Really Make Decisions*, BBC Documentary. See www.dailymotion. com/video/x3q4alx [Accessed 29 November 2023]. Toby Macdonald, 'How do we really make decisions?', BBC News, 24 February 2014. See https://www.bbc.co.uk/news/science-environment-26258662 [Accessed 29 November 2023].

10 RIBA Radio, Episode 3, Overview – Unconscious bias with Pragya Agarwal. See https://soundcloud.com/the-riba/riba-radio-episode-3-overview?in=the-riba/sets/riba-radio [Accessed 29 November 2023].

11 *The Cognitive Bias Codex*. See https://upload.wikimedia.org/wikipedia/commons/6/65/Cognitive_bias_codex_en.svg [Accessed 29 November 2023].

12 Ruby McGregor-Smith, *Race in the Workplace: The Mcgregor-Smith Review*, 2017. See https://assets.publishing.service.gov.uk/government/uploads/system/uploads/attachment_data/file/594336/race-in-workplace-mcgregor-smith-review.pdf [Accessed 29 November 2023].

13 Sean Coughlan, '"Unconscious bias training" to be scrapped by ministers', *BBC News*, 15 December 2020. See https://www.bbc.co.uk/news/amp/education-55309923 [Accessed 29 November 2023].

14 P.S. Forscher, C.K. Lai, J.R. Axt, C.R. Ebersole, M. Herman, P.G. Devine and B.A. Nosek, 'A meta-analysis of change in implicit bias', 2016, modified 2021. See https://psyarxiv.com/dv8tu/ [Accessed 29 November 2023]

15 Calvin Lai, Twitter, 2019. See https://twitter.com/CalvinKLai/status/1127958431-225262087?s=20 [Accessed 29 November 2023].

16 'What can you do to spot and stop unconscious bias', *BBC Radio 4*, 2019. See www.bbc.co.uk/programmes/articles/21wxrfj5S79pz6CMCdHmVL3/what-you-can-do-to-spot-and-stop-unconscious-bias [Accessed 29 November 2023].

17 Angela C. Bell, Melissa Burkley and Jarrod Bock, 'Examining the asymmetry in judgments of racism in self and others', *The Journal of Social Psychology*, 2019, 159(5): 611–627. DOI: 10.1080/00224545.2018.1538930.

18 I. Dror, J. Melinek, J.L. Arden, et al., 'Cognitive bias in forensic pathology decisions', *Journal of Forensic Sciences*, 2021, 66: 1751–1757. https://doi.org/10.1111/1556–4029.14697

19 Daniel Kahneman, *Thinking, Fast and Slow*, Penguin, 2011.

20 Ibid.

21 *Unconscious Bias Training: An Assessment of the Evidence for Effectiveness*, EHRC Research Report 113, 2018. See www.equalityhumanrights.com/sites/default/files/research-report-113-unconcious-bais-training-an-assessment-of-the-evidence-for-effectiveness-pdf.pdf [Accessed 29 November 2023].

22 'Unconsious bias training has no sustained impact on behaviour', *People Management*, 2019. See www.peoplemanagement.co.uk/news/articles/unconscious-bias-training-has-no-sustained-impact-on-behaviour [Accessed 29 November 2023].

23 Jennifer Y. Kim and Loriann Roberson, 'I'm biased and so are you. What should organizations do? A review of organizational implicit-bias training programs',

Consulting Psychology Journal, 2021, 74(1): 19–39. https://doi.org/10.1037/cpb0000211

24 Binna Kandola, *Racism at Work: The Danger of Indifference*, Pearn Kandola Publications, 2018.

25 'The "problem" woman of colour in nonprofit organizations', The Centre for Community Organizations, Montreal. See https://coco-net.org/problem-woman-colour-nonprofit-organizations/ [Accessed 23 November 2023].

26 Angela Fitz, Elke Krasny, Marvi Mazhar and Architekturzentrum Wien (eds), *Yasmeen Lari: Architecture for the Future*, MIT Press, 2023.

27 Robin DiAngelo, *White Fragility*, Beacon Press, 2018, p. xiv.

28 Jennifer Eberhardt, *Biased: Uncovering the Hidden Prejudices that Shape Our Lives*, Windmill, 2019.

29 Anna Carroll, *The Feedback Imperative: How to Give Feedback to Speed Up Your Team's Success*, River Grove Books, 2014.

30 Sheila Heen, Douglas Stone, and Bruce Patton, *Difficult Conversations: How to Discuss What Matters Most*, Penguin Books, 1999.

31 Timothy R. Clark, '7 psychologically safe ways to handle tough feedback', LinkedIn. See www.linkedin.com/posts/timothyrclark_7-psychologically-safe-ways-to-handle-tough-activity-7034591599544160256-GTOM [Accessed 29 November 2023].

32 Robin DiAngelo, *White Fragility: Why It's So Hard for White People to Talk About Racism*, Beacon Press, 2018.

33 RIBA, RIBA Radio Episode 7, CQ Drive. See https://soundcloud.com/the-riba/riba-radio-episode-7-cq-drive [Accessed 29 November 2023]

34 Generally, there are not just 'five levels of listening'. The levels here are extracted from the *Relational Dynamics 1st Training Manual* by Deb Barnard and references Carol Wilson's 'The five levels of listening'. See www.coachingcultureatwork.com/the-five-levels-of-listening/ [Accessed 11 November 2023].

35 Soon Ang, Thomas Rockstuhl and Georgios Christopoulos, 'Cultural intelligence and leadership judgement and decision making: ethnology and capabilities', Anna B. Kayes and D. Christopher Kayes (eds), *Judgment & Leadership*, Edward Elgar, 2021, p. 168.

36 Chris Turner, *Civility Saves Lives*. See www.civilitysaveslives.com/academic-papers [Accessed 29 November 2023].

37 Amy Edmonson, *The Fearless Organisation*, Harvard Business School, 2019.

38 Timothy R. Clark, *The 4 Stages of Psychological Safety: Defining the Path to Inclusion and Innovation*, Brett-Koehler Publishers, 2020.

39 Taken from the Japanese words *wabi*, which translates to less is more, and *sabi*, which means attentive melancholy, *wabi sabi* refers to an awareness of the transient nature of earthly things and a corresponding pleasure in the things that bear the mark of this impermanence. As much a state of mind – an awareness of the things around us and an acceptance of our surroundings – as it is a design style, *wabi sabi* begs us to appreciate the pure beauty of life – a chipped vase, a quiet rainy day, the impermanence of all things. Presenting itself as an alternative to today's fast-paced, mass-produced, neon-lighted world, *wabi sabi* reminds us to slow down and take comfort in the natural beauty around us. Andrew Juniper, *Wabi Sabi: The Japanese Art of Impermanence*, Tuttle Publishing, 2003

40 Gina Battye's 'Five pillars of psychological safety'. See www.ginabattye.com/5-pillars-psychological-safety/ [Accessed 29 November 2023].

41 Sarah Cartwright on 'Saying "No",' *Brave Conversations: The Key to Resilience*, Clore Emerging Futures, 2018. See https://youtu.be/y8BzKAdnz-0?t=506 [Accessed 29 November 2023].

42 John Amaechi on 'Yes, if…', LinkedIn. See www.linkedin.com/posts/amaechi_if-you-feel-like-youre-doing-the-job-of-activity-7062342335526760448-eQeQ [Accessed 29 November 2023].

ATTRACT AND RETAIN

Chapter Four

[A]s human beings, we are not problems waiting to be solved, but potential waiting to unfold.[1]

If you're a sole practitioner or micro-SME in the built environment then you may feel that some of this is not relevant to you, but I'd ask you to think again. No one in the built environment is creating spaces entirely on their own, whether you're a planning consultant, tiler or CEO of a major infrastructure firm. The EDI actions, measures and outcomes detailed in the next few chapters of this book, alongside the case studies of great practice, are opportunities to reflect on your own behaviours and policies, as well as how to support those who may need it, how you can collaborate well, and, consider, if you grow your own business, how you can do it as inclusively as possible.

My Inclusive Culture Pyramid in Chapter One describes the foundational behavioural traits of cultural intelligence, then how those are embedded organisationally, through role-modelling, talent and skills development, fostering of understanding and conviction, and creation of supportive formal mechanisms, then across the four areas of the business; how you attract the people you work with, how you treat, progress and retain them, how you create your design, products and services and how you engage with external stakeholders.

This chapter examines those first two areas of the business, how you **ATTRACT** and **RETAIN** people, as it connects with the 'talent and skills' development, and 'supportive formal mechanisms' – I've been referring to these things so far as the procedures, policies and practices.

But before we get to the point of hiring competent staff, a quick note on the whole built environment sector needing to look at how it attracts a diversity of people into its professions in the first instance.

DOI: 10.4324/9781003435747-7

OK, so this is a can of worms.

In some built environment professions attracting a diversity of students and apprentices seems to be less of an issue. Architecture, for example, attracts more than 50 per cent women; there are equitable proportions of racialised groups in interior design; there have been significant increases in engineering degrees of those who declare as disabled people.

There is no doubt that a lot more needs to be done to encourage a mix of people and backgrounds to enter these professions. We need a range of entry opportunities, apprenticeships being an obvious one. Not many people can afford the high cost of a full-time university education without reverting to the 'bank of mum and dad' or taking out significant loans, and that can feel like an onerous burden once graduated.

However, whilst in tertiary education, there can be drop off. Inherent here is the issue of culture in some of the built environment schools, departments and courses; the coloniality of curricula and concerns around sexual and racial harassment, bullying, fear and discrimination are the main drivers.

The damning Howlett Brown report of 2022 into the Bartlett Faculty of the Built Environment at UCL cited: 'an unhealthy culture of competition'; 'very few checks in place to ensure that the unit structure did not drive inequity or an abuse of power, is one of the systemic root causes of the concerning experiences'; 'unit structure has been a significant catalyst for allowing poor conduct and culture to thrive'. UCL has apologised, but the shame of it, of course, was that it took a significant amount of distress, a champion[2] to gather the stories and go to the press, and an independent investigation for it to do so, rather than original complaints being listened to.

TESTIMONIAL

The teacher approached a student of Caribbean ethnic minority and his first reaction to the student not having new work was to ask him if he was sure architecture was for him, and if he had pressure from his family to do this, and he might be better doing something else.

In the same session, a white student of English heritage had a similar problem, he approached that student and his reaction was quite different. He asked how can he support him, offered him some books, and offered some direction as to what could jolt the student making progress with the project.

Alumni from environments like these go on to form their own practices, and whilst these outcomes are not universal, the students who have spoken to me after various lectures I've given around the country sadly have tales of woe, where in their professional internships they have faced racism, sexism, ableism and poor working culture to varying degrees.

And so, all routes into education for the built environment professions need to engage in a similar inclusion strategy to that for organisations.

This is a specific area on which many people are working to bring about change. As part of the joint institutes Action Plan[3] there is a commitment to:

> develop a robust, evidence-based understanding of the disparity between the diversity of students that start on institute-accredited courses and those that join the workforce; and to build on existing good practice to improve our collective understanding of retention rates and awarding gaps in education.[4]

To address any findings this would require fundamentally addressing inclusive behaviours, the creation of psychological safety and robust whistleblowing support, also an inclusion informed curricula analysis, behaviour standards for tutors, schools' engagement programmes, and listening to the student experience in meaningful, inclusive ways.

This is a sizeable piece of work, and heads of schools and educators should find useful insight in this book, but I am aware there are particular strands to inclusion in higher education. I know professionals in built environment education are working on solutions, and organisations like Building People CIC are trying to join the dots between different initiatives in order to bring about an aligned and holistic change.

Meanwhile, I would encourage practices to also support the many projects and initiatives which promote built environment professions to non-traditional groups:

- HomeGrown Plus, run by Neil Pinder, who believes that only by including people from non-traditional backgrounds in fields like architecture can improvements be made in the built environment and other areas of society, and his inspirational programmes encourage young people to do so (see Figure 4.1).
- MATT+FIONA ask young people how their built environment might be improved and empower them to bring that vision to life.

Figure 4.1 Neil Pinder and the HomeGrown Plus alumni of the New York–London inspiration trip – NY-Lon – presentation.

- MOBIE is an educational charity inspiring young people to build the homes of the future.
- CSTT was established by The Worshipful Company of Chartered Surveyors to help individuals overcome the barriers they face in pursuing a career in surveying.
- The Built Environment Trust has a wide-ranging learning programme to inspire, connect and empower people to improve the quality of our built environment.

QR Code 4.1:
USE: Building People's network of networks.

These are just a handful of the many organisations doing incredible work in this space, and Building People CIC[5] can point you to many others (see QR Code 4.1).

WORKFORCE LIFECYCLE

Having got through their education, there's then the task for an apprentice or graduate of securing a job.

From the time someone looks up your job advert to joining your organisation, through to the time they leave your organisation, that's the workforce lifecycle. There are some key stages within that and it's your business' role to ensure that the structures and systems around that encourage diversity and support inclusion. These are: workforce planning, remuneration, recruitment, onboarding, learning

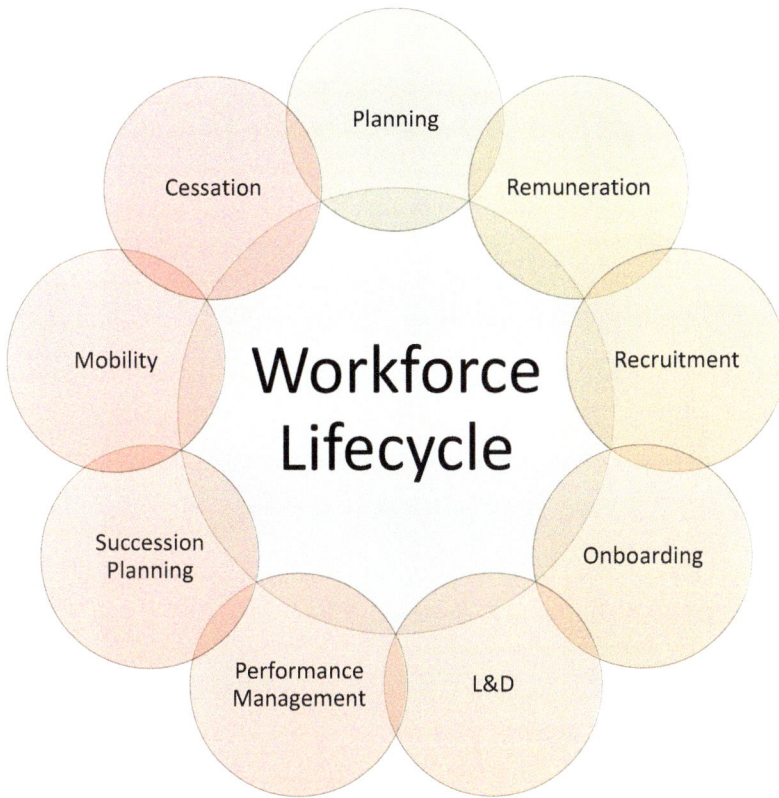

Figure 4.2 The workforce lifecycle.

and development, performance management, succession planning, workforce mobility, and cessation of employment (see Figure 4.2).

Just as people change, context changes, political, economic, legislative demands can all evolve, so too must your structures and processes. Strategic moments to reflect, evaluate and improve come after each hiring decision, and when someone chooses to leave. There's also the opportunity to review when new conversations are being had in wider society about menopause or race or gender identity, for example. Don't let it be only when something is going wrong that you take the time to look at your processes, procedures and practices.

It is more straightforward to embed inclusivity if you're an agile business with under 250 employees. And, I daresay there's a good argument for collaborating with others rather than growing an organisation beyond this number, fundamentally rethinking organisational development and economic structures to support that – but that argument is, perhaps, for another book.

Remembering the steps to success require you to STREAM your EDI, looking at the workforce lifecycle is one of those occasions when Time is required, to embed a culturally intelligent Strategy, to plan effectively, and anticipate change. The more practised you are, the more responsive you would be, and it would take less time and energy. However, don't underestimate what you may be doing already; a shift in culture is also a shift in mindset, and approaching any expended effort as opportunity creation, rather than issue solving, will help you see that some of these things really aren't that big a deal to implement.

The creation, implementation and enforcement of procedural changes to mitigate bias in workforce systems, and identifying and tackling bias within, requires transparency, trust and respect, as well an objective consideration of fairness.

In RIBA's Good Practice Guide for Business Resilience, by Mark Kemp, I contributed to remind readers that:

> Being fair in the workplace requires understanding that what you might think is fair, someone else may not. That doesn't mean either of you are right or wrong, you just have different perspectives. Coming to an agreement when perspectives are different requires emotional intelligence and cultural intelligence. Developing these skills is core to being inclusive, especially because we are all inherently biased, and it's a fallacy that by simply knowing we're biased we can mitigate it. So, we need to create procedural changes to mitigate the impact of hidden bias. This means having clear, objective hiring procedures; making progression steps and opportunities available to all staff; conducting independent exit interviews and acting on feedback, etc. Taking the time to do this work well pays dividends, ethically as well as financially.[6]

WORKFORCE PLANNING

Good business development requires you to have a workforce plan. Rapid expansion can result in a lot of 'people problems' if a day or two isn't taken to stop and consider the current and future supply and demand of the talent and knowledge you'll need, and what skills, experience, abilities and capabilities are likely to be required in the team. Bear in mind, though, as Laloux suggests, that dealing with these matters should be seen more through the lens that 'as human beings, we are not problems waiting to be solved, but potential waiting to unfold'.

If you flex, by expanding and contracting your teams for projects, clarity on these matters and the monitoring of demographic data will be crucial to ensuring the opportunities and risks around EDI are identified and tackled.

So, what do I mean by that?

- You need to have a plan that places EDI at its heart, in terms of values and goals.
- Do a SWOT analysis of how you're planning on growing the team.
- Factor in EDI opportunities and risks.

I've already suggested the huge opportunities of working and relating effectively across difference, of course the risks are around a diversity of people working within a non-inclusive culture, also how do you manage those whose values are very different to those of the organisation you're in, and there may well be belief systems involved in those value differences. There are ways to manage this, including bringing in cultural intelligence at the earliest stage with all new colleagues. However, there isn't always a blanket answer, and seeking expertise or experienced peer-to-peer support to advise may be a way forward.

- As you map the growth of the team in the plan, strategically consider the knowledge you'll need, and what skills, experience abilities and capabilities are likely to be required. Also build in cognisance of the demographics as that team is built.
- As a new job family is emerging, and as you plan for the future, ensure that the same kind of person isn't in the leadership position, similarly, consider this regarding who the reporting team are. Look at diversity holistically, and carefully monitor.
- Collect the data analytics of the wider built environment sector to plan to be more inclusive.

Data analysis work is being done by various organisations in the built environment, not least the ARB and the six professional institutes; RIBA, RICS, RTPI, ICE, LI and CIOB. As other institutes grow their work in this area, like CIAT, CABE or CICES, it would be my hope that they would align with the core data approach, so results can be usefully aggregated, and that infrastructure and property would join in with creating consistency.

The GLA usefully pulled together a Workforce Data Equality Guide in 2021 (see QR Code 4.2)[7] to provide a useful set of questions, alongside

QR Code 4.2:
USE: Workforce Data Equality Guide.

a benchmarking tool with demographic statistics of London, which can be sliced to provide intersectional data too. This can help London-based firms with comparative insight and help with targeting underrepresentation.

The Supply Chain Sustainability School (SCSS) runs an in-depth record of diversity data. The survey tool has been tracking progress in the construction and utilities sector annually since 2016. Employee data across 270 supply chains of eight major companies and two membership organisations was collected and analysed, including: HS2, National Highways, Network Rail, Transport for London, Environment Agency, Morgan Sindall, VolkerWessels, Cadent Gas, Infrastructure Client Group, and the Major Projects Association, comprising nearly 340,000 people.

SCSS says that despite increased engagement levels and sample size, diversity inequalities remain apparent (as notably highlighted by the attraction and recruitment statistics). Key takeaways from the 2022 survey[8] include:

- Gender: inequality persists, with women making up only 23 per cent of employees.
- Ethnicity: representation of ethnic minority groups increased to 13.7 per cent for 2022, but ethnic minorities representation was still 5 per cent below the ONS UK population average.
- Attraction and recruitment: the application to hiring ratio ranged between 21:1 to 78:1 for ethnic minority groups, 16:1 for white applicants, 16:1 for women, 22:1 for men and 22:1 for disabled people.
- Disability: the lack of data collection around disability persists, with 44.5 per cent of employees not disclosing whether or not they have a disability.
- Sexual orientation: disclosure is progressively increasing across the sector, yet only 1.7 per cent of employees identify as part of the LGBTQ+ community for the sector. While this is an increase over previous years, it is well below the ONS UK population average of 3.1 per cent.

Of course, data like this still needs to be interrogated, because we need to account for diversity within diversity, and those with intersectional identities. Visible versus invisible disabilities, for example, and Black women versus South Asian heritage men, those in manual roles versus leadership positions, are all hidden elements, and SCSS can provide that slicing.

That said, this context is important to understand, because, once the data has been collected, we need to carry out the comparison piece; with other industries within a sector, and then sector by sector, as well as with the wider working population. All will help with identifying and targeting your workforce opportunities, and any risks from not addressing any revealed underrepresentation. The professional institutes and other industry bodies can, and should, help with collective funding contributing to robust datasets and analysis. So:

- Compare gathered data with other data, for example, wider trends or previous information.
- Identify issues, gaps and opportunities from it.
- Create strategies to manage those.
- Review those strategies in an ongoing way.

As part of a workforce plan, in order to be inclusive in its development, the strategies you might consider include flexible working options, provision of prayer spaces, quiet rooms, allowing people to wear headphones, casual clothing, type of toilet provision, should you have childcare onsite, and so on.

I wouldn't want to generalise too much about what this means or should look like because the actions you need to target as part of your workforce planning will depend on many things.

As always, having the motivation and the systemic adaptable support to do so is key.

TESTIMONIAL

I remember at a particular time I had a line manager that wouldn't even say hello to me. He wouldn't talk to me. He would just walk past me. He was supposed to be my line manager and he just didn't want to have anything to do with me but was obviously talking to everybody else in the office.

> I wasn't sure what was wrong, why he didn't want to [talk to me] … It eventually got better, and on my last project, there was somebody that I had to speak directly to and tell him 'You are racist, if you have an issue with the colour of my skin, you need to tell me now' … it just got to a stage where I've had enough, I've been so quiet for the past five years and I just let everything slide no matter what people do or say – this particular one, I was like, 'No that's it, I'm sorry but you are being racist. If you have an issue with the colour of my skin, then you need to let me know.'
>
> He said 'No I'm not racist' but that was how I felt. I told him 'That's the way you are making me feel, like I'm not wanted here'.

Measures

In pursuing inclusivity and diversity, an organisation should delve into a comprehensive analysis of various measures that could significantly impact their overall success. These measures, viewed through both an aggregate and segmented diversity lens, play a vital role in gauging the effectiveness of EDI efforts.

Firstly, an organisation should closely monitor the data on available workforce supply and demand, in comparison to role requirements and EDI opportunities and risks. This includes scrutinising demographic representation to identify areas of over- and under-representation. By understanding the demographic landscape, it should aim to build a workforce that mirrors the diverse society it serves.

Additionally, it should track the number of job and progression opportunities offered to individuals from demographically underrepresented groups within specific timeframes covered by their comprehensive workforce plan. This measurement would be crucial in assessing an organisation's commitment to providing equal growth opportunities for all.

An organisation should also look for trends in adverse and disproportionate impacts to ensure their initiatives don't unintentionally exacerbate inequalities. Identifying any concerning trends allow to make targeted adjustments to strategies and actions, ensuring the pursuit of EDI objectives remain on track.

Lastly, assess the effectiveness of strategies and actions in achieving EDI objectives and address opportunities and risks outlined in the workforce plan. Regular evaluations allow for the refining of approaches to ensure continuous progress towards fostering an inclusive and diverse environment.

By meticulously analysing these measures, an organisation can pro-actively steer their EDI.

So, measure:

- demographics around workforce, noting over- and underrepresentation;
- demographically underrepresented groups regarding job opportun-ities and progression opportunities across timeframes;
- negatives trends;
- whether strategies and actions on achieving EDI objectives are working.

Reproductive Recognition in Workforce Planning

Specifically, inclusive workforce planning needs to be rooted in the dis-pelling of fallacies and myths.

For example, I am quite fascinated by the idea that it is women's 'choice' to have children. Individually, yes, it can be. Societally, definitely not. By that, I mean for humans, wombs are biologically required to ges-tate babies in order to continue the human race. If we could give that job to males, I am sure some of us with wombs would – but we cannot. That doesn't sound like a choice to me.

I have considered that humans with wombs could collectively choose not to gestate children – however, I suspect we could end up in a version of *The Handmaid's Tale* or *The Matrix*.

This biological requirement doesn't prevent us from being brilliant professionals who deserve to be retained and progressed. After all, it's not all we're good for. Very few of us who study and/or strive for years to develop our careers are willing to give it all up because of this human need, desire and genetic obligation. In her book, *Pregnant then Screwed*, Joeli Brearley highlights the multiple ways in which this plays out – that women are frequently sidelined, undermined and made redundant, including a chapter entitled 'I had a baby, not a lobotomy'.[9]

There may come a time when we can choose to gestate babies outside the uterus,[10] but there are concerns around ethics and process which need to be grappled with first. Meanwhile, biology being a determining factor impacting our culture in this day and age, and presuming about the facility of the 'working mother', is short-sighted, and unworthy of our evolutionary potential as a species. In (M)otherhood,[11] Dr Pragya Agarwal makes poignant and far more nuanced arguments on these matters, including around surrogacy, and I urge you to follow up by reading it.

To enable this human-species obligation, approximately half the global population have periods and then go through the menopause.

Speaking on RIBA Radio, Dr Annabel Sowemimo,[12] a sexual and reproductive health consultant, said that our whole working experiences have been designed centring men and those with male bodies,[13] and there's not enough research about navigating working spaces from different perspectives. In a satirical article written in 1978, Gloria Steinem mused on how 'if men could menstruate'[14] how different our lives and society would be set up:

> The answer is clear—menstruation would become an enviable,
> boast-worthy, masculine event: Men would brag about how long and how
> much. Boys would mark the onset of menses, that longed-for proof of
> manhood, with religious ritual and stag parties. Congress would fund a
> National Institute of Dysmenorrhea to help stamp out monthly discomforts.

Women, even in female-dominated environments, can hide when they're menstruating, secreting pads and tampons up a sleeve as they head to the toilet to make the necessary change. Not feeling free to do these things openly or feeling a stigma related to bleeding, is social conditioning related to shame, which can be reinforced with managerial behaviours and organisational systems.

But, to be fair, it's not just about that. We can be our own worst enemy on occasion. I tell this next story not to shock or trigger you (this is a warning, skip to the next paragraph to avoid), but to say sometimes we have to take responsibility for our own agency in some situations. When I was working in journalism, I was once responding to a breaking news story. Whilst I was out, I started miscarrying. I can even tell you the story I was working on: the death of Pope John Paul II. It was horrendous. I was probably in denial and just continued working, across the two days I was called in to work. When I look back now, I wonder why I didn't speak up – and it was due to shame. No one knew I was pregnant, I'd only just found out myself; my husband and I weren't married at the time and I thought everyone would judge me.

There are occasions when we can presume a lack of psychological safety, so we have to get over ourselves, and our social and cultural conditioning, as well trusting those around us to support, because, actually, quite often they will. To help with this, colleagues and managers in the workplace can ensure, every day, you're role-modelling compassion and acceptance of vulnerability, so that when needed, people feel safe to share.

Across heritage and cultures, normalising discussions in the workplace as to our reproductive health; the impact of IVF, the excruciating, debilitating pain we can endure with periods, baby loss, and so on, will help with these matters. If you're line-managing people who have the capacity to bear children, consider that my previous experience and fears may not be unusual, and be sensitive about having open conversations, and don't judge those outcomes either.

It is important to remember that, just as any of us might go through something temporary, uncomfortable or upsetting, it doesn't necessarily impact on our ability to do our jobs other than in the immediate or short-term. Checking-in with staff should be done with emotional and cultural intelligence, and never make assumptions about how someone is feeling or what might, or not be, any ongoing repercussions of their situation.

Asking 'when are you having children?' can be intrusive for those who, for example, might be going through IVF, or not want them – and why would you be asking that question anyway? There are ways to engage in these things, if necessary, with proper thought and care to navigate them well.

TESTIMONIAL

If I speak about pregnancy and my return to work: it's the lack of empathy and, to be honest, I don't think it's just across the built environment, it's the workplace in general. They don't seem to be prepared, or if they prepare, it's all on the surface. When someone comes back from maternity or from long sickness, it's the same. I had a time where I had surgery and I returned to work after one month. You return [to work] and you just feel like a stranger. You feel that they're not really including you, nobody tries to find out how you are – you return and it's just business as usual.

As a minority ethnic, you always have to go the extra mile, having this cap you wear because you have to show this performance act that you take when you work, when you are not part of the majority group, you tend to overdo it. I'm not doing it anymore.

Menopause

It's important that organisations and managers know how to provide support for employees who are on their journey through menopause. Again, culture and heritage will play a part here. Raising awareness on this topic, and reducing the stigma attached to it, is vital so that appropriate discussions can take place and inform the development of effective guidance and resources. According to the Chartered Institute for Professional Development (CIPD), women over 50 (that is, the majority of individuals who experience menopause) are the fastest growing demographic within the UK's workforce.

Fifty-nine per cent of working women aged 45 to 55 say the menopause has had a negative impact on them at work. Impacting both attendance and performance, it's clear that this is not just an individual issue, but an organisational one. And it's clear that this age group is off-ramping from built environment professions – so we need to ask if the menopause is a factor here.

QR Code 4.3 WATCH: RIBA discussion about the impact of menopause in the workplace.

QR Code 4.4 READ: RIBA Menopause Guidance for Colleagues and Managers.

By the time I started experiencing peri-menopausal symptoms, I long since abandoned any sense of shame, and felt no concern when my then boss had to, literally, carry me into a local hotel to sleep off some bizarre vestibular migraine symptoms I was dealing with, in the early days.

As the average age of women RIBA Chartered Architects is 44, it is important that as we develop guidance for our organisations and the built environment professions, like that produced at the RIBA,[15] that we begin by listening and learning from individuals who have lived experience (see QR Code 4.3).

I should be explicit here, that all of this advice, and the inclusive behaviours, extend to benefiting men as well as women. Men shouldn't have to hide when they and their partners are going through challenges due to hormonal issues. Everyone gains when a workplace culture has planned for these concerns (see QR Code 4.4).

Ideally, what is required is better systemic state and business support with, for example, childcare and associated impacts, so that we can all thrive. In the meantime, organisations can create workforce plans that eschew these biases, factor in these realities proactively, and put in place robust supportive policies which encourage all staff to succeed.

CASE STUDY: Workforce Planning

Clare Nash, Clare Nash Architects

What is the issue you were trying to address?

The first one that changed everything was sorting out my money mindset in relation to fees. At the same time, niche-ing so that I felt I represented more value to the client, which is a bit of an imposter syndrome thing, but also demonstrating, really well, what the client was getting that was unique to me. And then growing my team, making clear what we can offer versus what other architects can offer to make it easier for them to make a choice.

How did you do that?

I started that with blogging and then I just got brave one day and doubled my fees. I didn't do any proper calculations, I just decided it's not enough. Doubling it didn't actually work like that completely financially, but it just made sense in my head.

I thought I'd lose loads of clients, but I didn't. The same amount [of clients] kept coming in and I was in a situation where I was having too much work because of the success of the blogging. I went to a conference a while ago, and Tom Miller said that if you go after three clients, you expect those clients to be going after three quotes. It's highly likely that you're going to only win a third of those projects. So, if you're winning more than that usually means you're too cheap. I thought, in hindsight, that's probably a lot of what was going on, why I was winning too much work. Even when I doubled my fees, the work still came in. That was another big indicator of how low it was before. Since then, I've been a bit more accurate about pricing and because I've got the data now with the time sheets, how long things take roughly, what my staff costs are, and the overheads, over time I've become much more serious about the financial side of the business.

The other big eye-opening thing was when I worked with a developer client, and they made £200,000 pure profit from the extra design value that I added to that project. The estate agent said it was unique to the area.

It was really clear that my impact and the financial value of that on that particular project and my fees were just such a tiny fraction of it. I thought, that's enough. I'm not going to give it away anymore. I'm not running a charity.

We're authentically ourselves and so people are attracted to our kind of way of being, which is quite relaxed and informal and appreciating the world, the environment and nature.

It's all being massively positive and then a much better work–life balance as well, because I'm not having to work stupid hours to make reasonable money.

It's then the same for staff, because they want to feel like their work is going towards something beneficial. It allows us to not do any unpaid overtime. Sometimes projects do need a bit of extra work, but it's all paid for. It's not very often that we do that and, in those cases, we just all pull together. I'd say it's about twice a year. There's a few extra hours put into a project, the rest of the time you can go for a swim in the afternoon if you want to. It's more how real life works. Real life doesn't fit into the nine to five bracket.

When I was growing the business, I didn't want to commute, and I didn't want to go to an office. My very first employee was a student where I was also teaching (not my student). I thought if I'm going to employ students, they won't necessarily have a car and I live out in the countryside. In the first instance I was offering very part-time work because of financial reasons. I thought it's just too scary to take on a full-time salary straight away when you don't even know if it's going to work. I thought it would really suit students, they could do it around their studies and it is much better pay than bar work and they're getting content for their CV at the same time.

I just trusted them to do the hours when they could fit it in and then we'd have our meeting, to discuss any problems. I still really believe in face-to-face at least once a week, when it was Covid that went virtual.

Although not my preference, being virtual is really convenient. We still have virtual meetings occasionally because sometimes logistics are just against us or sickness or whatever. The vast majority of the time we meet in real life and now we have a meeting room. It's extended so it's a work together day rather than just a couple of us meeting and people pop in and out.

Slack is a really useful tool. We're always writing in it to each other about the projects because we are not sat next to each other. It's really handy for the Part IIs to see the project history and all the discussions and things all written down and handy if we ever need to explain timelines to clients.

The parents in the team all work flexibly around their child-care commitments. And those with children that need extra help, it wouldn't be possible in a typical office situation to work without that, but they are incredibly talented women and men.

I'm not monitoring what the staff do all the time, it's just based on if the invoices can go out or not, and progress. We upload screenshots of where we're at. We have design discussions on Slack and in real life.

What have been the outcomes of your approach?

I definitely advocate for planning and preparation, seeing how it works, adapting, going back to the beginning, if it doesn't quite work out – whatever it is, whether it's changing your fees, flexible working, growing the team.

I am quite good at strategy and thinking, big picture stuff. I tend to focus on the big overall aims. I work out the details as I go along. I do have backup from team members who are more detailed thinkers than me. I'm good at starting projects and doing the overall vision and things and I'll keep kind of popping in and out of stuff, but I'm not really the person who is best fully developing and detailing a project. So, I've a built a team that complement my skills.

What reflections and learning have you had on your approach?

I always reflect. I have consistent business coaching, sometimes it's an external coach I work with for a range of sessions until I achieve what I want to achieve. Other times, I'm part of a women's coaching group – about six of us and we all run different companies. We're all quite creative people. That's been going for years. I find that so supportive and helpful, just somebody else to talk to about business problems that you can't talk to the team about. Sometimes you need to work out your own thinking before you announce it to everybody.

Figure 4.3 Clare Nash Architecture Team. Photograph by Vivacious Mel Photography.

BEHAVIOURAL ANALYSIS

DRIVE: Figuring out what would drive you to make the changes so you can plan more successfully for the future, might start with sorting out fees, it might be something else. Consider what the factors are, intrinsic and extrinsic.

KNOWLEDGE: As you feel your way forward with your workforce planning, make proper notes of what you're learning and understanding from other practices, networking and experiences.

STRATEGY: Think about how you could implement changes as you wish to grow. What would be your priorities and ensure that you factor in inclusive measures to your growth plans and overall aims. Don't make assumptions about how this would play out but consider a variety of outcomes.

ACTION: Ensure your plans have some adaptability baked into them, so you can flex as necessary and remain agile, learning and reflecting with others to get good feedback on your approach.

Outcomes

The potential EDI outcomes for workforce planning encompass several essential elements that contribute to fostering a more inclusive and diverse organisation. These outcomes are instrumental in guiding and measuring the success of EDI efforts.

The articulation of clear and tangible EDI objectives in the workforce plan is a fundamental step. By setting specific goals related to diversity and inclusion, an organisation demonstrates its commitment to promoting diversity and inclusivity within its workforce.

We need to address gaps in knowledge, skills and abilities. This is essential in creating an inclusive work environment. Ensuring that all employees have access to the necessary resources and support to thrive is crucial for achieving EDI goals.

Also, an organisation's commitment to addressing demographic over- and under-representation highlights their dedication to building a workforce that mirrors the diversity of the broader community.

The ability to assess the outcomes of workforce planning in achieving the aim of becoming a more inclusive organisation is crucial for measuring the effectiveness of EDI efforts. This evaluation enables you to make data-driven decisions and implement necessary adjustments to continually improve inclusivity within the organisation.

By achieving these potential EDI outcomes, your organisation takes significant strides towards fostering a work environment where every individual is valued, empowered, and celebrated for their unique contributions. Embracing diversity and creating an inclusive culture not only benefits employees but also enhances the organisation's overall performance and impact on society.

TESTIMONIAL

It's so much better now than it was. We have facilities, we have welcoming and support, but sometimes what I find difficult in this industry now is challenging people in day-to-day life. If I want to get something done, if it's coming from me, they don't do it sometimes. I just have to talk to my boss and get things done through him. That needs to be addressed and changed.

I don't know if it's because I'm a woman or if it's because of something else? Is it because I just started? It could be anything else. It's just my experience at the minute, it's been one year for me already.

- Your business should have a workforce plan which places EDI principles at its heart across all nine stages
- Having the right data to plan well could be something you gather, but your professional body should be able to help.
- Consider the potential outcomes you'd like to see and plan backwards, taking into account the measures you'll use.
- In order to manage out discrimination, create a plan that's supportive of, for example, the inevitability of people starting and growing their families and the different needs of different bodies.
- Normalise discussions in the workplace about different experiences. Men as well as women benefit from this, as we're all impacted directly and indirectly by these issues.

REMUNERATION

What Is Remuneration?

Let's do a bit of defining: when people put in time and effort and deliver for an organisation, they get paid and may get other benefits too, based on what their role requires. This is remuneration.

The pay itself could come in lots of different forms, across different timeframes, be related to performance, and so on. This may be fixed or negotiated. Benefits include annual leave, which is paid, pension contributions, access to private healthcare, and a host of other perks, all of which cost the organisation money, but which provide value to both the individual and the business. A happy, well compensated person tends to be a more productive one.

It stands to reason, then, that all of these different elements need to be considered through the lens of inclusion to ensure equity and what can be objectively seen as fairness.

Transparency is the key to delivering this. According to the Fawcett Society, despite legislation, if we don't know what individuals are getting paid, how can women use the legislation to act on their concerns? The Society has been campaigning on the 'right to know' so everyone can be clear they are being paid fairly. Currently, women have to go to tribunal just to find out. This is where allyship is so important. Men can share with their women colleagues what they're getting paid to ensure gender pay equality.

Culturally, this is a significant shift. Being open about how much you are being paid inside and outside of work is not a conversation that people easily have, and so, if it is taken out of the hands of individuals and transparency is placed within a searchable system by job title and role requirements, then it is easier to determine if there are gaps to be addressed.

- Develop policies, procedures and practices that embed EDI into your remuneration processes and work collaboratively with teams when pay is under discussion.
- Review market rates themselves for fairness for roles, with due regard for percentage comparison with the highest earner in the organisation.
- Explicitly describe what range of salary and which benefits are offered for a role providing a defined list of activities.
- Where creep beyond the above occurs, be prepared for discussions around compensation.
- Any changes to pay, benefits, perks and ancillary remuneration should be overtly, explicitly and transparently communicated in as many ways and as many platforms as appropriate.
- Consider your Environmental, Social and Governance commitments and inclusive values commitments when deciding on perks to offer, for example, time off for volunteering.

Pay Gaps

It seems obvious, equal pay for equal work; in fact, it is illegal not to pay equally for equal work, and yet it happens. The perpetual nature of gender and ethnicity pay gaps, and the fact that they are widening in architecture and construction, according to 2022 figures reported in 2023, must be addressed.

Equal pay is when doing work of equal value, or the same work, men and women, whatever racial group or identity, all must be paid the same. It is illegal not to do so (Equality Act 2010, precursor Equal Pay Act 1970).

The **gender pay gap** is about average pay. So, the difference between the average pay of women and the average pay of men across bands and grades, as they compare. Pay discrimination, that is, not fulfilling equal pay, may be a contributory factor to the gap, but there are other factors, for example, how many more men are in senior leadership positions and therefore earning more, compared with women in those roles. Women have more interruptions to their career and aren't always supported to return at the same level as when they had to pause, and are structurally pushed by business and policies to take on more caring and juggling of career and other responsibilities.

The **pension gap** is about average provision for retirement for women as opposed to men, caused by the fact that as women go through life and careers they are structurally financially disadvantaged with maternity leave and part-time working which accumulates and catches up with them.

The **ethnicity pay gap** is the difference in average pay between white people and racialised people in your workforce.

Why Do These Gaps Exist?

Below is a closer look at the gender pay gap, rather than racial pay gap, because there's more evidence and research done into the disparities, and the issues around systemic racial discrimination are wide and varied.

The gender pay gap is a long-standing feature of labour markets across the globe. There are many theories that explore this[16] and include the ideas that:

- Differential gender roles are adopted early on in life.

Men and women often end up taking different paths in education and work, and this leads to variations in how much they get paid. It's not like anyone consciously decides to stick to traditional gender roles. Instead, these choices are shaped by social pressures and expectations, and they tend to get passed down from one generation to the next. I was speaking to a woman who now runs a construction company about her path into the profession. She said that when she was given careers advice at school, she was told about secretarial roles, hairdressing and so on, this was within the last 20 years.

- Women having lower 'human capital' than men.

Due to historic lack of access to education, opportunities and skills development, men had a comparative advantage over women and were supported to develop careers. When it comes to getting an education, especially in terms of which college you attend and what you study, men still seem to have the upper hand.

- Men occupying higher positions within an occupation.

Due to the above, other arguments already cited, and a number of other biases, men are progressed more easily in careers.

• Women tend to be overrepresented in low-paid jobs.

Jobs with lots of women in them are often called 'feminised', for example, cleaning, caring and clerical, and so on. What researchers have noticed is that when there are more women in a job, the pay tends to be lower on average. This means that both men and women in feminised jobs end up with lower pay. But since there are more women in these roles, they're hit harder by this pay gap.

• Work done by women is socially and economically undervalued.

The fact that the gender pay gap still exists hints at the idea that there might be a sort of stigma around jobs that are mostly done by women. There are theories that suggest that some types of work are seen as less important or less valuable simply because they're traditionally associated with women.

As built environment professions are more associated with men, plus the other theories in combination, could be seen as reasons for pay gaps persisting.

We have known about the issues for many years and have been recording the statistics, however, the pay gaps are not only continuing – they're widening. My view is that this is due to:

• Complacency around the issue, every year everyone says, 'we must do better' but rarely do.
• None of the issues described are being tackled systemically, because people don't investigate how.
• COVID-19 embedded some biased opinions and responses, due to people being in enforced cognitive bubbles.
• Fallacy of unbiased behaviour, because people think they're not biased they then embed the behaviour around, for example, hiring and salary decisions
• Lack of accountability – despite the news articles, no one is facing any consequences for not making progress.

Whatever your size, your firms should be looking at these things. Any widening of pay gaps, gender or ethnicity, should be cause for concern and serious introspection, as it is indicative of systemic discrimination and a failure to consciously act to prevent or mitigate it.

I like to remind you, as I've suggested earlier, it's a fallacy that simply by knowing we're biased, we will act in a less biased way. We need to create, implement and enforce policies, procedures and practices to mitigate the impact of hidden bias. Bias will show up in widening pay gaps.

When the RIBA Benchmarking report came out in 2022, it uncovered increases in both the gender and ethnicity pay gap among practices with 100-plus employees who volunteered their metrics. I commented at the time:

> Having the data is an amazing opportunity. It's an opportunity to dig behind it and look at the behaviours, processes and policies that are leading to e.g. staff from underrepresented groups leaving, attracting different groups at senior levels, and how you are treating, retaining and progressing your talent. It's an opportunity to listen more acutely and plan for a different future. It's an opportunity for change. I hope leadership will take, with both hands, these opportunities for reflection – if necessary, bring in the expertise they need to help them – and do this better.[17]

Of course, I stand by this, and I am grateful to have this opportunity to suggest strategic ways forward.

Measures

As always, collecting data to track change helps keep you accountable for the values you purport to hold and promises you may make to staff. For smaller organisations, those responsible for payroll have to keep their organisations honest when publishing the details would reveal personal information, and therefore it's not possible.

- Gather input on employee approval or discontent with the fairness of the actual compensation and benefits they receive.
- Monitor and document the number and nature of grievances and disagreements related to compensation and benefits within the organisation.
- Examine workforce compensation and benefits data to uncover any discrepancies and disparities in pay and perks. This includes assessing variations across job categories, geographic locations and pay structures.

- Collect feedback regarding employee satisfaction or dissatisfaction with the fairness of our organisation's compensation and benefits policies, processes and practices.

Kirsty Howard of Gratton Construction (see case study) in her exemplary approach to pay, ensures the data is robust around market rate, constantly doing the checks and balances to be fair, and being explicit about the process and progress across bands. If a construction firm can manage it and thrive, I'm sure any profession can.

TESTIMONIAL

Ultimately if I'm wanting empathy, I'm wanting my needs to be met, I can't just expect that other person to understand me and meet my needs. I also have to try and understand them and meet their needs.

I've got that back quite a lot more in construction because a lot of the behaviour (particularly the negative behaviour) is much more on the surface. That's always been one of the positive aspects of construction that I've noticed and seen, that if there's something untoward, you can see it. It's very, very direct and it's clear. Whereas in the corporate environment, it's fundamentally different, it's a lot more under the table. It's a lot more under the surface and in many ways can be a little bit more devious because of that and it's harder to spot.

One has to be a lot more guarded in a different way. At least on a construction site, if I didn't like being around someone or in a certain space, I can go and work somewhere else, wait until that person's finished what they're doing and then go back. In a corporate environment it's much harder, if not impossible to do that.

Government Guidance on Ethnicity Pay Gap Reporting

The UK government's new advice on ethnicity pay gap reporting[18] agrees that:

> Ethnicity pay reporting is more complex than gender pay reporting. While gender pay analysis only involves a comparison between two groups, ethnicity pay analysis can potentially involve many more ethnic groups, depending on how ethnically diverse a workforce is.

This is where the issues start to unravel. Race is a completely made-up idea, unlike the gender pay gap, which is rooted in extremes of biological sex, so allowing you to make some clearer distinctions.

> Unlike gender pay reporting, employers may also have to make decisions about how best to combine different ethnic groups to ensure their results are reliable and statistically sound and to protect confidentiality.

Do this, and you may end up hiding issues, because, of course, what if only Brown men are holding leadership positions and being paid fairly, but Black women are nowhere to be seen, what about those who have mixed racial backgrounds? The grouping together of racialised groups starts to get fraught.

> These complexities also mean that employers should carefully scrutinise and explore the underlying causes for any pay disparities.

However, the government guidance also says (italics are my emphasis):

> There *could be legitimate reasons why there are variations in pay across ethnic groups.* It *should not be assumed* that any disparities are necessarily a result of discrimination. Where pay differences arise, further analysis is recommended to help employers understand the *real* causes and decide whether further action is needed.

This is problematic to find in government guidance, giving employers a backdoor to claim legitimacy for issues. It is worth noting the government that produced this guidance is the same government that produced the Sewell Report,[19] insisting that systemic and institutional racism didn't exist and that slavery benefited Black people.[20]

They claim that pay disparities may be due to a number of reasons. For instance:

> lower pay among a particular ethnic group may be because that group disproportionately applies for lower paid, more junior positions in an organisation.

It does go onto say:

> On the other hand, it could be because the company does not provide
> adequate progression opportunities for people from that ethnic group. It
> is up to employers to do further work or collate other available data (for
> example, staff surveys, data on recruitment and progression) to identify
> and understand the underlying causes.

This latter part of the guidance I can more easily get behind. Although, I
would insist employers actually 'do the further work', rather than suggest
to employers they can if they can be bothered.

'VICARS' OF THE BUILT ENVIRONMENT?

One of the key concerns amongst built environment professions is the
poor pay for time invested return for those becoming architects.

In researching this book, I have been considering that, of the built
environment roles, architecture may have been considered more of
a vocation, more than anything else, because of the pay. The average
salary after 7–10 years of training to become Chartered is around
£40,000.[21] Comparative training times, also for vocational work,
might be junior doctors, whose salary ranges hugely as there are a lot
of 'it depends' factors, from about £35,000 up to £80,000.[22] Overtime
tends to be paid. However, the closest I found for this level for training
and salary, unpaid overtime, and so on, was becoming a Church of
England vicar, which takes about eight years to become fully ordained,
with an average salary of about £30,000. There are other benefits however, as you can get a house and some bills paid as part of the job,
and the Church of England describe the 'Total Value of the Package' as
£50,000.[23]

However, the vocation argument would consider a more social focus
in the work produced. And, whilst I'm with Dr Flora Samuel, who in
her book *Why Architects Matter* (2018) suggests 'all architects are supposed
to be working in the public interest', and RIBA's stated mission on the
Charities Commission website[24] is to 'advance architecture by demonstrating public benefit', we know there's a great deal of diversity in
approaches and motivations for those who engage in the discipline of
architecture. Although a privileged and paternalistic view of benevolence

may well have been the motivation of some in pursuing the profession, it's not always the case nor feasible to afford to do so.

Overtime

It was quite insightful to see this kind of clause in architecture employment contracts:

> By entering into this agreement you waive your rights under the Working Time Regulations 1998 to a maximum weekly working time of 48 hours for each 7 days. Consequently, you agree that your working time may exceed 48 hours in any 7 day period. This waiver will apply indefinitely, but may be terminated by you giving to the Employer three months' prior written notice. If you decide to terminate the waiver, the Employer must ensure that it does not offer you work which would result in you working for more than 48 hours in any week. Therefore, you must keep the Employer informed of the hours that you work for third parties so that it can comply with this obligation.

Overtime should either be paid or granted as a matter of individual choice of goodwill. Whilst the need to work additional hours may vary by role and may fluctuate depending on project workload there needs to be a cap on working hours. If it is likely to be a regular or frequent requirement to work overtime, employees should talk to their line manager if they regularly find it impossible to do their role in the standard 37.5-hour week as this may indicate that they need support (perhaps additional training or help with time management), or there is more resource required in the team; in all cases such a clause would be unnecessary.

Whilst clauses like this continue to be standard fare, it is impossible to ensure employees have rights. The Working Time Directive was introduced to protect from the unscrupulous. Only the unscrupulous would want to usurp it and require new staff to surrender it.

The fees and compensation debate in architecture continues to rage, and it remains fundamental to issues of inclusivity in the profession.

As the keynote speaker at RIBA London's 2023 Regional Awards ceremony, Peter George, Strategic Director of Economy and Sustainability at Ealing Council (see Figure 4.4), had this to say on the matter:[25]

> I felt really uncomfortable when, on an Open London tour that I was leading, I was asked by two Black parents whether I thought their daughter should go to architecture school.

Figure 4.4 Peter George, Strategic Director of Economy and Sustainability at Ealing Council, delivering the keynote at RIBA London Regional Awards ceremony. Photograph by the author.

What could I say?

I couldn't not mention the fact that the gender pay gap in the architectural industry is actually getting worse. I had to say that pay relative to years of study was poor. And how could I not mention that the number of Black architects has declined to only 1%? I hated the fact that I could not in good faith recommend this once great profession of yours as a good career option for their daughter. It genuinely makes me sad.

A profession that has an Architect Benevolent Society and a podcast called the Broke Architect is a broken profession. And RIBA are campaigning on their website for architects to earn over the London living wage. For us non-architects in the room it's unfathomable that you can study years, too long, to become a qualified architect and then not earn the living wage.

So, until the question of architectural salaries, and therefore fees is addressed, and architectural practices, you stop this race to the bottom, until that ends, you will continue to have a diversity problem in your industry. So, instead of campaigning for minimum salary pay perhaps industry bodies like RIBA could lead on the restoration of fee guidance to restore respectable salaries and restore a sense of pride in the architectural profession.

As Clare Nash notes in her case study, and across many practices and studios I've come into contact with, it is perfectly feasible to pay fairly, live well, work reasonable hours and win projects. As I keep reiterating, other practices just have to trust that inclusive actions work, and demonstrate the behaviours that lead to them.

Outcomes

As you consider what good looks like, you should first look at your organisation's policies, processes and practices to strive to embody the principles of fairness, inclusivity, equity and transparency. This entails ensuring that every employee, irrespective of their background, feels that the way they are compensated is just and clear-cut.

The compensation structure should be designed to uphold the principle of equal pay for work of equal value. This means that individuals performing roles of equivalent significance are remunerated on an equivalent basis, irrespective of their personal characteristics.

Any existing disparities in pay that may be linked to diversity-related factors are acknowledged and proactively addressed. No one should have to go to tribunal if you've got things wrong. Fess-up and do the right thing. Anomalies should be scrutinised, and steps taken to rectify them to ensure that compensation is not influenced by factors unrelated to job performance.

Your organisation should actively cultivate a reputation among stakeholders as an inclusive employer that adheres to fair and equitable remuneration policies, processes and practices. Be known for striving to be recognised for its commitment to EDI values, ensuring that its remuneration approach aligns with the broader goal of fostering diversity and inclusivity within the workplace.

Again, please note, the behavioural piece is fundamental to success. I can suggest what to do, but you still have to use the right behaviours to follow through on doing it.

Whilst I reference the impact on certain groups, you may have noticed I very rarely say, 'do this for women', or 'do that for Black and Brown people', this is because an inclusive approach is inclusive of all, not just specific characteristics, and I refer you again to the intersectionality issue. Those who are discriminated against often have many layers to their identities.

So, when it comes to issues of fair remuneration when the systems are robust, whether you're a woman, Black, disabled, gay, tertiary-educated, all or none, the system will support an equitable outcome.

Kirsty Howard, Gratton Construction

What was the situation you were trying to address?

I was 17 when I entered the construction industry, working for a contractor in a clerical role. I found it really interesting. Every day was different, and I wanted to develop my career. I initially built up my career through experience, going through the roles and progressing through experience and formalising those with the qualifications. As I was doing that, one thing I noticed was that, in the industry, males who were in the same roles as me were being paid considerably more than me.

There didn't seem to be a clear reason as to why, when you do all the things, you could argue about the qualifications, but I went and studied, I got the formal qualifications and I was doing everything I could do in my opinion to get the experience, to get qualified, and do my job to the best of my ability. The firm didn't have any issues whatsoever with my knowledge, with my role, with my expertise in what I was doing. But it seemed as though, the more I progressed, the more there was a salary gap. So, at a more junior level you'd only notice a salary gap of £2–3k, but actually, when I was trying to push to get into these more senior positions, I was only being marginally crept up in terms of my salary. Whereas when they were recruiting males into that role they were getting paid far more money. Sometimes it was £10k more a year. So that really struck me. I was quite determined to succeed anyway. It wasn't just about the money. I wanted to succeed in the industry and display perseverance, but I had days where I would get very frustrated, at the pay situation anyway.

So, I know how that feels, and I can only imagine how it would put people off continuing in their construction career. So, once I started my own business, one of the things I was passionate about, through working in construction and, and through all the research I did for my dissertation too, was making equality, diversity and inclusion a really big part of the business. And one of the focuses, you can say it's on gender pay gap, but my approach to it is less about focusing on there being a gap if that makes sense.

It's less about 'let's focus on what men are paid, and let's focus on what women are paid' and more to try to remove the demographic approach to that completely. Just look at face value: What are their skills, what are their experience, how do they fit into the role? And I think that is the approach I'm taking.

How are you doing that?

We're trying to remove any of the demographics in the selection process. You know, are they a male or female? How old are they? All these things that people have done in the past, either on purpose, consciously or subconsciously, and made that a real thing.

I'm not positively discriminating and going out there to recruit women on purpose, we've got a good divide. So, at the moment, in terms of the male and female split, all sorts of head office or non-trade staff, 70 per cent of the people that work here are female.

In terms of directors, there are only two of us, so, senior wise it's a 50/50 male/female split. In terms of the middle management layer, that's where there's a higher percentage of women. It's just taking people for face value. When they have the qualification that's relevant, they have the skills, they've got the experience, they've got the persona for the role – those are relevant, as opposed to meeting people with a preconception that they might not be suitable because they're from a certain demographic or something like that.

The whole approach here is around culture anyway. That's how we've tackled it. In terms of pay, I don't look at anything other than pay on market value. I look at market irrespective of age or experience or anything like that. I focus a lot on what the market rate is paying for a role at the time.

If the market is paying a certain salary for that role at that time, that is the salary we offer somebody. We set our salary band on the market as opposed to kind of bringing anything else into it, which keeps it completely fair.

Childcare, for example, we have a colleague who lost her job when her previous employer found out she was pregnant. When her baby was six months old and she wanted to come back to work, we made her a role that would fit her lifestyle. She's got good skills, she's got the experience, she's got the personality, and she's got the buy-in.

She does a couple of days in the office and she does the other days at home, she has flexible hours. I say to her, as long as you do your core hours between eight and five, you can do the hours around your home life. She wants to do the work, so, does it matter to me when she does it? Not really. So why would I make it an issue for her?

What have the outcomes been from this approach?

We haven't had recruitment issues. When we've advertised for roles, we've had good candidates apply and we've always been able to fill positions. We like people to feel like they want to work here. People do better in their role if they feel they are being paid fairly. We don't want them to look at what else is out there, or if they do, they see the pay is fair.

We also look at other benefits; we believe a lot in annual leave. Our annual leave allowance is quite a bit above the guidelines because we want people to feel that they can have a decent amount of time off a year. We have quite a flexible culture because we believe that if you've got the right person in the role and, very lucky that everyone is actually like this, that they are so bought into the business and they're so genuinely invested in the business. I know they're committed and, does it really matter anyway, if they're a bit late, if they're doing their best? feel like that helps with the culture in terms of managing it all.

What learning and reflections have you had about your approach?

We haven't been as successful with on-site roles, where we don't have women applying. There is a supply issue. If I do, I will still stick to my principle, if you are the best for the role, you'll get the role and just be fair to everybody. It wouldn't be fair to get picked for a role because you fit a demographic.

BEHAVIOURAL ANALYSIS

DRIVE: Rather than driving wages down, to get good people who feel valued requires you to develop the intrinsic and extrinsic motivators to push you to pay well even if you feel profits will take an initial hit. What other outcomes can you imagine from paying people better?

KNOWLEDGE: Do the research – what do you need to know about pay and market rates for different levels of expertise, and what can you do to support the best options?

STRATEGY: Plan for how your organisation will cascade pay and the ratio of the top paid versus the least and other benefits that you could use as compensation to attract great people.

ACTION: Having a wider flexible culture around work life means it's possible to have adaptability built in too, even when you can't have a pay system that's flexible.

REMUNERATION: KEY TAKEAWAYS

- Understand different gaps and investigate them whatever your size of practice.
- Government guidance isn't always robust, do what's ethical instead.
- A cultural shift towards transparency happens in systems, rather than with individuals.
- Allies can help address pay gap issues.
- Architects can choose to pay fairly rather than 'race to the bottom' with fees.
- Equitable systems work for all, no one is disadvantaged in them.
- Taking a robust approach to fair pay is indicative of a culture where people thrive, and so productivity tends to be higher.

INCLUSIVE RECRUITMENT

What is recruitment?

Recruitment is … attracting, sourcing, assessing, selecting, employing.
People with … knowledge, skills, abilities, capabilities.
In order to meet … business objectives and budget.

In theory! In practice, it can be getting your mate in to help out, and you end up employing them, because you're sure they'll be a good laugh and generally get the job done. Or putting out an advert, but then a colleague says, 'Oh, I know someone who'll be good for that', and you blindly go through the perception of a process, knowing you're going to hire them anyway. It can work out because those people 'fit'. More on this in a moment.

What is *inclusive* recruitment?

Inclusive recruitment is … attracting, sourcing, assessing, selecting, employing.
People with … knowledge, skills, abilities, capabilities.
In order to meet … business objectives and budget.
With procedures … that mitigate unhelpful bias at every stage of this process to ensure equitable outcomes.

Taking yourselves through an entirely different approach to recruitment will be a challenge to your biases, and so require clear procedures which you shouldn't be consciously trying to manipulate, in order to reach different outcomes.

Once you hire differently, the organisational culture must support the inclusion of difference. This shouldn't be about trying to mould someone to 'fit in'.

The Danger of 'Culture Fit'

When we hear the term 'culture fit', this should ring alarm bells. This is completely soaked, permeated through, with unhelpful bias. So, we need to stop thinking about culture fit, and start thinking about 'culture add' (see Figure 4.5).

When we talk about culture fit, we usually mean hiring people that will magically fit into a company's culture. We see it all the time in architecture practices and surveying firms, as well as on construction sites. It works in theory, but what you're really doing is hiring for a homogeneous team.

Teams are effective if they're diverse and inclusive. We need to create that culture of inclusion when we have lots of different ways of doing things, backgrounds, perspectives, values, and so on. So, the problem with hiring for culture fit is that you end up hiring the same kind of person over and over again.

If you want to do that, that's fine. Go ahead and have your homogeneous team over there. And you will be very effective and you will get

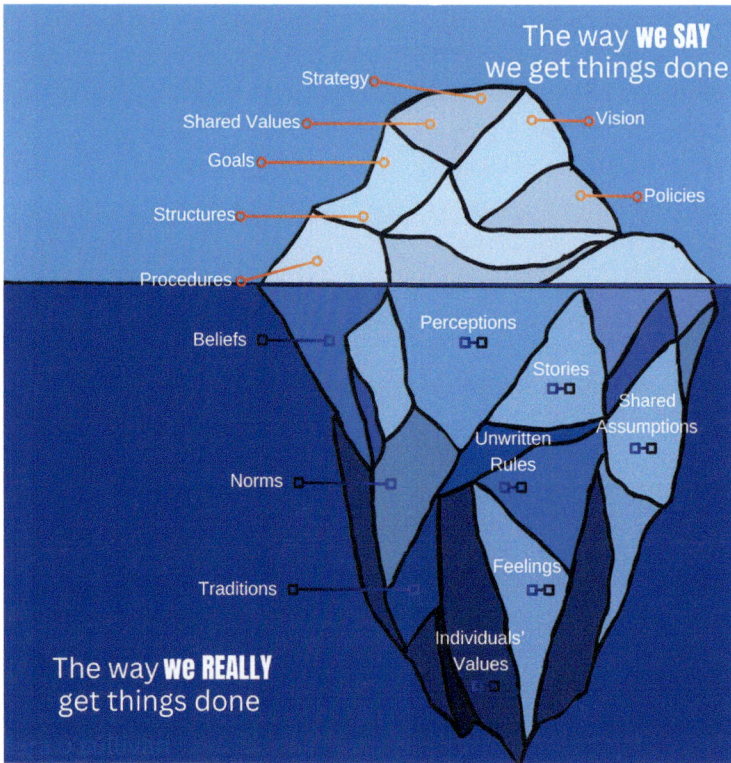

The way **we SAY** we get things done

Strategy
Shared Values
Goals
Structures
Procedures
Vision
Policies

Beliefs
Perceptions
Stories
Shared Assumptions
Unwritten Rules
Norms
Feelings
Traditions
Individuals' Values

The way **we REALLY** get things done

Figure 4.5 The culture iceberg. Image by Tara O'Sullivan.

stuff done, but you're in danger of groupthink. You're in danger of not innovating. You're in danger of not actually moving forward with the world. You will fall behind, essentially. And no good business wants to fall behind.

The better thing to do, and all the research shows, that having a diverse team and inclusive culture is the better outcome.

When you're hiring for 'culture fit', this feeds into concerning matters like confirmation bias, affinity bias, and all those biases that leave you with the sense 'this feels comfortable to me', 'I would happily go to the pub with this person'. All of these things play out when you're talking about culture fit.

One of the dangers, too, around 'culture fit' rather than 'culture add', especially when only addressing representation and targets, is the initial false sense of security that you 'got the hire right' – there's a honeymoon period for all parties. A person feels welcomed and everyone enjoys having the novelty of the new person. Then, the new person settles in and they start to raise the issues, and bring their different perspectives, and they start to point out all the ways things can be done differently. And they push for accountability. That's when things start to go wrong, not just for the team, but for that individual, especially if they are the only person who looks like them or has their background, brought in to answer the 'diversity question'. I refer you back to 'The Problem Woman of Color [sic] in the Workplace'.

If you're going for culture add, but you are not willing to embrace the new different perspectives, you could create poor cultures amongst the team. People getting ostracised. What you really need to do as leaders in an organisation, which is shaping the culture, is to then to demonstrate the best behaviours the cultural intelligence piece I've been reiterating, and work on improving the culture of your organisation.

A reminder too about the point I made about representation. Just because someone might look different doesn't mean they're going to think differently as well. There are a range of things to think about.

TESTIMONIAL

My first job as a Part 1 in London, I'd not been asked to continue after my probation period because they said 'We don't have a lot of work, but if you had fitted in better, it might have been different.' That was when I learned my job is not to be an architect – my job is to fit in. It had been Ramadan and I'd been fasting, and I still went for drinks with them and stood outside in the rain while they smoked. But I was freezing, I was cold. I wasn't eating or drinking and I still went. Then I just went home because I didn't really want to do that. When I'm fasting, even then I was trying to be social.

I'm an incredibly social person – when it wasn't Ramadan, I do drink alcohol, I went out for a drink but they just binge-drank beer from a jug, and that's not what I do. So, I wasn't fitting in, I wasn't part of the group in any way, however much I try to be.

You may well have seen images like Figure 4.5 before, of the overt and implicit nature of organisational culture. What is apparent and above the surface isn't always what's actually going on. The purpose of recognising this and challenging the bias inherent in your culture is to bring that which is below the water line, above, and create those procedural changes to mitigate bias, so the unsaid and unwritten are not prevalent.

Hiring for Values

Values are very personal. People should be able to bring their values and beliefs into work and be entitled to hold those beliefs and values, even if they're very different to your own, as long as they do no harm to others through expressing them. If there is harm through that, then they need to keep expressions to themselves. People can know that they hold them, I am not advocating for hiding who you are, I'm advocating for acknowledging difference and creating cultures that work. For example, if some people have a faith, and other people are not people of faith, and it is not integral to you achieving organisational outcomes, that you have faith or not, then you can know, acknowledge and respect each other's difference without it getting in the way of team goals.

Having clearly stated organisational values are something candidates should be aware of, and new recruits should be onboarded with, so they're clear that working within a company comes with aligning with these stated values. Where, for any reason, organisational values are in conflict with personal values, this should be addressed at the earliest opportunity. It could be some rewording is necessary to make your values more inclusive, or if that isn't the case, the new recruit can decide if the organisation is one they still want to join (see Chapter Three and how Arthur Mamou-Mani describes this in the case study).

Creating an Inclusive Culture and Inclusive Recruitment

Inclusive recruitment is about having clear procedures for describing and assessing skills, abilities, experience and capabilities, in order to bring people into your organisation to achieve business outcomes. Recruiting for values is subjective and deciding whether someone's values are going to fit into an organisation would be a biased decision based on assumptions. Inclusive recruitment requires us to make policies, procedures and practices that are as objective as possible. Describe the role. Detail the requirements for that role. Can your candidate do those things? Yes? Great.

Then, there is the candidate who has all the role requirements you need, but they come with all these additional things, their background, their perceptions, their values, their beliefs. All the things that make us human. This human now is going to be working amongst all these other humans. How do we ensure that not only is everyone getting their jobs done, in an effective respectful environment, have a laugh too; we know that these things lead to good productivity.

This is something that we shouldn't recruit for. We recruit around objective criteria, but there's an additional HR and leadership piece, which is about that culture. We're full circle, because, how do you create that? It is through having cultural intelligence and making sure that the values of an organisation and the values of an individual can come together to create a third way that will drive results. That's an optimal way where everybody has to be culturally intelligent, not just the organisation, but individuals coming in as well.

Assessing people for cultural intelligence when they join a team should not be judgemental, but a tool to help them be part of the inclusive culture, and I'll describe this more under onboarding.

How Do You Do It?
Managing inclusive recruitment in organisations is about more than seeing more people from racialised backgrounds in your shortlists. It's about more than improving other areas of underrepresentation. It's about more than hiring someone who isn't your 'usual' candidate. Inclusive recruitment is about you changing the thoughts, behaviours, actions and processes around the attraction, selection, retention and inclusion of others.

That starts with assuming that, unless you are fundamentally doing your recruitment in different ways, prioritising finding great people with the right skills, over cost, convenience, speed and presumptions around educational background, then you are doing it in a biased way, and that categorically needs to change.

Going through the motions, having done some training, and simply believing you're doing the interviews differently, is not enough. Your staff demographic data will show you who you have in your workforce now and where your gaps are. Strategically looking to fill those gaps is part of the solution, but it's very important that you do so in a fair and inclusive way. The reason why those gaps exist is because of inherent bias in the hiring process and systems, and issues of inclusivity in your organisation to retain, and progress, people from a variety of backgrounds.

Aspects of Attraction, Recruitment and Selection
As outlined by Dr Binna Kandola in Racism at Work: The Danger of Indifference,[26] recruitment processes should be driven by the following considerations:

- Identifying the best selection criteria.
- Validity and reliability, the effectiveness of the process.
- Legality and fairness, there should be no adverse impact or disparity between how people are treated in the process.

- Convenience and practicality.
- Cost and development time.
- Applicant reactions.
- Evaluation.

You need to examine how you expend effort on each aspect and the order in which they're prioritised. Reflecting on our approach will help us identify what needs to change in order to eliminate bias.

Attracting a Variety of Candidates

Outward-facing presentations of your organisation have to look and feel like it would be a great inclusive place to work, so when you produce your job description and the advert people looking at your organisation feel there's a congruence between what you say you're asking for, and who you propose yourselves as being. This goes beyond images of a diversity of people on your website, this is about policies and messaging being consistent with inclusive values, as well as its inherent accessibility.

The reputation of your organisation in terms of media coverage and reaction to important inclusivity issues on your social media platforms needs to be explicit. You also need to think about where you're advertising and what your job advert says.

Relevant jobs boards are a great place to start, but it's not enough on its own. Other industry job boards are also worth looking at, but only insiders know about them. If you're only advertising on LinkedIn, that's not inclusive, as it may only be visible to those within your social network. Individuals who have not attended higher education are less likely to use it, as they are not plugged into professional networks, and this may mean people who could have the skills you need might miss out. This is particularly important if you are going to be proactive about supporting new routes to practice, such as apprenticeships. Referrals are also useful. However, a variety of biases can come into play if this isn't mitigated during selection processes. Reaching out to people at jobs fairs is also good, but where, when and who you have representing your practice makes a difference as to who you'll attract. So, you need to be prepared to invest in a variety of places and approaches to get a variety of people to know about your vacancies.

The details you include in the job requirements – are they really skills, or are they a wish list of traits and values? Levels of experience and educational background can exclude competent people who don't have exactly the degree you're looking for or are not old enough to have the amount of experience, but could still be developed and rise up to fulfilling the role. Unconsciously gendered wording can lead to fewer women applying. Check out 'Gender Decoder' to run your language through the system.

When it comes to values and traits, how those play out for people of different backgrounds varies and so it's better to stick to the core skills and capabilities required for a role, than traits. For example, 'we work in a competitive environment and strive for the best results': 'competitive' can be interpreted in a number of different ways and some people may prefer to achieve results collaboratively and the result is still a great outcome. Individuals from certain backgrounds may even have been criticised for their competitive approach, despite an environment claiming to value it, so that can lead to people not responding for that reason.

Focusing on skills, rather than behavioural traits, will help. So, if you need 'data analysis accurately turned around quickly', it is better than 'eye for detail'. 'Understanding of how to engage a variety of clients' is preferable to 'can build rapport easily'.

CASE STUDY: Inclusive Recruitment

Jess Littlewood, Programmes Manager, Public Practice

What's the issue you're trying to address with your approach?

First of all, there's a whole chunk of marketing and campaigning that comes before the actual recruitment side of stuff to make sure that we're reaching and engaging qualified people who may be interested in shifting to a purpose-led role in the public sector. We work with our Alums network to share their journeys and day-to-day experiences to inspire the next generation of place-makers to apply to the programme. If we are lacking in certain areas, we make sure that we're going to our partners or to certain geographical locations, to ensure that we do have a good diversity of people coming onto the programme that are right to apply, for us to then go through the recruitment process.

We want to ensure that each stage of our recruitment – online applications, assessment days, which consist of a presentation, a group exercise and interview – are all as inclusive as they can be.

How do you do that?

It starts with an online application; we don't ask for CVs at the first point. We know that the correlation between how well someone performs in a job and what their CV looks like does not represent how well they can work in that job. In online applications we ask for details about themselves.

We've started collecting CVs just as part of the eligibility check to ensure only those with a minimum of 3 years' experience in the built environment sector are being assessed. The CVs are not seen by anyone assessing at either the online assessment or assessment day stage.

We then have four competency-based questions, and that's it for our online application. Super simple. They've got a couple of hundred words to answer those. We've got little prompts in case the question itself is not clear enough. We're measuring against values and different competencies, looking at motivation to work in the public sector, interest in politics, an understanding of place and all the things that we think are the baseline that we need in terms of making a good public practice associate.

We then have a panel who independently review all the responses against defined scoring criteria.

We provide guidance for the panel – they have tips on how they can reduce their own bias. So not comparing, say, answer two with answer one, just marking against the criteria for that question.

With our assessment days, we know that people process information in different ways. So we give briefings ahead of time. Sharing the questions ahead of time with candidates allows everyone the same access to information and a better chance to prepare.

We can offer things in alternative formats as well and have, for example, visual adjustments. There are a lot of different adjustments in place for both online assessment days and the online applications as well.

Assessors are trained to try to eliminate any bias.

Where there could be differences in how people experience the day, we try and ensure there's a mix of activities, because we know that people might be better at presenting and other people might be better at the teamwork and the group exercise. So ensuring that we've got that kind of diversity of activity as well, so all can play to their strengths in the activities that they do.

We recognise it can be a bit hard for assessors that are used to traditional hiring, as we don't do prompting in the interviews. That's just to ensure consistency across the board, which sometimes might feel a little unnatural, but we also warn all of our candidates that that's in place and why that is in place as well.

After the assessment day, we ask for feedback from people that are successful and those who are not successful as well.

We review that every single time, so each time it is very iterative, and we look at what we could do differently based on the feedback from both assessors and also the candidates as well.

There is then another recruitment stage for people that are successfully matched. They then go and have an interview directly with the authority that they have been matched with. So at that point, we are not in the room with them. We are not leading that interview, but we can give guidance, if asked, on what that might look like.

People who come to us have applied to our programme as opposed to a specific role, which throws up its own challenges.

How does that then segue into the recruitment with others?

Our CEO and Partnership Manager can have interesting conversations with local authorities about qualification requirements (see Figure 4.6). Some organisations can say 'Oh, you need this qualification in order to do this role', but they don't necessarily need that at all. So we're having conversations about trying to be more open to different educational backgrounds as well, and the potential of removing some of those qualification requirements, but that side of stuff is a little bit more outside of our control because it's directly with the authority.

What learnings and reflections have you had on the process?

We have increased the amount of criteria that people are marked against for each of those activities to try and be more fair to allow a larger set, to ensure that our scores are relevant and reflective of the competencies that we're wanting to mark against.

We have changed some of the questions in our online applications. We did some work with the Work Psychology Group and they helped us review some of our questions. There were certain small things, like removing double barrel questions because it might be harder for certain groups of people to answer.

It's constantly changing, and we have to get that balance right in terms of different people's adjustments and whether we make that adjustment to the entire programme to try and be more inclusive, but considering if that is then excluding other people by bringing in that adjustment?

We like to remain open to the fact we still have a lot of learning to do. We need to continue to be experimental as well.

Figure 4.6 Public Practice CEO Pooja Agrawal delivering an EDI talk.

BEHAVIOURAL ANALYSIS

DRIVE: Wanting to address historic disparities in who is hired and needing to tackle the bias in the process has to be a fundamentally understood position before designing a process like this as otherwise you could find yourself trying to game your own system.

KNOWLEDGE: Gather the data to understand where the demographic gaps are and use these as part of your Positive Action process to attract a good range of candidates from a range of backgrounds.

STRATEGY: Check any assumptions you might have about why gaps might exist and challenge them, preparing and training yourself and the others involved in the recruitment process.

ACTION: Make sure those who need adaptations and assistance with the process are given it. The skills required to apply for a job are different to those required to do it. Don't deny yourself access to those skills by not opening up your process.

Positive Action

Positive action is not positive discrimination. Positive action is allowed under the Equality Act 2010. It is about taking specific steps to improve equality in the workplace. For example, to increase the number of disabled people in senior roles in which they are currently underrepresented. It can be used to meet a group's particular needs, lessen a disadvantage they might experience or increase their participation in a particular activity.

You must be able to show that positive action is an appropriate way for the organisation to achieve one of these aims and the steps you are taking have been carefully thought through.

Six examples of positive action:

1. Placing job adverts to target particular groups, to increase the number of applicants from that group.
2. Including statements in job adverts to encourage applications from underrepresented groups, such as 'we know some women applicants can be discouraged by not meeting some criteria, please put yourself forward anyway'.
3. Offering training or internships to help certain groups get opportunities or progress at work.
4. Offering shadowing or mentoring to groups with particular needs.
5. Hosting an open day specifically for underrepresented groups to encourage them to get into a particular field.
6. Favouring the job candidate from an underrepresented group, where two candidates are 'as qualified as' each other.

> **TESTIMONIAL**
>
> When it came to job offers, on quite a few occasions I would be shortlisted. It would be down to me and one other person – most of the time it would be between me and one other white person and for some reason I'd be told that they had to go with the other candidate.

This needs to be properly thought out, diaries blocked out and prioritised, and a good length of time put aside to go through the process without dragging it out for the candidates. Have a template; as soon you have a vacancy, inform the necessary people with timeframes attached for reviewing and dates suggested for relevant activity.

When it comes to shortlisting, being aware of how bias can creep in, in terms of names and education background, is crucial. If someone attended your alma mater, then there's a chance you can consider them more favourably. There are ways you can negate this, by simply asking competence-based questions, and removing names and educational background. However, there is research that shows when the identity of someone is implied in terms of background or education, this heightens the bias response. So, it is better to have a framework scoring system. Ask a few people to score the same candidates and compare scores with no individual having a greater say in the process.

Using psychometric testing has some value, depending on what it is and how it's used. It shouldn't be a make-or-break element of recruitment, but a source of discussion with the candidate. It's important to note that if someone is hugely self-aware, they can honestly respond but this doesn't mean they don't know how to mitigate their own behaviours. It's also worth noting that for a variety of reasons, from how these tests are created to other cultural issues, women or racialised groups are less likely to perform in such tests compared with white men.[27]

Interviews can be a useful part of the process, but they need to be clear, fair and consistent. Creating scoring criteria with a panel of people from a range of backgrounds, again, with no individual having a greater say in the process, is crucial. There shouldn't be more than three people in a panel otherwise that can be intimidating, depending on the level of role. Better to have two rounds of two, than one round of four. Ensure, if you're making adjustments for candidates, that they're properly comfortable. Each person should be asked the same set of questions. Listen to answers rather than having a 'perfect' answer in mind. Give people a good amount of time to explain their answers and clarify. Remember, the skills required to get a job can be very different to the skills required to do it, so it's more important to try to test skills to do in the process.

The panellists should have time to individually consider the candidates and score before the overall discussion. Put aside time for this. Give candidates realistic expectations and stick to those timeframes.

Communicate with them, if they change. Be sure to evidence your decision-making and provide proper feedback to all candidates, so you know it's not a gut (biased) decision.

After completing your process and making your offer, ask all candidates, including the successful one, for feedback on the process so you can learn and improve.

There is no one fixed way of doing inclusive recruitment well, what is important is that you approach it with the mindset that all aspects of the process need to be done consciously, inclusively and with high levels of emotional and cultural intelligence.

When you consider what makes a great built environment that delivers on ideals, the onus should be on ensuring that you have a diversity of voices and an inclusive environment in which staff can thrive. Unless you consider actively pursuing a different tack that will support a variety of people coming into your practice, can you ever hope to reach your full potential as a firm? What about having full empathy with those you're placemaking for?

If you don't reflect the communities you serve, are you effectively serving them? Inclusive recruitment is just one part of a holistic inclusive approach to organisational culture and practice, but an incredibly important one.

TESTIMONIAL

As soon as I got to the interview, I was waiting in the reception – as soon as the director came out and saw me, he looked at his watch and said he only had 30 minutes. It was clear I wasn't who he was expecting me to be.

Measures

Data collection will be crucial in helping you manage gaps, target them and track change. There are all sorts of pieces of data you can acquire, with Monitoring Forms. The process should engender trust. I refer you back to Chapter Two and STREAMing your EDI; data as a resource and how you collect it is something that will determine your efficacy in being able to interpret it and address the resulting narrative appropriately.

Information you can collect around demographics include:

- The range of people wanting to work for you.
- The mix progressing through recruitment stages.

- How you are responding to making adjustments in the process.
- The mix of people recruited addressing current demographic gaps in staffing diversity.

QR Code 4.5:
LISTEN: RIBA Radio episode 17, 'Inclusive Recruitment'.

Outcomes

When you do these things well, you'll find that your workforce plan starts to come together and a range of people will start to come into the organisation. You'll iterate and continue to manage your processes to identify and mitigate bias, and people will feel like it's a fair and inclusive place to work – which will be identified in formal and informal ways (see QR Code 4.5).

ONBOARDING

Congratulations! You've selected your candidate and they're excited to start. They'll be chomping at the bit to get started and to understand what their role is and how it all fits into the wider context. But you must be mindful of the difference between 'the way you say you get things done' and 'the way things really get done' (remember the iceberg, earlier in this chapter?). This is the difference between overt and inferential organisational culture, so deeply considering the needs and support of the new starter will make the difference between a successful onboarding experience and a poor one.

Check your organisation's shared assumptions about language, values, traditions and ensure there is someone the new person can go to to ask all the questions they need to and feel safe doing so. Asking questions isn't a sign of incompetence – you can normally determine this through the type of question.

Plan the process. We tend to overwhelm new starters with tons of webinars, training modules, organisational charts, meetings with teams … you need to give them a good amount of time to bed in. Also, bear in mind, as a result of hybrid and remote working, people can't get a feel for a new organisation and its culture. Building rapport with others isn't always straightforward on Teams or Zoom.

When making adjustments, do so openly, willingly and generously, so new starters can feel like they are valued and respected, rather than awkward and problematic.

Make sure you support your candidate fully, regardless of their background or identities. If they're struggling, ask yourself first if it's you, rather than them.

You should review new starters' progress up until the time their probation is due to end and encourage inclusive behaviours by demonstrating them as well as being explicit about expectations, calling people in for the conversation as they adjust to the new environment.

Reviews should be noted, regular and constructive feedback taken into account so that the starter can feed into improved systems for anyone else in future.

CASE STUDY: Welcoming Students

Rachael Sayers, Architect and Partner, FeildenCleggBradley Studios

What's the issue you're trying to address with your onboarding process?

We recognised we needed to get a variety of people through our door, so we invite a broad range of courses to get their students to apply through our online portal and they get to upload portfolios anonymously. So we try to see the work first. We also have up to three apprentices a year. We have a variety of tools to select people inclusively.

Once we've recruited a diversity of people, we try to support them to be themselves in the organisation.

How do you do that?

Everyone has a buddy so that you can have somebody who, just day to day, is probably sitting quite close to you and is somebody who helps you 'socialise' into the office, and find your way around. But also if you are new to a particular software that you are having to use, then they'll be the person that you ask and can be generally supportive.

Then there's an opportunity to either be a mentor or to have a mentor. That's a system that people sign up to voluntarily. That's a slightly more formal process. It varies quite a lot regarding what people want to get out of that mentoring.

We have a set of inductions which people go through. They're often part of a cohort, and they learn about everything about being in the office to filing systems to holiday, to HR, all sorts of things.

And, importantly, they can always ask.

Then we have a three-months-in chat with somebody which tries to uncover if there are any particular strengths they have or questions they have, and they can always ask at any time.

We're split into groups within each studio. In the Bath studio we have three groups of architects who work on a range of projects together. We have about 20 people in a group. There's a sense of belonging to a smaller group within the larger whole, so you're not lost in that. Hopefully that means you have a voice because every other week that group would have a group meeting.

We talk about some design issues. We ask students to present their portfolio work, they have a voice there. We might have a digital design crit, and everyone's genuinely welcome to express their thoughts around design or ideas for what's going on in the office at any one time.

What reflections or feedback have you had on the process?

Over time we have had an employees' forum who feedback to the formal process of the partnership. I think people genuinely think that that system works. Also, when students leave, and when anyone leaves, they have an exit interview and they have the opportunity to provide feedback through a survey if they want to, if timing doesn't work for a chat.

We also talk informally to students because they're our fastest turnover by quite a long way. People tend to stay for a long time in the practice generally, and we want to firstly make sure it's the sort of place that they want to come back to.

They're often a different generation to many of us, and we want to make sure that we're listening to the things that matter to them because they're the future of the work of the profession. So we had, for example, an informal discussion with the students who just left us in our group. It's overwhelmingly positive. I don't think they always read the structures that we put in place. They may not have worked anywhere else to compare it with, though. They really enjoy the project work. They really find people very helpful on a one-to-one basis. I think we do have a culture of people respecting each other and working well together. That doesn't mean that there won't be some hard work involved around deadlines and some real focus, but people are basically there to help those at the beginning of their working lives.

We all remember what it was like to work with people who did that for you. The cohort of students who just left, they really loved it, and in part they love it because they've got a group of others around them who are doing the same thing as them. Partly because they get to work on really quite extraordinary projects. The new Bristol Zoo Eden project, some senior living, some competition work.

It's quite a strongly pastoral environment for them.

BEHAVIOURAL ANALYSIS

DRIVE: Realise what you can gain from ensuring that new joiners are given a great experience, even if they're only with you for a short time.

KNOWLEDGE: In addition to inviting new joiners to ask if they have any concerns or feedback, loop in regularly to check-in so you have the understanding you need to make adjustments, especially if they're feeling concerned about raising issues for fear of coming across as incompetent.

STRATEGY: Plan as much as possible, trying to remember what it was like when you were first a new joiner and all the questions you might have. Plot in that support, but also make sure you don't assume your experience would be the same as anyone else's in your effort to be supportive.

ACTION: Patience and consideration allow you to be pastorally supportive, however, if this isn't your default nature, practice it, and give way to others who might be better at supporting new joiners.

In the den of iniquity that exists in some architecture practices, the Future Architects Front[28] (FAF) has told me that students and early career architects can be prevailed upon to use their own computer equipment, their own subscriptions and software, and their own funds to support commercial projects (see Figure 4.7). This is not ethical.

Within employment and internship contracts, specific reference should be made to the provision of equipment. There are other issues around data governance, cyber security and intellectual property which leaves any employer wide open if they do not provide company equipment, pay for, for example, OS maps and up-to-date CAD subscriptions.

Students can and should refuse to use their own equipment on these grounds, not least because of storage and memory issues. Architecture schools should intercede to protect their students from these environments and call out these practices to governing bodies.

Good inclusive onboarding should leave people feeling welcomed, included and valued, not exploited. New starters should understand where to get the information they need, or who to go to if they don't. They should see and understand what it means to be part of an inclusive culture and also contribute to it with their own inclusive behaviours.

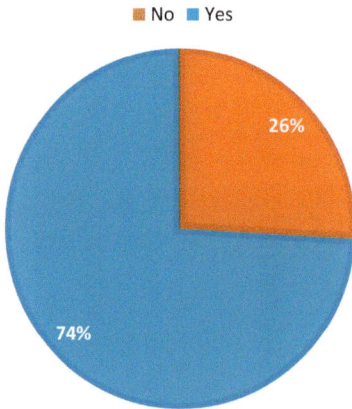

Figure 4.7 A pie chart showing the percentage of FAF survey respondents who said they felt exploited in architecture practice.[29]

Hani Salih, Senior Researcher, Quality of life Foundation

Every now and again I think back to my first year of architecture school. I had a whole lot of energy and passion but nowhere to put it. It wasn't long before I had grown accustomed to catching the train from Manchester to London once every couple of weeks to attend events at the RIBA – the world-famous 66 Portland Place. I remember feeling very happy and excited to be in that space. But as I kept attending events and lectures there, I slowly felt like I was growing more and more distant from the conversations that went on.

I found myself walking away from each event wondering why I was feeling more depressed about the prospects of architecture as a meaningful tool for positive social change. As I grew more critical, I remember feeling incredibly excited to meet people that shared the same sense of growing frustration gnawing at our already tested, poor architecture student psyches. Every once in a while, we'd desperately seek each other out in a sea of white faces at these events, laughing amongst ourselves at how ridiculous we felt.

'If you want to go fast, go alone. If you want to go far, go together' (African proverb)

As people who were trying to find our place within an industry that had so clearly thought of us as fringe voices, the 'other', we learned to lean on each other for support. And as our frustration boiled over, we realised that instead of waiting for the industry and the institutions to change, we should just start. Instead of being satisfied by the incremental, arguably tokenistic, changes granted to us by those in power, we decided to figure it out ourselves. F*** it. Instead of complaining about how things are why not just figure it out ourselves?

Regardless of your position as a minority or a disenfranchised person, you should always look to see the status quo critically. This relationship to power and the institutions that wield and protect it.

In a profession like architecture, there is so much emphasis on doing things the 'right' way. But following this rigid path to accreditation has lost its lustre for many people of colour – we're all aware of this 'mysterious' drop off in the number of BAME architecture students from Part 1 through to Part 3. Just from a financial perspective, how is it possible to justify spending roughly 60,000GBP on an education? For what? A title? Someone, please explain this to me.

There is a lot of value thinking beyond the existing infrastructures. Changes in the way we learn, work and socialise are already shaking up how we think and live beyond just washing our hands regularly and taking Zoom meetings in our pyjamas. As we find ourselves seeing off the last vestiges of the age of the 'starchitect', maybe it's time to rethink our role in all this.

Yes, there is value in engaging with institutions and existing structures, there is no need to throw the baby out with the bathwater. But we need to stop thinking that they hold all the cards when it comes to making change. Learn a skill, put it to use. If you don't have the time or the resources, maybe you can pool both with a few friends. For the first time in history, it is possible to make things happen without being in the same physical space. The tools for making a change have been democratised, there is no paywall, no membership fee and no endowment fund.

Find people that inspire you, people that are equally passionate, angry and curious as you are about a cause. Find people that challenge and inspire you to turn this whole thing on its head. Because if you're looking for radical change, maybe you need to look around you. By building networks and carving out your own space, you can start to question why things are the way they are and begin to imagine new ways, all your favourite revolutionaries started by finding their people and asking questions.

I promise you; no one is going to give you permission.

Just start.

(First published in *Now You Know: A Collection of Sound Advice to Challenge Spatial and Racial Inequality from 60 Architects and Urbanists*, Sound Advice, 2021)

PROFESSIONAL LEARNING AND DEVELOPMENT

Organisational learning and development (L&D) activities aim to enhance individual, team and organisational performance by improving knowledge, skills and abilities. Inclusion should be a fundamental principle in all learning and development efforts. To identify organisational learning needs, look at the workforce plan. Individual learning needs can be pinpointed during recruitment, induction and performance management reviews.

Offering development opportunities fairly can increase participation, challenge biases, prevent discrimination and boost individual potential. To promote inclusive behaviour, learning and development with a focus on EDI should raise awareness of the organisation's EDI principles, as well as the experiences of others. We know that some people get access whilst others do not. Be open about what opportunities might exist, or ensure you have funds set aside for annual development of each person in the organisation. Skills that move on quickly like digital, AI, inclusion, sustainability, fire safety, and so on can all be business-enhancing skills and areas to develop your offer, and so pay back dividends.

Both formal and informal methods can be used, such as a mix of face-to-face and online training, coaching, mentoring, temporary assignments and secondments.

There was once a very prestigious external leadership programme that my organisation's EDI lead wanted me to participate in, so he adjusted the entry criteria so I could do so, opening it to others too, but this was a positive action move to address underrepresentation in the organisation's pipeline. However, my direct line manager then went to her boss, who also went to his boss, all of whom then put in barriers preventing me from accessing the opportunity – I was told that I 'wasn't ready' and I wouldn't be supported. Apparently, according to my manager, I wasn't the 'kind of person they wanted on the scheme. The scheme was for people like HT [a white woman]'.

I ended up circumnavigating the whole process, and after I 'smashed the interview' according to the course leaders, and once accepted on the scheme, my managers couldn't say no, but my removal from that department was arranged so I could (and did) thrive elsewhere – whilst suffering from reactive high-functioning depression and then going through a very disastrous psychological implosion, which was the result of the wider situation. In order to try to protect others from going through a similar predicament, I felt it necessary to raise a complaint.

It was entirely unnecessary, of course, the whole episode, which then ended up (also unnecessarily) being dragged out over years. The point being that this kind of situation is not unusual for racialised women in white-led workplaces, so frequently a number of things can be done differently.

In my case, there were some wider cultural issues as well as individual personalities at play, however, if learning and development programmes are available and accessible to all members of the workforce, there should be no question that suitable people would be barred.

TESTIMONIAL

We were given the opportunity to gain a career grade level upgrade and I applied for this. However, when I did apply for this (this is when the real pushback happened), at this point I realised that this was a form of systemic racism that I was experiencing, and I needed to get out of this organisation.

It was the behaviours, not the policies, procedures and practices, that caused discrimination in this instance, and it became systemic when multiple layers of the hierarchy conspired in the process, believing the people placing the barriers, not the individual facing them.

This is an example of needing to ensure a transparent and fair process to provide access to opportunities, and once on those opportunities, that they're accessible themselves.

All L&D opportunities should espouse EDI principles within them, crafted to enhance awareness and cultivate an understanding of the advantages derived from diverse perspectives, abilities, values and beliefs. It's equally crucial to emphasise the significance of fostering inclusive and respectful behaviours. Images, language and outcomes from all programmes should support the wider inclusion agenda.

INTERNATIONAL CASE STUDY: In-House Learning

Ellen Bensky, Partner, CEO and CFO of Turner Fleischer Architects, Canada

What's your approach to learning and development?
We always struggled with the question 'when you finish your formal education, who's responsible for investing in continual learning?' My philosophy is that we are responsible for providing formal learning opportunities for our studio members. Our industry is

changing rapidly and we need to not only get the new tools and technology in our studio but we need to get them in the hands of our studio members. I cannot ask someone to take a night course on something new because those courses do not exist. I realised years ago that I needed to create a formal learning platform so people could continue to keep up with the advances of our industry.

Another factor in our decision to invest in learning is time to learn. In the past architects could work for 10 years, gain project experience, lived experience, and move through their career. Now young designers do not have that kind of time. They are expected to graduate, start working, get through a project and know everything.

Our multicultural studio is another driver for our focus on learning. How do we get the tacit knowledge from the people, who I call the 'greys', into the heads of the people I call the 'greens' and vice versa. The 'greens' have technological knowledge, and the 'greys' have experiential knowledge.

We also have a multicultural studio. I believe that if you are new to Canada, and you are an architect from another country, you are still an architect. Newcomers often face the concept that 'you cannot get a job in Canada without Canadian experience'. I believe it is our responsibility to offer people the opportunity to learn. The concepts of architecture are the same. We are just building with different materials. We have different bylaws, different zoning, different approvals, processes. But if I can teach all that, then what is the difference?

How do you embed learning?

Our most robust learning platform is TF Academy. It has two terms per year and offers a variety of courses, electives and workshops, taught by studio members to studio members. Our January 2024 term has 61 unique learning opportunities which translates into 164 individual sessions over a five-month period. We not only cover practice related learning we also have a deep health and wellness stream. As we have grown as a studio, I knew we needed to bring experts in adult education into our learning programmes. We now have two professionals with Master's degrees in adult education working within our Knowledge Management team to ensure we are providing professional support to our teachers and our learners and that we are continuing to grow and develop the Academy and other supporting learning programmes.

In what way did this help you grow your business over COVID?
We were able to pivot to working from home very quickly both in terms of work and the TF Academy. There was no break in learning. I believe we grew during this time because we already had a culture of taking care of our people. We did not have create this culture under pressure. I wrote to the studio every single morning for a year. We cared and they knew we cared. We kept them informed and continued to learn together.

I had the business infrastructure to scale quickly. As others were failing to take care of their teams, we were recruiting. We were winning projects from other architects as well as gaining new clients and projects because we had the capacity.

We renovated our studio over the pandemic. We asked our studio members what they wanted most in our new space and we designed based on their feedback. Our main objective was wellbeing and as a result we have trees, a double-sided green wall that integrates with our mechanical system, intelligent windows, skylights, a reflection room, a gym, stand up desks, double monitors for everyone and so much more. We also manage our studio space utilising a fully operational digital twin.

We're a hybrid studio, but my partners and I believe in the importance of leadership being here every day to ensure our studio members receive the support that they need in order to be successful when they are in.

I believe when we invest in and genuinely care about our people, together we will be able to provide amazing service to our clients and truly make a difference in our communities with the designs that we create and get built.

BEHAVIOURAL ANALYSIS

DRIVE: Work out what motivates you to support others in their learning and development. What can you gain? What niche can you carve out for your practice?

Figure 4.8 The TF Academy. Photograph by Turner Fleischer.

KNOWLEDGE: Recognise how the industry is moving on and consider how you can, maybe, work with others to develop and deliver wider understanding and knowledge-sharing.

STRATEGY: Check how learning experiences are being used and support their implementation across the business with peer-to-peer support.

ACTION: Ensure people outside the business know that you support your people's development, which will enhance your reputation as a good employer.

Measures
- Tracking who gets access to L&D opportunities and how often will be crucial to continuing to gauge how well you are delivering on inclusion.
- Look at evaluation following the delivery of any programme, act on feedback.
- Ensure there is implemented change and support people to embed learning following courses.
- Ask trainers for feedback on staff engagement.

Outcomes

The ways in which inclusion filters through thriving inclusive cultures are manifold. Teams would be clear as to why EDI principles and objectives matter; it would be demonstrable that inclusivity is a big part of everything you do, whether it's your programmes, resources, interventions or events; everyone would feel they have a fair chance to develop their potential within your organisation.

In the end, all these efforts are about making everyone, your teams, and your whole organisation perform better. This will give you a great edge in the competitive game.

TESTIMONIAL

I had to ask HR at my current practice to review a company policy that prohibited 'BAME' staff from returning to the office due to concerns that 'BAME' people are more likely to spread COVID-19.

PERFORMANCE MANAGEMENT

It once took me two years to manage out a poor performer. He'd been in the organisation nearly 10 years and it was considered just too difficult to bother. So, whilst he continuously let the team down, delivered a substandard product and demonstrated poor behaviours, when I took on the leadership role, which was a very exhausting and demanding job in itself, I also diligently stuck to the process in order to get to the outcome the business and team needed. I named my early grey hairs after him.

Inclusive performance management is about setting clear expectations, robust processes and fair procedures. It should never have got to the stage where he was simply allowed to continue.

Timely, fair and constructive feedback conversations are a prerequisite to give people a chance to perform better. There should be, in any case, regular conversations between team members and leaders about progress on stated personal and organisational annual objectives and any external pressures. One-to-ones on a weekly, fortnightly or monthly basis (depending on role and context) would avoid issues building up. Prioritising and committing to a regular half-hour check-in is a crucial part of tracking performance.

When we weave EDI principles and goals into how we manage performance, it helps create a culture where we all share responsibility. If you're in a management role, it's important to lead inclusively and make sure your team's and individual goals for EDI are set and reached, all while aiming for constant improvement. In our day-to-day management, we should also acknowledge and reward inclusive actions and deal with any bias or discrimination.

To make sure we hit our EDI goals when it comes to performance management, it's important to let everyone know about the inclusive behaviours you expect. These should be integral to performance management policies and practices so that everyone can play a part in building an inclusive workplace. To keep things fair, clear and unbiased, criteria for performance evaluations should be shared as policy.

Giving feedback is key. Use the frameworks described in Chapter Three. You need to praise inclusive actions and, when needed, address non-inclusive behaviour. If there are areas where someone can do better or where someone isn't following your stated values, there needs to be a fair and gradual approach to address it.

As always, all processes should be subject to continuous evaluation, so you'd know if teams are happy or unhappy with how performance management is going. You should keep an eye on how performance management is working out. This helps you see if there are any biases in how people are being evaluated and if there are any problems you need to fix.

Maria Grazia Zedda, Senior EDI Manager, Workforce HS2, told me that they have a system to reward good performance, bearing in mind HS2 is a project, and there isn't necessarily the opportunity for promotion. They have a system that will track how people are evaluated in order to try to prevent bias with a bell curve. They have, for example, 5 per cent who are exceptional people, then 20 per cent who are top talent, then people who meet expectations, and 5 per cent who need improvement or not sufficient evidence, and so on.

They monitor this closely to avoid bias. They know that people tend to favour people who are more similar to themselves. So they work with line managers, not to focus just on the people who are similar to them, but also seek out the diversity that will give them the advantage that they need.

The more experienced the hiring manager, the better decisions they make in terms of promotion and talent, recognising talent and advancing talent.

> **TESTIMONIAL**
>
> Just after qualifying at my end of year review, instead of creating some targets and goals to assist me in the next stage of my career, I was greeted with an extremely hostile situation of blaming and accusations, and it was proposed to put me on a performance review for three months. This essentially put me back on probation without an expected pay rise after being there for a whole year, having no prior conversations about my performance and being blindsided completely, at a time when I should be celebrating and gaining more confidence.
>
> It's these types of scenarios that knock your confidence and make you question whether you belong in this industry.

Measures

It's really important as you move ahead with performance management that you're not disproportionally targeting underrepresented groups. The only way you'll know this for sure is if you track and monitor the demographics of your process. Remember, as per onboarding, if people haven't settled in, think why might that be – and think about the introspection you might need to do first before looking at the performance of the individual if they succeeded in coming in via a robust recruitment process. Has there been clarity around expectations, role and delivery? What other questions can you ask? So:

- Look at who is going through processes.
- Any trends in performance management ratings and outcomes, and if there is any disproportionality in that.
- Seek feedback about performance process.
- Track good and exemplary inclusive behaviour.
- Track and tackle promptly poor behaviour.

Outcomes

Managers need to step up and showcase inclusive leadership. They're the ones making sure that we nurture and keep our talent while creating an environment where everyone feels like they can thrive.

As per your Workforce Plan you should be exemplifying the goals tied to EDI, demonstrating all have to take responsibility for great performance.

When it's evaluation time, it should feel fair and friendly. So, the way managers and team members interact during these assessments should be impartial, positive, and, most importantly, inclusive. When done well you'll spot and address any EDI-related learning and development needs. That way, you will keep growing and contributing to your inclusive culture.

If you see any bias or discrimination in how you do performance management, you should not let it slide. Take action to keep your workplace free from those issues and make it a fair and equitable place to be.

SUCCESSION PLANNING

A major issue across a lot of built environment professions is the pipeline. In a few cases we don't necessarily see underrepresentation at entry level, it's in senior-management and leadership positions where we have a prevailing white and male demographic.

This can be tackled with conscious planning to recognise our great performers and set them on a path to be retained and progressed within our teams and organisations. Hopefully, you can start to see how all the pieces of the Workforce Plan fit together.

Through inclusive recruitment, paying fairly, developing and performance managing, you can be sure of having a decent breadth and depth of staff choice for succession planning.

The approach would be similar to that of inclusive recruitment, at every stage ensuring you don't fall foul of the Peter Principle. The Peter Principle is often summarised as 'Employees rise to their level of incompetence'. In practice, this means that an employee who excels in their current job may be promoted to a higher-level position, even if they lack the necessary skills or qualifications for that new role. As a result, they may struggle or fail in their new position, leading to a decrease in overall organisational efficiency.

The Peter Principle highlights the potential pitfalls of basing promotions solely on an employee's past performance in their current role, without considering their ability to perform in the new role, and what new skills and capabilities can be trained for in advance. For example, if a great surveyor wants to take on a partnership, having effective business acumen is an additional set of skills.

To return to the running analogy, you wouldn't graduate to running a 1,500m race if you're a great sprinter, without preparing for it first, even though you can put one foot in front the other very quickly – it's a different set of skills to do so effectively.

Clear objective criteria to determine who should be progressed, what benchmarks need to be met, how they will be met, over what time periods, can all be explicit and shared so there's transparency about what is being asked of them and why, if they want to be considered for promotion.

Bias can be an enemy here, and so it is crucial that you are certain objectivity is baked into procedures, mitigating subjective outcomes.

As Oprah is known for saying, 'there's no such thing as luck, it's about being prepared for your opportunities', so it is with succession planning. If you want to build in business resilience, knowing who is ready to come next, or the kind of person you're after, when people leave, needs to be an inclusive process.

TESTIMONIAL

I was told to choose, because of some perceptions that pursuing my interests meant I wasn't loyal to the profession. Eventually, I did choose, and at that point in time I didn't choose architecture.

WORKFORCE MOBILITY

People move around a business all the time, but who gets to do so, especially if there are prestige visits abroad, requires there to be an inclusive approach to this too.

Also, you may choose to move an HQ to a different city or part of a city, a good deal of inclusive planning should go into this too.

When you're thinking about dishing out new tasks or asking someone to pack their bags and move, it's a good idea to look at what the job involves, how the person is growing, and whether the job can be done remotely, especially with the access to technology we've got these days.

If the job or the person's development means they've got to relocate, it's important to take a smart approach. That means thinking about things like being flexible, keeping people safe and healthy, making sure they're well, dealing with immigration matters, and considering all the other important factors in a careful and organised way.

In approaching how you move people around in the workplace, you have to be fair and inclusive. Everyone should be able to learn about job opportunities, have a fair shot at them, and be judged on their skills and abilities, not on anything else.

When it comes to these job moves and possible relocations, there are a number of practicalities too. Some aspects can be a bit tough, so you need to be ready with the right support and resources.

People also have their own situations and families to think about. So, if someone says 'no' to a job move, it's not the end of the story. Be clear you will still think about them for other opportunities or find ways for them to do their job without having to uproot.

Don't ever assume who would and wouldn't move. Recently, someone mentioned to me that they were only seeking candidates from London because they required people to be in the office three days a week. I said, 'Hang on a second!' I live in Derby and travelled to London to work in RIBA offices as a TWaT (Tuesday, Wednesday and Thursday), because it suited me to escape my family. I hope they went away and opened the job up nationally, or they could be missing out.

Keep an eye on the costs and benefits of moving people or trying out new ways of getting the job done. You want to make smart choices that work for everyone.

Measures
- Take a look at the demographics of who is accepting and who is declining roles and check out why people are saying 'no'.
- Make sure you've checked if you *need* to do the relocation.
- Listen to and review complaints.
- Look at trends and assess any disproportionality in who is affected.

Outcomes
As with all other areas of the workforce lifecycle, when inclusion is done well you see a mix of people benefiting from relocations and similar changes, and mitigating impacts on those who don't want the change. It's done well and the inclusive culture benefits the wider outcomes for the business.

> ## TESTIMONIAL
>
> Being a woman on site has changed a lot over the years. The times inclusion was most effective was when it started from the very bottom and it went all the way up to the top. Something as simple as having a proper changing room, and proper welfare facilities rather than just being given someone's office to change in. Having

your own space really felt like I belonged there – that was the beginning of it. I visited a site recently – they've got free sanitary products in the changing rooms there and that was the first time I'd ever seen that.

The times when it hasn't worked well is when I've been told by my supervisor or my manager – the person who I'm relying on to give me work and to be having my back as it were – they're telling me they don't believe that women should be in construction. When you have managers who are supportive and they really understand that you need everyone in the workforce in order to allow it to be diverse, but also to fill the need of the industry by tapping into every resource possible. They feed that down and they impose that on the supervisors and managers that work below them.

There's a general voice going across that feeds out to all of the workers, that everyone belongs there.

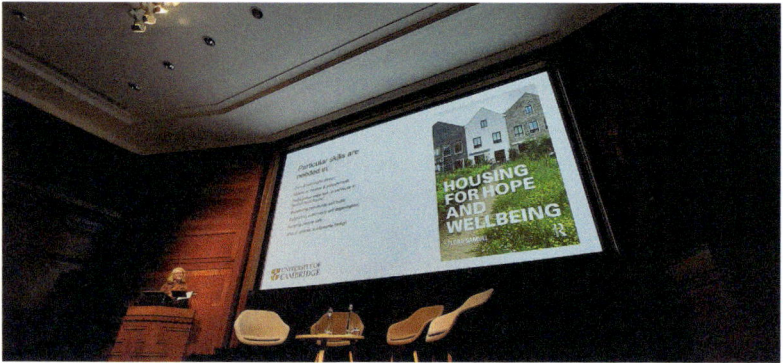

Figure 4.9 Dr Flora Samuel presenting at the RIBA VitrA talk on Shaping Integrity – New Forms of Architecture. Photograph by the author.

EMPLOYMENT CESSATION

In pulling together this book, it has been hard to find examples of good cessation practice, because not enough places give it enough thought.

Ending employment, whether someone decides to leave or it happens for other reasons, like retirement, redundancy, performance issues, or even ill health or passing away, is what I mean by 'cessation of employment'.

When organisations are parting ways with an employee, it's important to do it thoughtfully. This might involve providing information, access to support services, and resources, as well as giving them a chance to have a chat or appeal if they need to. They should also have a way to share their thoughts or concerns.

Leaving a job can be a tough and stressful time for some people. So, when organisations are wrapping things up, they should be clear about what they're doing, treat everyone fairly, be considerate and respectful, and make sure everyone's privacy, health and wellbeing are looked after.

In all cases an exit interview should be offered.

> ## TESTIMONIAL
>
> This experience is something I find really difficult to talk about. I still experience a lot of trauma and fear from that time. I worked for a company for a number of years, however there was a bullying culture in the management. I decided to leave and find another role – and that was not dealt with very well. I spent a horrible number of weeks working out my notice with a lot of tension, being ignored and being mistreated. To this day I still can't reference that company because they've decided not to acknowledge the hard work that I put in.
>
> The sad thing now is I see online that particular place talking about how they support Black Lives Matter and how they're going to do better, but I've never had an apology. A lot of Black women's labour taken, and no acknowledgement of it, but here they are at the forefront talking about Black Lives Matter; and yet my Black life was not significant to them and neither did they support me, so it's really difficult because a lot of companies are paying the lip service, but it would be really interesting to scrutinise whether that's being practiced, whether their past injustices have been acknowledged and whether they are really changing.

Exit Interviews

If you are not asking people why they're leaving, the likelihood is you'll continue to make the same mistakes and suffer retention problems. For instance, if an employee leaves your organisation because of a perceived toxic culture or a lack of growth opportunities, chances are they're not the only ones to think so. Unless you address these issues, you'll soon see others, your best people usually, head out the door.

Exit interviews are a significant tool to provide valuable intel into your workplace culture, daily operations and management approaches. Furthermore, they facilitate an understanding of the reasons behind employees' decisions to depart from your organisation.

Although receiving feedback, which is likely to be negative, can be challenging, it is a constructive process. Not having an exit interview process is a missed opportunity for enhancing the overall employee experience and increasing employee retention.

Cover why they decided to leave, what it was like whilst they were working there, anything you need to know about the role, and any other thoughts they have about the business overall.

Listen to understand, not to respond. They're already leaving and, actually, they're doing you a favour.

Other Things to Think About

In any approach to handling the conclusion of an individual's employment journey, you should establish a set of practices that reflect your dedication to equality, diversity and inclusion.

Check your bias and ensure that criteria for redundancy and severance are entirely fair and free from any form of discrimination. This ensures that the process remains impartial, giving everyone an equal opportunity.

There needs to be comprehensive support during this transition. This shouldn't be done in platitudes. There should be mechanisms in place for consultation and appeals. If there are workforce representatives or unions, collaborate with them as well. Proper time and listening are necessary.

If any complaints arise regarding bias and discrimination in decision-making processes, you should investigate them thoroughly and work towards resolution.

It remains all about the data. Make sure you are clear on who is being affected, track resignations, retirements, redundancies and dismissals. This helps you stay informed about any trends and patterns.

People should always feel their contributions are valued. This includes recognising those who champion EDI, as well as those who set an example by demonstrating inclusive behaviour, and those who achieve significant milestones and accomplishments during their time with you.

Even after someone leaves our organisation, you should allow them to stay connected. Provide channels for them to maintain relationships with their former colleagues because you value the bonds that were formed.

Continually evaluating the impact of your cessation of employment policies, processes, and practices on your workforce diversity. This helps you identify and address any imbalances or negative effects that may arise.

EMPLOYMENT: KEY TAKEAWAYS

Having an inclusive approach to your workforce brings about better engagement from your staff, higher productivity, greater goodwill, a happier environment overall. These things needn't be time-consuming, but they do require conscious effort.

Across the built environment, attracting, treating well, progressing and retaining a good mix of staff is a significant pain point. Rather than focusing on different diversity dimensions, see diversity as the output, and focus on improving your culture instead.

- Each part of the employee work life cycle is interlinked.
- Track data of the demographics impacted by each area of policy and how it's implemented.
- Keep seeking feedback so you can evaluate and improve.
- If things aren't working out, check yourself first, and seek feedback before looking to the employee.
- Listen and make sure you provide ample opportunities to listen to team members, even if what they have to say is difficult to hear.

NOTES

1 Frederic Laloux, *Reinventing Organisations*, Nelson Parker, 2014, p. 46.
2 'Ex-students complain of sexism and racism at UCL architecture school', *The Guardian*, 31 May 2021. See www.theguardian.com/education/2021/may/31/ex-students-complain-sexism-racism-ucl-architecture-school [Accessed 23 November 2023].
3 Joint Built Environment Institutes Action Plan, 2022. See www.designingbuildings.co.uk/wiki/Three_year_equity,_diversity_and_inclusion_action_plan [Accessed 23 November 2023].
4 Ibid.
5 Building People CIC Networks. See www.buildingpeople.org.uk/Home/Network [Accessed 23 November 2023].
6 Mark Kemp, *RIBA Good Practice Guide: Business Resilience*, RIBA Publishing, 2022.

7   Workforce Data Equality Guide. See www.london.gov.uk/programmes-strategies/communities-and-social-justice/workforce-integration-network-win/workforce-data-equality-guide [Accessed 23 November 2023].

8   Supply Chain Sustainability School, 'Largest-ever employee diversity survey in the UK'. See https://www.supplychainschool.co.uk/diversity-survey-results-2022/ [Accessed 23 November 2023].

9   Joeli Brearley, *Pregnant then Screwed: The Truth about the Motherhood Penalty and How to Fix It*, Simon & Schuster, 2021.

10 'Human trials of artificial wombs could start soon. Here's what you need to know', *Nature*, 2023. See www.nature.com/articles/d41586-023-02901-1 [Accessed 29 November 2023].

11 Pragya Agarwal, *(M)otherhood: On the Choices of Being a Woman*, Canongate, 2021.

12 RIBA Radio, Episode 10: CQ Knowledge – Women/Gender pay gap/Reproductive health/Flexible working. See https://soundcloud.com/the-riba/riba-radio-episode-10-cq 14'30" [Accessed 29 November 2023].

13 Norah Vincent, in the early 2000s, conducted an experiment in which she spent a year disguised as a man, living and working as one, in order to understand the different lived experience and documented this in her book, Self-Made Man (Atlantic Books, 2006). It is a fascinating read for anyone who would like some insight into the fundamental difference in life experienced as a man, especially a white man, versus that of a woman. A note that Norah is not trans or otherwise a cross-dresser.

14 Gloria Steinem, 'If men could menstruate', reproduced in *Women's Reproductive Health*, 2019, 6(3): 151–152. DOI: 10.1080/23293691.2019.1619050 [Accessed 29 November 2023].

15 RIBA, 'Menopause and work: why it's so important', *RIBA*. See www.architecture.com/knowledge-and-resources/resources-landing-page/menopause-and-work [Accessed 29 November 2023].

16 Malcolm Brynin, 'The gender pay gap', *EHRC Research Report* 109, 2017. See www.equalityhumanrights.com/sites/default/files/research-report-109-the-gender-pay-gap.pdf [Accessed 29 November 2023].

17 Greg Pitcher, 'Worsening ethnic and gender pay gaps show "systemic discrimination"', *Architect's Journal*. See www.architectsjournal.co.uk/news/worsening-ethnic-and-gender-paygaps-show-systemic-discrimination-warns-former-riba-chief [Accessed 29 November 2023].

18 'Ethnicity pay reporting: guidance for employers', Government Guidance, 2023. See https://www.gov.uk/government/publications/ethnicity-pay-reporting-guidance-for-employers [Accessed 29 November 2023].

19 Commission on Race and Ethnic Disparities: The Report. See https://assets.publishing.service.gov.uk/media/6062ddb1d3bf7f5ce1060aa4/20210331_-_CRED_Report_-_FINAL_-_Web_Accessible.pdf [Accessed 28 April 2024].

20 'UK Race Commission amends line on slave trade after criticism', *The Guardian*, 30 April 2021. See www.theguardian.com/world/2021/apr/30/uk-race-commission-amends-line-on-slave-trade-after-criticism [Accessed 29 November 2023].

21 The Fees Bureau, Architect Earnings, 2023. See https://www.feesbureau.co.uk/architectsfeesdigital [Accessed 29 April 2024].

22 BMA, Junior Doctor Pay. See www.bma.org.uk/media/5504/bma-junior-doctors-contracts-pay-tables-apr-2022–2023.pdf [Accessed 29 November 2023].

23 Church of England, Salaries of Vicars. See www.churchofengland.org/sites/default/files/2023–04/csa_report_2022_final.pdf [Accessed 29 November 2023].

24 Charity Commission for England and Wales, entry for RIBA. See https://register-of-charities.charitycommission.gov.uk/charity-search/-/charity-details/210566 [Accessed 29 November 2023].

25 Peter George, RIBA London Awards Keynote. See www.linkedin.com/posts/peter-george-he-him-83b1b710_riba-speech-activity-7063050362059943937-s5TV [Accessed 29 November 2023].

26 Binna Kandola, *Racism at Work: The Danger of Indifference*, Pearn Kandola Publishing, 2018.

27 Council of National Psychological Associations for the Advancement of Ethnic Minority Interests, Testing and Assessment with Persons & Communities of Color, American Psychological Association, 2016. See www.apa.org/pi/oema [Accessed 29 November 2023].

28 The Future Architects front is a grassroots a campaigning group for worker rights, inclusion and sustainability in architecture practices. See https://fafront.co/about/ [Accessed 23 November 2023].

29 Open Letter from FAF to RIBA. See https://drive.google.com/file/d/1RqqvgV-LBb WToAXmy136x2PZ8D3fUj5R/view [Accessed 29 November 2023].

CREATE

Chapter Five

The best way to predict the future, is to create it.
Abraham Lincoln, Peter Drucker and others

Humans have always designed, shaping the world around us to interact better with it, and, generally in harmony with it too. It's only comparatively recently that that interaction, and design outcomes, have been having a net detrimental effect.

Speaking of the 2022 Stirling Prize winner, the sitting RIBA President Simon Allford said:

> We must build 'forever architecture' … A unique setting with a clear purpose – The New Library at Magdalene College is sophisticated, generous, architecture that has been built to last.
>
> Creating a new building that will last at least 400 years is a significant challenge, but one that Niall McLaughlin Architects has risen to with the utmost skill, care and responsibility.[1]

Undoubtedly, it is a supremely beautiful, well-designed building. However, my first thought was not about its aesthetics or environmental performance, it was about its exclusiveness and permanence – and, in 2422 who will need a 400-year-old library anyway? (I can hear your sharp intake of breath, so stick with me.) Even today, as technology changes, we're consuming information in entirely new ways to even 20 years ago. Who is to say, by the end of this century, we're not putting on VR headsets, haptic gloves and olfactory sensors, and flicking through material in that way as a means of avoiding deforestation and providing greater universal access to more knowledge from across the centuries? Or, (for fear of sounding like an episode of *Black Mirror*)[2] even having small chips embedded in our brains to access the information we need, when we need it?

The 2021 Stirling Prize winner, Kingston University Town House, by Grafton Architects, has an entirely different remit: open; for the

DOI: 10.4324/9781003435747-9

community; variety of uses; a flow through the space; clearly built with adaptability in mind; and an intention that anyone can access it, which suggests it can transform as the people around it do.

> Many of the students at Kingston are the first in their family to attend university and this building sends an important message to them, their educators and the local community, that this is a place where everyone is welcome and valued … Generous volumes allow people, light and air to flow naturally through the building, which also uses a thermally-activated concrete frame to reduce operational energy use. This highly-adaptable building will stand the test of time and provide an inspiring environment for students, residents, and visitors for years to come.[3]

The way we experience space informs how we inferentially conceive our ideas about the world. As humans, individuals don't experience our built environment in permanent ways to a time scale of hundreds of years. As the planet faces crisis and the movement of people becomes ever more inevitable, I argue that the spaces we should be lauding might even need to be biodegradable. Certainly, they should be hugely adaptable, with the potential to sustainably biodegrade. As a result of advancements in technology, the way we use a space now may not be the same in 50, 100, 150 years, let alone 400.

I was at the Parthenon (in Athens, obviously) for the first time, recently (see Figure 5.1). Incredible, in so many ways. I happened to be messaged by an architectural historian when I was there. His response to me telling him where I was? 'Ah! Back to the source!' I laughed, but in seriousness,

Figure 5.1 The Parthenon, Athens. Photograph by the author.

I can see why ideas about proportion, beauty, dimension and longevity have been inspired by that impressive site.

I reflected, however, that what we know less about, and are not as influenced by, is how other, now biodegraded, ideas may have existed about how our spaces can be designed. As we have less evidence of them, there might be more wide-ranging, shared ways of building and living which would promote better approaches to inclusion and sustainability. Those approaches may have biodegraded along with our own capacity to ideate inclusive lifestyles, as church, state and colonialism sought to impress status, grandeur and a particular way of being (see QR Code 5.1). Ideologies, literally – and deliberately so – cemented into our unconscious. When developing what have become the norms and traditions that have shaped the prevalent approach to our built environment today, we have relied on what is still standing, not what we never saw.

Is there not an element of availability bias here?[+]

If we physically want to keep things rooted in the same thinking, what impact does this have on our societies, our ideologies, our psychology, our perception of the status quo? If we're to argue for a sense of permanence, 'forever architecture' with a view to 'keep to tradition' for 'longer life', 'to delight and inspire for generations', I beg you answer, why? Who does that, actually, serve?

Coming back to Einstein, 'a new type of thinking is essential if [hu]mankind is to survive and move toward higher levels', means that the architect's obsession with their own legacy and permeance needs to take a back seat. Planners need to be agile and consider agility too. Engineers need to be more innovative. And how we design and think in this way is fundamentally existential and pertains to matters of inclusion.

Ever since the agricultural revolution humans have been shaping and imposing on and extracting from the planet to create built environments. With the industrial revolution, those who had the power and influence to do so failed to listen to the voices who raised the warning signals, and now we're at the tipping point of climate catastrophe. We're paying the price of this in manifold ways. It's here, in design, that the intersection of sustainability and inclusion is clear.

The demographics of those who have encouraged the inexorable growth of human domination on the planet – the white male of the global north – are the same demographics of those who have influenced the academy of, who run and determine the outcomes of, the built environment professions today. So, this fundamental rethink must not only come from new schools of thought but also a multitude of backgrounds, looking for solutions, for example, by harking back to indigenous practices – many of which have been brought to the brink of extinction though colonialism – and may need to be refound through oral traditions, where they exist.

Yasmeen Lari has described how when she travelled to England from Pakistan to study, her country had only been independent for about a decade, after 150 years of colonial rule. 'We had been told that our culture was really nothing, and that everything in the West was something to be emulated.' When she came back, she saw her country with new eyes, 'It is really like a relearning of your own self, as to what you are. And, looking at people, really understanding what made Pakistan.'[5]

This is why the 'people' piece of the inclusion puzzle has been described first in this book – it's the nature of the inputs that determine the outputs (so too with artificial intelligence) – and so who, the backgrounds and thinking, and what we're feeding into design, is as crucial as the processes themselves that we're using to get there.

I have heard many a young person and student from an underrepresented background tell me that their approach to design has been dismissed because what they present is culturally rooted in their heritage. When arguing for a different approach to design they have to explain ideas that are fundamentally misunderstood, or tutors and practice leaders don't want to understand. There's a role here for educators to engage in some 'relearning' themselves.

As Peter Drucker and others say, 'the best way to predict the future, is to create it'. Sometimes this requires a fundamental move in thinking how to do so. What we do know is that we need a central shift in order to be inclusive, safe, sustainable, ethical and innovative, because far too often the sector fails on some or all of these counts.

INTERNATIONAL CASE STUDY: Referencing Indigenous Practices

Sandeep B. Menon, Landscape Architect and Lecturer in Landscape Architecture, Manchester School of Architecture, UK

How can indigenous practices be useful?

Indigenous practices are rooted in time and space. For example, the sacred groves in Kerala (a state in the southern part of India), are patches of land that have been left untouched for centuries within the homestead plots. They are usually located in the south-west of the built houses and are often associated with a waterbody. In a landscape where everything else has been modified by humans, these are the only ecological patches that hold the bio-gene pools of the actual floristic compositions which were there in those regions. Kerala is a lot like the UK in that aspect, a lot of what may seem as natural maybe in reality be modified by humans completely.

The inherent idea of these sacred groves is that they are in fact not protected by fences but by the sheer power of faith and a string of superstitious canons. The reliance on superstitions, obviously, has a flip side to it especially when one looks at it from a Euro-centric, 'enlightened' scientific lens. But one should imagine that these were imposed at a time when there were no bylaws. There were no rule books or approving authorities. Maybe, the canons were made to protect the sacred groves from being encroached upon but, unfortunately, with time the logic behind protecting these groves as ecological bio-gene pools has been forgotten yet the superstitious narratives and the illogical canons stayed on.

It is evident that there is quite a distinct ecological thought inbuilt into the ideas of sacred groves. Especially because the 'owner of the land', or the 'owner of the house', was not seen as just responsible for their family, but were seen as being responsible for everything that lives within their plot, including the reptiles, the birds and all the other life forms. So, even before one decides to build a house, the idea was that one ought to 'request', metaphorically, the reptiles and the other animals to relocate to this designated forested patch, which is called the *Kaavu* in the local language Malayalam, loosely translated as the 'Sacred Grove'.

The trees are cut down with a lot of rituals. They use axes which are coated in honey. This may seem absurd to our twenty-first-century modern minds, but the idea was that it was an exercise which was designed to be conscious and to be emphatic in the minds of the agents wanting to cut down a tree. One is aware, one understands and consciously reiterates that 'yes, I'm going to cut a tree; it's going to hurt that living being and I'm going to ask some beings to relocate to the sacred grove designated for them for posterity'.

There was a sense of sensitivity in that exercise, which I believe we've lost in this age of instant construction and modern byelaws.

In today's world, in many of the cities, we have the provision of compensatory planting. 'I can cut down as many trees as I want in the city because I would probably do compensatory planting somewhere else, or in some other nation', for example. That goes against any principles of ecology. Life that was dependent on those vegetative patches are lost forever and frequently in urban areas where fallow lands are increasingly built over.

However, don't get me wrong, these sacred groves are not bereft of problems. I speak highly of them from an 'ecological lens' but from a 'socio-cultural lens' they have been problematic because it is only the rich landowning communities in the past that have had these. They traditionally functioned as places of worship for the marginalised communities in these areas where entry to the built temples was only allowed for the upper-caste populace. This is also something which I need to acknowledge when I speak about these. This practice was abolished in the 1930s.

There are also some bizarre rules that women even today cannot enter these spaces during the period of menstruation. To think of this as an acceptable cultural practice in today's day and time is also problematic. This is also something I need to acknowledge while listing the ecological wisdom behind the groves.

But they're not very permanent. How do indigenous practices view permanence?

Many of these indigenous practices are designed in a way wherein the impact on the landscape or on the larger environment is meant to be very minimal.

If one reflects on the impact of many of these indigenous practices, they are meant to cope with the environment rather than leave a new mark on the landscape. The end goal was never considered to be a statement of human ingenuity, unlike many of the colonial or post-colonial projects in the global south, for example, if one looks at the frenzy of 'Capital City' building in the post-Second World War independent erstwhile colonies, you'd see the difference. Le Corbusier, who designed Chandigarh, India, created a modern city for the cars. However, it is interesting to note that India in the 1950s, a newly formed country, gaining independence after centuries of colonial rule, with a chance to reinvent its urban legacy and create a new city in the northern plains, invites an architect from Paris and asks him to design it. Pakistan followed with Konstantinos Apostolos Doxiadis, a Greek architect, designing Islamabad. Bangladesh had Louis Kahn designing the Capitol Complex. In short, it is always a white man who is invited to design these spaces, invariably these cities are cast in concrete. They are meant to stay for a very, very long time and are meant to be the beacons of the global identity of these newly independent countries. But the truth is that they literally cement coloniality, as foundations to their newly found post-colonial identity.

However, there are examples of local practices that have carried on. For example, in Bangladesh, where a large proportion of the population still live in flood affected areas, they have this innovative way in which they ingeniously use a floating weed, *Pontederia crassipes* (formerly *Eichhornia crassipes*) to help make these floating rafts on which they practice agriculture (see Figure 5.2).

'*Pontederia crassipes*', also known as water hyacinth and 'the Terror of Bengal' because of its highly invasive nature, is a colonial import from the Amazon basin into the Indian subcontinent via Kew Gardens and the British Raj. Originally brought in as an ornamental plant to the water gardens of the rulers, it is now an assertively invasive weed that out-competes the native flora. It is a highly problematic plant because it covers the waterbodies aggressively and does not allow any sunlight to pass through into the underwater zones thereby adversely affecting underwater flora and fauna.

What is unique about the water hyacinth plant is that its stem has a buoyant bulb like structure that helps it stay afloat. It also has an ability to withstand a bit of salinity. In Bangladesh, there are local communities in flood affected areas, who create floating food gardens using water hyacinth and bamboo rafts. They take the water hyacinth, which is abundantly available, and tie them up onto the bamboo rafts, so that it becomes a floating platform (see Figure 5.3). The plant rots and releases nutrients and the rafts are planted with locally found vegetables and leafy herbs. Hence, even when there is a flood, while the land may get submerged, these agricultural rafts would stay afloat protecting the crops.

Figure 5.2 Water hyacinth, *Pontederia crassipes*. Image by Sandeep B. Menon.

This type of cultivation, known as 'Dhap', has been identified by the Food and Agricultural Organization as a globally important agricultural heritage system (2015). This is a significant acknowledgement since this is emblematic of how the world is finally waking up to accepting such unconventional ways of coping with what is locally available, like these local, community-created ingenious ideas.

What are the issues about how these ideas might be replicated?

In today's world, there is a marked impatience around wanting to see immediate results. It does take time for many of these practices to bear results. But our modern ways of production and building pushes for the need to constantly measure and have a metric, to determine impact.

There's no room to wait, see and assess. The immediate and instant seeing of results is a hindrance for advocating towards these indigenous practices. For example, the 'living root bridges' of Meghalaya, India are crafted over generations by training the aerial roots of the Ficus *elastica* trees, planted on the sides of the valleys, enmeshing them to form 'living bridges' that can conduct pedestrian travel across the gorges. These living bridges may develop over a generation but once established they will live for hundreds of years. The Ficus trees also help stabilise the soil on the edges of the river as well as provide refuge for the local biodiversity. This is context-specific.

However, indigenous practices do allow us to think 'out-of-the-box'. It allows one to reimagine a future wherein one can cope with the ever-changing climatic conditions with locally available resources. Everything does not have to be factory produced. Everything does not have to be tested and approved by organisations who are probably hand-in-glove behind our backs [with political systems].

What's also remarkable is that most of these indigenous knowledge practices are initiated and carried forward by community members who are not trained in any architectural or engineering backgrounds, still they dare to innovate. They work as a community, through generations, and generate resilient solutions that have helped them navigate their day-to-day lives without any significant ecological footprints!

Figure 5.3 Bangladesh planting rafts. Image by Sandeep B. Menon.

BEHAVIOURAL ANALYSIS

DRIVE: Consider how much do you want to know about methods you've never seen and may have died, or that are present in communities you've not experienced or studied. Look at a map, and ask yourself, why have you not explored the built/natural environment of those areas?

KNOWLEDGE: And then explore them – find out what you can, but also be aware of the lens with which they have been presented. Is it a local voice or a colonial one?

STRATEGY: Think carefully, not about replicating like-for-like, but what principles can be applied to a local perspective you are working in. What assumptions might you make that need to be checked? How would you tackle the incredulity that a fundamentally different approach adopting an 'indigenous' approach might encourage?

ACTION: What adaptations to your design approach, using indigenous inspiration, are effective and which ones may not be? How can you flex a design approach that will incorporate such an approach without being incongruous?

QR Code 5.1:
LISTEN: RIBA
Radio episode 22,
'Decolonisation'.

DELIVERING INCLUSIVE DESIGN

Inclusive design endeavours to establish fairness and equality in how individuals experience the world around them. Its core objective is to create safe and accessible environments that cater to the diverse needs of all community members. While accessibility primarily concentrates on providing basic physical access, inclusive design surpasses these requirements by incorporating thoughtful consideration, active engagement and innovative thinking.

The essence of inclusive design lies in its profound focus on people. Also, the essence of sustainable design lies in its profound focus on planet, and shouldn't be considered separately from inclusion, but alongside. Inclusive design acknowledges and celebrates the unique differences among individuals, recognising that various abilities, backgrounds and challenges are present within our society. Compromise is not a dirty word, but I dare say that collaboration is a better one. Compromise suggests having to give something up, but collaboration suggests you have something to contribute. In both circumstances it's about finding a middle way forward, but inclusion isn't about winners and losers, it's about forging a good next set of steps, by listening, learning and reflecting together. By accommodating diverse age groups, acknowledging the religious requirements of local communities, and addressing hidden needs, such as chronic pain or fatigue, inclusive design seeks to foster an environment where everyone can participate fully in the built environment.

In her book *Are You an Inclusive Designer*,[6] Julie Fleck references how design of our spaces influences how we are with each other and the process: 'Understanding the barriers to inclusion may help to change our attitude and our behaviours so that inclusive access becomes standard practice, an integrated and normal part of any planning, design, construction and management process' (see QR Code 5.2).

Dr Bridget Snaith, Lecturer in Landscape Architecture Design Practice at the University of Sheffield, found that while we might assume that parks equally offer everybody a space that's open for use, her research shows that actually park spaces are contested and that people do not have equal access to parks where they live for a variety of reasons.

QR Code 5.2:
LISTEN: RIBA Radio episode 21, 'Inclusive Design, featuring Julie Fleck'.

The focus of her work has been around the underrepresentation of racialised people. This isn't just to do with access to these spaces, although that is the case sometimes, but some of these outdoor spaces are in places populated by the global majority.

She surmised from her wider research that it's not about the park not being where you live, it's about the 'fit' between the groups and the parks not working quite right and experiences of racism.

She wondered if the vast majority of the people making the park space, or almost everybody making park space is white, are our parks actually whiter by design? (A reminder that there is a statistical 0 per cent of Black landscape architects according to the Landscape Institutes demographic survey of the profession published in December 2022 (see Figure 5.4).[7]

LANDSCAPE WORKFORCE DISTRIBUTION BY ETHNICITY (2022)

■ White (93%)

■ Asian or Asian British (4%)

■ Other/ Did not declare (2%)

■ Mixed or multiple ethnicities (1%)

■ Black, African, Caribbean or Black British (0%)

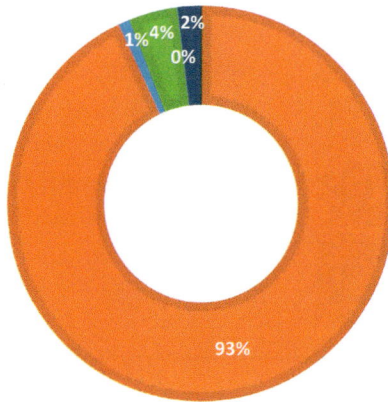

Figure 5.4 A pie chart displaying the racial demographics in landscape architecture.

TESTIMONIAL

Low expectations, very very low expectations of you. You walk in and people just assume that you're a lot younger than you actually are. It becomes degrading when someone five or six years younger than you thinks that you're younger than them, with less experience than them.

This lack of diversity ultimately hurts everyone. The progression is not really welcoming, almost monoculture.

She had 3,000 participants taking part in her engagement and equality's impact measures and what she found is that there is evidence of exclusion due to place-makers' cultural preferences.

> Those preferences are seen as being legitimate, that they are moral, that they are rational, and the other views that are associated with different cultures or religions, or people who don't subscribe to this particular world view, their views can be trivialized or even denigrated, and might even be expected to be 'educated out', such that people who don't share the legitimate view need to learn it.[8]

Open space professionals are not then reliably providing for people who have different ideals or different social needs. So, a crucial part of delivering design has to be about who is leading the process and listening to a variety of voices.

Also, inclusive design places a significant emphasis on accommodating individuals with varying sensory abilities. Addressing issues related to vision, hearing and other senses, it seeks to create designs that are intuitive and usable for all users, irrespective of their sensory capacities.

The inherent advantages of embracing inclusive design are not restricted to those with specific needs alone. By incorporating a broad spectrum of perspectives and considering the needs of a broad range of people, designers can create spaces that are not only accessible but also enjoyable and functional for all users. Inclusive design fosters a sense of wholeness, respect and dignity for every individual, leading to stronger, more cohesive communities.

Inclusive design is a holistic and purpose-driven approach that celebrates human diversity. By surpassing mere accessibility and factoring in the multifaceted aspects of human existence, it enriches lives and nurtures a more compassionate and harmonious society. Embracing inclusive design is not only a responsibility but also an opportunity to create an environment that truly values and embraces the uniqueness of every individual.

Ideas about these things continue to flex and need to remain agile. Human life is constantly changing.

GENDER INCLUSIVE = INCLUSIVE FOR ALL

A chapter of feminist author Caroline Criado Perez's *Invisible Women*[9] recounts the story of the sexist snow-clearing schedule of the Swedish town of Karlskoga: since driving routes were prioritised, women, who are more involved in caring responsibilities and making use of pavements and public transport to accompany those they care for, were put at a disadvantage. The changed schedule prioritised the needs of pedestrians over motorised vehicles and revolutionised the local area, saving millions of pounds in healthcare (fewer falls and injuries) and creating positive domino effects, with those not injured able to continue with their economic contribution to society.

Vienna's City Administration declared that 'gender equality is such an important issue', it needs to be considered 'when planning new measures'.[10] Since 2014, all aspects of public life in the Austrian capital are thought to contribute to an 'inclusive and gender-neutral destination': government bodies use gender-sensitive language to communicate, public transportation includes illustrations of men with children to signal seats reserved for parents, pavements are wide for pedestrians navigating the city with prams or children, and a large proportion of the city, including the whole public transportation network, is wheelchair accessible.

The core urban plan for the city's new Aspern neighbourhood, for example, prioritises short distances, pedestrians and cyclists, wide streets, and high-capacity public transport, creating streets (including some named after Janis Joplin and Zaha Hadid) and public spaces that are fundamentally public, human, lively, intimate and secure. While initially approached from a gender equality perspective, the result is inclusive of all.

Inequalities run so deep in our lives and cities that they are often difficult to see. No one would have viewed historic Vienna as inherently unfriendly to women and, as Criado Perez recognises, no one in Karlskoga designed or set out to create a sexist snow-clearing schedule – so no one thought of improvements either.

It takes a diverse group of people to gather, bringing their many different thoughts, voices and experiences to the table, to imagine alternative and better ways forward. Having them informs a hive revolution in cognition, and therefore design.

The lived experience of the broad diversity of people, and in particular women's lives, has in these instances revolutionised the public realm in ways we are only starting to think about. Those who traditionally hold positions of power in our societies tend to not want to work across difference because the status quo suits them; they don't have any problems, so why does it need to change?

It's clear, though, that when you include one group, invariably it's inclusive for so many others – be there inclusion of race, sexuality, disability, caring responsibilities, age – wide open spaces are effective for those who are usually physically disabled, and for gender and racial safety.

Vienna shows that inclusive design in the built environment can be legislated for – and in a really intersectional way. There's no sense that men are excluded from using these spaces, just because they've become inclusive and designed for and by women.

The UN advocates for involving girls in urban development, stating that doing so will make the city better for everyone. Their guidance, *Her City: A Guide for Cities to Sustainable and Inclusive Urban Planning and Design together with Girls*,[11] suggests that girls plan and design with diversity and different needs in mind.

> Participatory processes are key for planning a city that works for everyone. If we let citizens that are rarely heard be the experts, our cities and communities will become more inclusive, equal and sustainable.

The purpose of this initiative is to make methods and tools available to urban actors and cities globally. It supports cities to scale up and mainstream girls' participation in planning as a part of long-term strategies to build sustainable cities and societies.

By letting *Her* guide you through the urban development process, you will improve the participatory urban planning, design and implementation that are key for building a city that works for girls and young women, and ultimately for everyone.

In 2022, the *Landscape Journal* ran an issue entirely dedicated to gender equality in design, marking 100 years of women in landscape architecture.[12] In a variety of articles it sought to discuss the structural barriers holding back women in the profession, covering design, experience and impact on women. In a report on a panel she led about Gender Inclusive Design, Eleanor Trenfield, founder of EDLA, described a variety of different approaches to space and materials, stating, 'These design elements not only serve young people, but also increase … biodiversity gains'.[13]

It's inclusion for all, or it's not inclusion at all.

TESTIMONIAL: Architecture: Queer in Identity and Action

Gem Barton, author, academic and founding chair of QuEAN (Queer Educators in Architecture Network)

Architecture, one of oldest and most conservative of disciplinary traditions, is frequently resistant to creative critique, activism and subversion of its hegemonies – the very opposite of queer theory and thinking. From the outside Architecture and Queerness are very unlikely bedfellows, binary opposites even. If architecture is to be *just*, if architecture is to be for *humanity*, then architecture needs Queer-ing.

A cursory look at the ARB diversity data in August 2023 tells you the profession is still the domain of the self-serving straight, white, male; Straight/hetero = 78 per cent, White = 80 per cent, Male = 68 per cent. But *identity* and *action* here are not exclusive; one can *be* queer and not *do* queer, equally one can be straight-identifying and still embody queer practices. Queer in *action* means to unsettle, to unnerve, to bother established norms, exactly what architecture requires in unprecedented times of inequality, waste, exclusion and injustice.

Too often the 'labour of change' and the responsibility to educate others falls to the marginalised – those whose queer identity often brings with it a subversive desire, born from repression, to deform and reform mainstream standards. It is time for the privileged majority within the architecture profession to do *the work*, to reconcile past failings, squash the hostile ego and to consider those who are different to them, as harbingers of hope.

RIBA INCLUSIVE DESIGN OVERLAY

In July 2023, a small group of motivated professionals, led by Pareisse Wilson, an inclusive design and access consultant, launched the Inclusive Design Overlay to the RIBA Plan of Work,[14] after more than two years of collaboration across the built environment (see QR Code 5.3).

The Overlay incorporates inclusive design principles into five essential team roles: Client, Project Management Team, Design Team, Construction Team, and Asset Management Team.

These roles are pivotal in shaping the inclusive design strategy, application and success of overall outcomes. It also provides guidance on involving an Inclusive Design Lead (Consultant or Champion) and defines their role and responsibilities. Inclusive design enablers, like an inclusive design strategy, form the foundation for its effective implementation throughout the project.

KEY RESOURCE: RIBA Inclusive Design Overlay

Lead Author: Pareisse Wilson

What is the issue that the overlay is trying to address?

The inclusive design overlay is seeking to address a few main problems.

- Creating confidence to discuss the topic of inclusive design and to know when to appoint an inclusive design consultant or champion.
- Having a singular framework that all built environment professionals could work towards.
- Provide support for why inclusive design expertise is necessary.

What's exciting about this overlay is it gives everyone a bit of a baseline in terms of a definition of what is an inclusive design consultant, what is an inclusive design champion, what is an inclusive design audit? And what's an inclusive design review? When does it happen? Why does it happen? And who is it done with? And what it does is it takes the, I think there has been a natural pressure and worry going back to the first reason why we set this up, a pressure to have all the answers regarding inclusion.

This overlay says you don't have to figure it all out, specialists can do that. The overlay provides the definition of what their role is and what they're supposed to cover. The whole overlay itself encourages all the different roles to work together.

How does the overlay work?

There are five roles and it maps, according to the roles, what should be done at each RIBA work stage regarding inclusive design and how they're interlinked and who to connect with to develop a space or design.

The inclusive design strategy is not siloed by the client. It's done with the inclusive design lead and the asset management team. It's a strategy that's developed in partnership with other people. This is a theme throughout the overlay, the design team in one of the work stages might be encouraged to engage and consult with the user group.

They do that in partnership with the inclusive design lead, or it might later in the work stages that we, for example, need to develop a building manual. That building manual needs to have element sections dedicated to inclusion and access within the building from a facilities perspective. Now that would be done and informed by the client, asset management team and the inclusive design lead.

The design team might have provided insights based on what products they chose to go into the environment. They might feed into it as well. What you find is these regular moments not just doing things by yourself. It's a team effort. It breaks down so many of the silos that take place when creating environments and encourages people to do it together.

What outcomes do you hope to see from its use?

A clear strategy for inclusive design on projects that is given the same attention and weight and budget that a sustainability strategy gets, that a net zero strategy gets, that a social value, social impact strategy gets. I'm looking forward to projects where clients approach us, or clients approach inclusive design consultants, and EDI practitioners who, have put aside a budget for this.

A budget that runs beyond the strategy, a budget that runs applicable throughout the RIBA work stages just for inclusive design. The second thing is I think we are going to see far more user engagement. I think community and user engagement is going to go up, and I think it's also going to go up with a new lens.

There is an engagement overlay from the RIBA. We know that for social value practitioners, community engagement is like bread and butter for them. The difference is for the inclusive design overlay is that we talk about user groups, and this is a key section in the overlay called *enablers*. This is where we cover some of the core enabling actions or tools that you need to make this overlay come to life.

In there, you've got a definition of an inclusive design strategy in there, you've got a definition of what a user group is and how to mobilise it. There's an understanding of equality impact assessments and we say that equality impact assessments can be used in tandem with built environment projects.

They no longer must sit with organisational change only. User groups are all about the protected characteristics and beyond, and thinking about who is impacted by your designs. Get a group together that reflects those that are impacted and consult and engage and consult and engage regularly throughout the design process.

I think we're going to see more environments where people have genuinely co-created, co-shaped, the design of a space and feel far more bought in as a result because they were so engaged.

There would be more stewardship of environments because of people who have just been engaged with that.

QR Code 5.3:
INTERACT: RIBA Inclusive Design Overlay and Guidance.

DELIVERING INCLUSIVE PRODUCTS AND SERVICES

Practices and organisations should prioritise the integration of EDI principles across everything they produce. To achieve this, the design, development and delivery teams must focus on incorporating inclusivity into products and services while ensuring respectful customer service. Advocating for inclusive working practices, safe conditions and fair treatment of all workers, including contingent staff and supply chain partners is also part of ensuring inclusivity across the piece.

In pursuit of proper inclusive approaches, organisations should extensively research current and emerging – especially underrepresented – markets, seeking insights into a full range of user requirements and unmet demands. To ensure comprehensive perspectives, input from various stakeholders, including the workforce, should be actively solicited during the design, development and delivery processes.

Recognising the impact of marketing and advertising communication, organisations should look to use positive images of a full range of individuals and use inclusive language to reflect their commitment to EDI principles.

CASE STUDY: Delivering Inclusive Design

Ed Warner, CEO, Motionspot

What's the issue that you were trying to solve when you set up Motionspot?

When we first set up Motionspot in 2012, we were very much trying to blend function with form to design more beautiful accessible spaces. Motionspot started initially as a company supplying beautiful, accessible bathrooms to people's homes because it's the bathroom where people want the greatest independence (see Figure 5.5). It's also where the biggest 'design crimes' tend to happen. Whilst the business has grown considerably over the last 10 years in our 'for home' business, the main part of our business now, and the problem we're trying to solve is how do we encourage clients and their design teams to understand how to design more beautiful, accessible and inclusive spaces for their employees, visitors and customers.

Figure 5.5 Inclusive bathroom design at The Londoner hotel in Leicester Square by Motionspot.

So how did you go about addressing these issues of 'accessible design crimes'?

Firstly built a really talented team of inclusive designers who know what needs to be done in this area of inclusive design. What's fascinating for us at the moment is the world of inclusive design is moving so quickly. A really great project is one where we can draw on best practice and global standards, but also research, pair it with our own inclusive designers' knowledge and experience of what works.

But really importantly, we talk to the people who are ultimately using these spaces. And that is what so often gets missed from the design process when designing accessible and inclusive spaces. Predominantly the designers of those spaces are not facing the same challenges that people using those buildings and spaces are. Not taking those perspectives into account is what's causing the barriers and challenges. So for us, it's all about evidence-based design, listening to people who are using the spaces and thinking creatively that accessible design doesn't have to look medical and institutional.

What have been the outcomes that you've seen to date for your clients?

The positive outcome is when we can get a client to understand that they shouldn't be just ticking a box to meet minimum standards of building regulations. The best outcome we deliver for clients is to help them raise the bar beyond minimum standards and design spaces to suit not just physical disability, but also sensory, cognitive disability. We see a lot of our outcomes being really great spaces designed for neurodiversity. Also, as our business has progressed and the industry has progressed, we're not just designing for disability, but we're designing for faith, ethnic background, culture, age, gender, all protected characteristics.

The type of work we do with clients is to help them understand what are the key principles that they need to embed in their developments. We put together bespoke inclusive design standards for clients to help them say, this is the benchmark we want to hit for all of our new builds and refurbishments.

Figure 5.6 Inclusive design by Motionspot at Hotel Brooklyn. Photograph by Henry Woide.

But that isn't a successful outcome unless the designers and operations teams implement those guidelines. So for us, we call ourselves an inclusive design golden thread that runs through a project, and we're there at each RIBA stage being able to fly the flag for inclusive design and ensure it's being thought about in the right way, but also being integrated really sensitively into buildings and spaces (see Figure 5.6).

The outcome that drives us as a business is the impact we can have on the people ultimately using these buildings in spaces. We are really keen to continue to measure and track that impact and report it back to clients and demonstrate just what an inclusive building means to their business, to their employees and their customers.

And that's so connected to the messages in your book about recruiting the best talent, retaining the best talent, improving health and wellbeing, productivity, it just being the right thing to do.

What reflections have you had across your 10, 12 years of business?

The world of inclusive design is still in its infancy. It has a long way to go. People are still just at the very early stages of understanding what it means. There is still a prevalence in the industry to tick a box when it comes to accessibility and not challenge the thinking beyond that.

We want to see inclusive design embedded across all roles within the built environment. And the recent inclusive design overlay for the RIBA Plan of Work published in July is a great starting point for that. We'd also like to see inclusive design embedded into architectural courses and interior design courses as part of learning. This shouldn't just be a specialism that sits with an inclusive design consultant.

Everyone in the built environment has a responsibility to design inclusively.

Importantly too, a building or space is only as inclusive as the people who operate it. You can have the most beautiful inclusively designed building, but if it's not operated in the right way and people aren't aware of the inclusive design principles that have gone into it, it's not going to be accessible and inclusive for the people using the space.

So ensuring that training is there after a new build or refurbishment is completed is really important.

BEHAVIOURAL ANALYSIS

DRIVE: How responsible do you want to be for 'design crimes' for those requiring accessible spaces? Consider this as a motivator to be thoughtful about inclusive design.

KNOWLEDGE: Gather all the information you can about who you think might use the space, but also who could use it too.

STRATEGY: Don't make any assumptions about those who might use a space, but be collaborative and design with users, planning every stage of the project in alignment with the Inclusive Design Overlay.

ACTION: Work towards an outcome that reaches a higher bar than legislation requires.

Feedback from stakeholders should be highly valued. Practices and firms should gather feedback on user and client experiences, interactions with representatives, and overall satisfaction and dissatisfaction with design and other relationship matters. Data on market opportunities and risks should be collected, too, to assess impacts on diverse market segments.

As part of inclusive design, internally, a company should place significance on understanding the work environment and treatment of employees. Information collected in this regard facilitates the nurturing of a respectful workplace culture, and this is a matter of integrity that internal behaviours reflect on external outcomes with proper alignment between the two.

There is a wealth of further information and resource around inclusive design available. It remains your personal responsibility to think widely about inclusive design, not just accessibility, to seek to achieve a bar far higher than the legal requirements, as legislation is not adequate in order to do this properly, and start with the right inclusive behaviours.

A final note for now on design: 'Architects wear black', said Jason Boyle FRIBA in his podcast *The Broke Architect*. 'Why do you like the colour orange so much?' he asked me. It's not just orange, although (if I may take this moment to sound pretentious), it is my signature colour, I do love a rainbow. I love the vibrancy and joy of colour. It turns out, so does designer Ingrid Fetell Lee who advocates for more colour in architecture. 'School administrators say that attendance improves, graffiti disappears and kids actually say they feel safer in these painted schools. And this aligns with research conducted in four countries, which shows that people working in more colourful offices are actually more alert, more confident and friendlier than those working in drab spaces.'[15] So, when it comes to inclusive design, rethinking informed by colour – perhaps even in what the professions wear – might help.

KEY TAKEAWAYS

- Inclusive design is significantly less about the architect, and much more about impact architecture for social benefit.
- Rethinking human-centred design happens alongside planet-centred design.
- Human + planet-centered design can be found in some indigenous sustainable practices.
- When you design inclusively for one group, invariably it includes so many others.

- The Inclusive Design Overlay to RIBA's Plan of Work provides in-depth guidance to help with every stage.
- The delivery of other products and services involve inclusive behaviours informing every part of the production stage of those products and services.
- Access the many sources of research and support to deliver inclusive design.

NOTES

1 The New Library, Magdelene College, Stirling Prize winner 2022, Naill McLaughlin Architects. See www.architecture.com/awards-and-competitions-landing-page/awards/riba-regional-awards/riba-east-award-winners/2022/magdalene-college-library [Accessed 29 November 2023].

2 'The Entire History of You', *Black Mirror*, Episode 3, Series 1, written by Jesse Armstrong. Zeppotron Production for Endemol, Channel 4.

3 Kingston University London – Town House, Stirling Prize winner 2021, Grafton Architects. See www.architecture.com/awards-and-competitions-landing-page/awards/riba-stirling-prize/RIBA-Stirling-Prize-2021 [Accessed 29 November 2023].

4 Availability bias is a cognitive shortcut where people rely on readily available information to make judgements, often overestimating the likelihood of events based on their recent or vivid exposure. This can lead to skewed perceptions and inaccurate decision-making.

5 Angela Fitz, Elke Krasny, Marvi Mazhar and Architekturzentrum Wien (eds), *Yasmeen Lari: Architecture for the Future*, MIT Press, 2023.

6 Julie Fleck, *Are You an Inclusive Designer*, RIBA Publishing, 2019.

7 *Landscape Skills and Workforce Survey*, Landscape Institute, 2022. See https://landscapewpstorage01.blob.core.windows.net/www-landscapeinstitute-org/2022/12/773450-Landscape-Institute_INTERACTIVE.pdf [Accessed 29 November 2023].

   The sector is predominantly white, at around 93 per cent of the workforce, compared to 86.8 per cent nationally. Ethnic minorities are most pronounced across the design sub-sector at 8 per cent of the total. Sub-sectors with the lowest levels of ethnic minorities in the workforce are protection (1 per cent), research, education and policy (2 per cent) and implementation (2 per cent); 93 per cent white, 4 per cent Asian/Asian British, 1 per cent mixed/multiple ethnic groups, 0 per cent Black/Black British.

8 Dr Bridget Snaith, Green Space or White Space, Festival of Place Bytesize event. See www.youtube.com/watch?v=EkdtBNpZf4I [Accessed 29 November 2023].

9 Carline Criado Perez, *Invisible Women*, Chatto & Windus, 2018, Chapter 1, pp. 29–46.

10 'The five principles of gender mainstreaming', City of Vienna Politics and Administration website, Austria. See www.wien.gv.at/english/administration/gendermainstreaming/principles/five-principles.html [Accessed 29 November 2023].

11 *Her City — A Guide for Cities to Sustainable and Inclusive Urban Planning and Design together with Girls*. See https://unhabitat.org/her-city-a-guide-for-cities-to-sustainable-and-inclusive-urban-planning-and-design-together-with [Accessed 29 November 2023].

12 'Designing for gender equality: Celebrating 100 years of women in landscape architecture', *Landscape Institute*, 2022. See https://issuu.com/landscape-institute/docs/12954_li_journal_3_2022_v16_issuu_1_ [Accessed 29 November 2023].

13 Eleanor Trenfield, 'Gender inclusive design, landscape', *Journal of the Landscape Institute*, 2022, 3: 60–61.

14 *Inclusive Design Overlay to the RIBA Plan of Work*, RIBA. See www.architecture.com/knowledge-and-resources/resources-landing-page/inclusive-design-overlay-to-riba-plan-of-work [Accessed 29 November 2023].

15 Ingrid Fetell Lee, 'Where joy hides and how to find it', *Ted Talk*, YouTube. See https://www.ted.com/talks/ingrid_fetell_lee_where_joy_hides_and_how_to_find_it [Accessed 29 November 2023].

Chapter Six

> I invited public bodies to demonstrate where and when they had appointed Black architects. It was so vanishingly rare in London that instances ended up being conspicuous.
>
> Architect X, 2023

You can't have spatial justice without racial justice, or any other kinds of social justice. This can be found through economic empowerment.

> If the global economy chose to dissolve the economic obstacles facing women, an unprecedented era of peace and prosperity would follow.[1]

Addressing issues of intersectional racial underrepresentation through procurement in the built environment is particularly relevant when managing approaches to diversity, because of significant racial underrepresentation in leadership across built environment professions. 'Survey after survey shows a greater propensity amongst non-white minorities for self-employment, the number of ethnic minority-owned SMEs will continue to grow in the coming years and become increasingly important to socio-economic growth in Britain', according to the Minority Supplier Development UK (MSDUK) report, *The Road to Inclusive Procurement*.[2]

SMEs (small and medium-sized enterprises) account for 99.9 per cent of the business population,[3] and according to MSDUK, in the UK alone, one in six businesses are minority-owned. This covers three million people, which accounts for 10 per cent of the UK's workforce and contributes £78 billion to the British economy. However, less than 1 per cent of corporate spend currently goes to the minority community.[4] This is a massive missed opportunity, because, not only are smaller businesses more agile, but they add value in many ways, including to the reputation of an organisation[5] and feeding back into their local economies (see Figure 6.1).

Of course, an intersectional approach requires us to look at our behaviours, motivation, knowledge, strategy and action, to create procedural

DOI: 10.4324/9781003435747-10

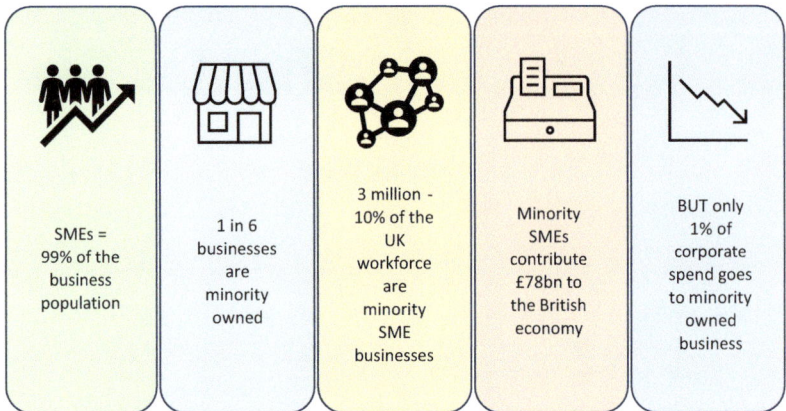

Figure 6.1 Infographic with SME statistics.

change, so attempts at inclusive practices are meaningful and not token-istic. Monitoring who is benefiting from being part of your supply chain will help you track who has access and who does not so you can take targeted action to address gaps in demographics.

In his critique of how architects can work through their profession, rather than within it, to demonstrate justice, Charlie Edmonds, of the Future Architects Front, argues that it's through organising a collective long-term approach to campaigning and political economics, not just through design, that equitable outcomes are more guaranteed.[6] I would say that procurement is one of the levers to do this, so even if you don't see yourself as an activist, you can still bring about a levelling of the economic playing field.

Inclusive procurement is the activity. Supplier diversity is the demographic factor you address with that activity.

The accepted definition of **supplier diversity** is 'an organisation that is at least 51% owned and operated by a group or individual that is traditionally part of an under-represented or under-served demographic. This includes Indigenous people, women, veterans, LGBTQ+ individuals, people with disabilities, and those from ethnic minorities'.[3] Whilst this is the accepted definition, it's always worth considering other groups that are discriminated against that aren't listed here, for example, those who are forcibly displaced/refugees, faith groups, neurodivergent and ex-offenders. Because of the intersectional nature of identities, the future may well hold a greater emphasis on access and equitable outcomes, than on the identities themselves.

In the realm of built environment practices and collaborations, procurement comes into play for acquiring goods or services. The entire procurement process involves various stages, such as tendering, supplier selection, contracting, and contract management. It's crucial that the organisation's EDI principles are integrated at every step of this process.

When discussing the suppliers that a project relies upon, they collectively form its supply chain. This supply chain can consist of vendors or subcontractors of different sizes, sectors and locations. To strengthen their position, many businesses adopt the strategy we call 'supplier diversity' in order to broaden the range of suppliers. The goal here is to enhance organisational resilience. However, often there is an inherent bias against doing so, allied with perceptions of risk.

There is no evidence whatsoever for not engaging with underrepresented groups in your supply chain. Research by the Hackett Group[7] shows that nearly all 'diverse' suppliers meet or exceed expectations in the delivery of products and services. If you've got talent that shows up, does the work and meets or exceeds expectations, and with that you can create a positive economic impact for a community, and with that you can encourage that community to engage more with your services, and perceive your organisation more favourably, really, there is no objective reason not to.

The only barrier would be individual and structural bias around perceived risk, which has no basis in reality according to the research. Engaging in supplier diversity is not about picking up just anyone who fulfils a particular characteristic, of course you'd need to procure a competent supplier, the point is, there are a lot of them available, and the only thing stopping you from accessing that competent supplier would be unhelpful bias.

So, demonstrating cultural intelligence, and creating policies, procedures and processes to access these groups, will assist with mitigating it. Also, create an environment of psychological safety where, when all procedures are followed, if something does go wrong, it's considered not as an issue of identity but, clearly, it would be something else where you can promote learning.

DEMONSTRATING INCLUSIVE PROCUREMENT

The Social Value Act requires public sector agencies to consider social and environmental benefits when commissioning a public service. The social return on investment through inclusive procurement and using supplier diversity can be difficult to quantify, however the ripple effects of supporting a community by delivering spend within it can be fed back to you via narratives and surveys; so, more qualitative data.

Ensuring that EDI principles, objectives and expectations are seamlessly incorporated and effectively communicated throughout every stage of the procurement process is something you can do with an explicit code of conduct.[8] The Chartered Institute of Procurement and Supply has some useful examples which you can use as templates.

There really is no such thing as 'hard to reach communities', only the will and motivation to reach those communities and engage with them. Many women and ethnic-minority owned businesses (EMBs) are in various supplier diversity portals and networks, and supported by frameworks, such as the Architecture + Urbanism Framework put together by the GLA. So, actively participate in supplier outreach activities to discover a diverse range of potential suppliers, generate occasions for businesses owned by underrepresented individuals or groups, strengthen stakeholder contacts and enhance organisational resilience.

Procurement processes can be complicated and unwieldy, making it difficult to navigate for smaller organisations, so the use of portals and pre-determined suitability for work will help provide opportunities to the range of groups you need in order to address underrepresentation.

CASE STUDY: Inclusion in Supply Chain, Heathrow

Jenny McLaughlin, Project Manager and Disability Network Lead

What is the situation you were trying to address?

My role at Heathrow is Project Manager. I'm also currently the lead for the disability network and I very strongly believe that the two hats should go together. So, understanding how we have unintentionally created barriers through our supply chain, through our procurement, to not enabling everybody to be able to access our airport, be they passengers, be they colleagues, or be they what we call 'Team Heathrow', which is our other companies that work in and around Heathrow Airport.

What I came to acknowledge is my own barriers that I hadn't acknowledged in myself. I have ADHD and dyslexia and I was starting to be aware, also as a female within a construction industry space, that's an anomaly.

I started to notice there were moments where, in my gut, I knew I was unsafe. I wasn't brave enough to talk about it because I didn't want anyone to believe that I wasn't entitled to be in that space, or I should be removed from that space because it was my fault that I was unsafe and not a fault or a fact of the design. I spoke to both our health and safety managers and advisors and also the procurement team and said that I wanted to hold a workshop looking at how do we better draw out what it means, and what do we need to do, in order to ensure that people have a voice within this space to say, 'this wasn't designed for me'.

What did you do to address the situation?

We linked that with something within our procurement strategy, which is called The Balance Scorecard. The Balance Scorecard is there to help incentivise our suppliers through procurement to deliver against the Heathrow Values. Now Heathrow Values are things like 'keeping everybody safe', 'working together', 'improving every day'. What I started to talk about, to the supply chain, within this workshop, is that that has to mean everybody. If it doesn't mean everybody, we are not living our values.

I started to draw this out with a number of examples, to bring to life for them what it meant. I got them to understand their own safety and to recognise that they are also not equitably safe within all spaces. That this is the problem that we are trying to solve. Through that, we have now designed a couple of things to start that journey.

We created a model where you answer a question and it creates a circle of possibilities. The questions get them to think about what things have they assumed or what things have they not looked at in terms of 'is the design built for everybody?' What it's very easy to do is only go on your own lived experience and not recognise that there's a lot of matters that have not been considered. What that's really started to draw out is that more of our supply chain and in our procurements, we are beginning to think differently, behave differently, and ultimately start to recognise where the gaps are in knowledge. Also, working with us collaboratively on that journey to improve.

What I say to individuals when this all sounds very, very scary is, these are incremental small steps. We are not going to go from A to Z in one go. We are going to make little steps and some of them will work and some of them won't and that's fine. But unless we start on this journey to start making those incremental steps, we will never get to the point where I can walk on site and I am as safe as the person next to me. And I know that anybody on that site feels safe, psychologically safe, enough to stick their hand up and say, this wasn't designed for me.

How long has it taken from the time you first started the workshops to the outcomes that you are seeing now?

It's probably taken between two and three years. If I think back to where we started to where we are now, the biggest difference is that I don't have to explain what equitable safety is when I go into the room. That's a massive change in terms of behaviour and culture to understand that not everybody experiences safety the same way.

It's like fire safety. I would say there are a big percentage of fire safety doors out there that I am not strong enough to open. And is that, actually, a fire safety door if I can't escape through it?

What learnings and reflections have you had about your scheme?

If I was starting again, I would have created more collateral to start off with so momentum could be improved upon. A lot of time was taken creating learning materials as we went. I think we almost needed to start with something that people could see and understand earlier on, so that they knew they had something to take away and start trying.

Until we're brave enough to say 'that's incorrect', it's not going to change. Somebody's got to be brave enough to say, that standard only suits this particular demographic, or even worse, we have no idea what the demographic is that that standard suits. We are just, none of us, brave enough to disagree with it because 'it's not my fault, it's the standard's fault'. But you are choosing in that moment to not question the standard, which could be wrong.

That's why the workshops have been so important, because we created the safety to question the basis of design.

BEHAVIOURAL ANALYSIS

DRIVE: Apply the principles here by asking what is the inherent value in encouraging your supply chain to join you in your inclusion journey? The procurement frameworks you want to join, are they asking about EDI when scoring?

KNOWLEDGE: What examples can you give to your supply chain about different lived experiences that can make EDI relevant to them? Build in empathy where you can.

STRATEGY: Create small steps and interventions to help them with aligning with you on inclusive practices, be aware of what they might think is too big a leap and plan accordingly.

ACTION: Reflect on how conversations go, know you can have the same approach with each supplier and adapt for each as appropriate.

MEASURING INCLUSIVE PROCUREMENT

The ISO for Human Resource Management,[9] which looks at EDI, suggests a range of generic measures to track inclusive procurement practices, which are relevant across all sectors including the built environment. These include:

- the number of organisations, by ownership, progressing through each stage of the procurement process, including those registering an interest in contract opportunities;
- the amount of spend with organisations in the supply chain;
- the number of people working for supply chain partners;
- the number of complaints, incidents and allegations relating to bias or discrimination to determine breaches in EDI contractual clauses; and
- the effectiveness of procurement and supply chain activities at different stages.

'BAME WASHING' AND WINDOW-DRESSING

Some white-led architecture firms have been accused of 'using' EMBs in a tokenistic way to boost EDI credentials when entering competitions or trying to procure public sector work. This is known as 'BAME washing'.

There are a variety of opinions on how this affects EMBs,[10] however, I would always advocate more a more thoughtful approach to inclusion, rather than a knee-jerk reaction to a competition criterion which has you scrambling for your contacts list if you're a white-male-led organisation.

> ### TESTIMONIAL
>
> In an award application, amongst other attributes, my practice claimed to be diverse and supportive to all. I emailed the studio member who had said this, to explain that the studio is not diverse. We have no Black people and I am one of the few people of colour, and I don't have any support from anyone senior with experience of dealing with consequential issues.

I was once live in a – thankfully, online – panel when my phone and watch started buzzing madly; when it's on 'Do Not Disturb', if you try me three times or more within 15 minutes it starts to ring. Clearly, it's an emergency, right? It was an architecture practice wanting to know if they could use my name in their bid for some public work. The deadline was imminent. I had a ton of questions, when I eventually got back to them, and as we spoke I thought, 'Oh yeah? Hmmm. Let's just see where this goes…' knowing exactly how I was feeling about it, as I handed over my CV. As I expected, precisely nowhere is the answer, and they haven't been back in touch since. Great procurers, who are weighting EDI, invariably have good staff who will see through tokenistic gestures.

In order to be properly mindful of EDI when approaching scored public sector procurement or when being assessed for it in competitions (something I would promote all competition holders did, with an automatic strike off if not addressed suitably), these are the following areas I suggest you address in bids (see Table 6.1).

Table 6.1 EDI criteria for architecture competitions.

	Area of EDI	
1	Understanding of EDI.	Describe and clarify what you mean about the words you're using in the bid.
2	Champion of EDI.	Biographies of team members need to show how you've demonstrated a commitment to EDI.
3	Evidence of working with diversity of people in the past and calling on expertise again.	Clarify who you've worked with in the past from underrepresented groups and get testimonials about how involved they were in the project, and how they might be involved again.
4	Treating collaborators well in key project roles.	Co-authorship and co-design voices centrally placed as pertaining to context and community engagement.
5	Thinking about source materials' impact and colonialism.	Where relevant, acknowledging coloniality and describing praxes to achieve decoloniality across the project.
6	Accessibility.	Beyond simply meeting legislative requirements, thoughtfully strategising how different visible and invisible disabilities can enjoy and benefit from the space.
7	Inclusive procurement procedures.	Demonstrating use of supplier diversity across the supply chain in potential choices and how you'll quantify the impact.
8	Building user inclusivity.	A wider description of inclusivity beyond disability, for example, gender safety, child access, faiths.
9	Referencing use of external expertise.	What kind of inclusion and accessibility support you've approached to assist with these matters if you don't have an in-house expert.

For those running competitions and procurement bids, be explicit about wanting these areas addressed in the brief. Each area should be scored between 0 and 5 to determine how strong it is in each area, and then translate that score into the overall weighted percentage. If any area is not addressed sufficiently, that is, scoring 0, it would be feedback for future submissions, and an automatic rejection. Overall, any score below 25 should be an automatic rejection. Any score between 25 and 34 should be marginal with strong guidance on developing these areas in the next phase of the project. If there are no entries that score enough, go back out to competition again, encouraging firms run by those who qualify as diverse suppliers and those with a history of inclusive work.

For the supply chain to function effectively, and for inclusive procurement to be done properly, all partners, including the supplier involved, should show a continuous commitment to EDI principles. Additionally, they need to implement proper HR management practices to ensure that the work provided is decent, with safe and secure working conditions, and fair and respectful treatment of all people involved.

CASE STUDY: GLA Architecture + Urbanism Framework

Rae Whittow-Williams, Principal Project Officer and Architecture and Urbanism Framework Manager, Regeneration Team

What is the situation you were trying to address?

We know that the built environment industry isn't representing the people of London in terms of ethnicity, gender, sexual orientation, ability and more. We had patchy data on that as well. It's not easy to get London-specific data on architects and urban designers. The data that we did have from a piece of work that we did through the Good Growth by Design programme showed the real issue with the diversity of London's architects, the architect sector. Comparatively, we also have the more up-to-date Architects Registration Board data, which is UK-wide, but still paints a pretty shocking picture. The Mayor believes that as people designing and making decisions about our city, the architecture and design sector should reflect the diversity of London itself.

We knew global majority architects continue to experience discrimination in workplace, homophobic experiences of LGBTQ+ architects, work on site, so we had this data as well as around ethnicity and gender and representation in general.

The Mayor says that for progress to be made, we all need to do our bit. He put a call out to everyone working in the built environment sector to consider how they can contribute to making the industry more diverse and take action. With that, and from the data that we have, the kind of experiences that we have working within our projects, we know that the built environment can actually exclude groups and create new inequalities if it's not designed and managed in an inclusive way.

So how we design and who is involved in that process is kind of really important to create inclusive outcomes to create a safe city for all Londoners to live in.

What did you do to address this situation?

When we set out to develop the procurement strategy for the new framework we set a series of strategic objectives and we had one which was to address the underrepresentation of women and people from minority groups in public procurement processes and promote equality opportunity in access to public sector work.

That includes looking at how we might broaden the range of suppliers that we work with and how we can also hold larger practices to account on their diversity commitments.

We acknowledged internally that political leadership was required to realise the full potential of public procurement to achieve better social impact. We had to take really practical action to ensure that our policy objectives to create a more representative framework wasn't going to be undermined by the bureaucratic typical habits of something like public sector procurement, which is quite challenging in itself. There are not, necessarily, specialists in the procurement team that deal just with built environment procurement. They deal with multiple other goods and services.

Procuring pens is very different to procuring around the optics of designers, architects etc. This required a significant piece of internal stakeholder management.

We've now post-rationalised that into our 10-step Supply Diversity Action Plan.

What have been the outcomes of this work?

Launched in 2023 the Mayor of London's Architecture + Urbanism (A+U) Framework provides a diverse, pre-approved panel of built environment consultants, making it quicker and easier for organisations like councils and housing associations to commission expertise for a range of built environment projects.

The Framework can be used by public sector commissioning authorities across the UK to appoint high-quality architectural, place making and urban planning design services. It has been established to support high-quality city making at both the strategic and detailed ends of the design process, support the Mayor's mission-led approach to the recovery of London, and create a panel of consultants more representative of London's diverse population.

There was a particular strategic objective to address the under-representation of women and people from minority groups in public procurement processes and promote equality of opportunity in access to public sector work, which including broadening the range of suppliers we work with and holding larger practices to account on their diversity commitments. Acknowledging that,

- Political leadership is required to realise the full potential of public sector procurement to achieve better social impact.
- Practical action being required to ensure policy objectives are not undermined by bureaucratic habits.
- The potential for procurement to be the greatest tool for achieving change.

What reflections and learning to you take away from the process:

From the research undertaken in the procurement strategy scoping phase it became clear that the need to develop a strategic case would be key in being able to achieve the relevant stakeholder approvals from GLA and TfL decision makers. This process included working with the Collaborative Procurement team at TfL, alongside GLA Responsible Procurement and commissioning teams across the GLA Group to reshape the existing procurement process, strip away unnecessary perceived barriers and devise an innovative procurement strategy to guide the overarching process. The 10-step Supply Diversity Action Plan now exists to serve that need.

BEHAVIOURAL ANALYSIS

DRIVE: What value could you get from developing your EDI policies so you can get on the A+U Framework (or similar where you work)? What are the consequences for you not attempting to get up to speed? How can you develop your confidence around the criteria listed, so you can be sure your approach is robust?

KNOWLEDGE: Look out for courses and support to help you develop your EDI credentials so you can make it onto these frameworks. Listen to the supply chain and do the data analysis of who you currently use to deliver projects.

STRATEGY: Check any assumptions and mitigate bias when perceiving risk about working with underrepresented groups in order to present yourself successfully for frameworks.

ACTION: Be prepared to listen to take on feedback if you're not successful making it onto frameworks where EDI is scored. Do the introspective piece of work to adapt, improve and try again.

BUYING SOCIAL JUSTICE THROUGH PROCUREMENT

The Buying Social Justice Through Procurement research team state that:

> Only 12% of those working in the construction industry in the UK are women and only 5–7% are from ethnic minority backgrounds. The picture is even starker in the building trades, where women account for just 1% of the workforce. Such low numbers persist despite numerous equality and diversity initiatives in the sector in recent years. There is plenty of evidence to suggest that the problem isn't that women or ethnic minorities don't want to work in construction, but instead the low numbers are a result of traditional and often discriminatory recruitment practices. As well, the workplace culture can be unwelcoming to women and minorities.[11]

The group has been exploring whether public procurement can overcome these barriers by setting equality objectives in the contracting process and monitoring the progress of contractors (see Figure 6.2). They say that early evidence suggests that this can work, where the client – or public body in charge of a project – sets ambitious objectives from the start. They add that the construction of London's Olympic Park and the HS2 rail infrastructure project are just two successful examples.

In addition, they launched a toolkit to assist firms wanting to pursue 'buying social justice through procurement'.[12] The practical advice,

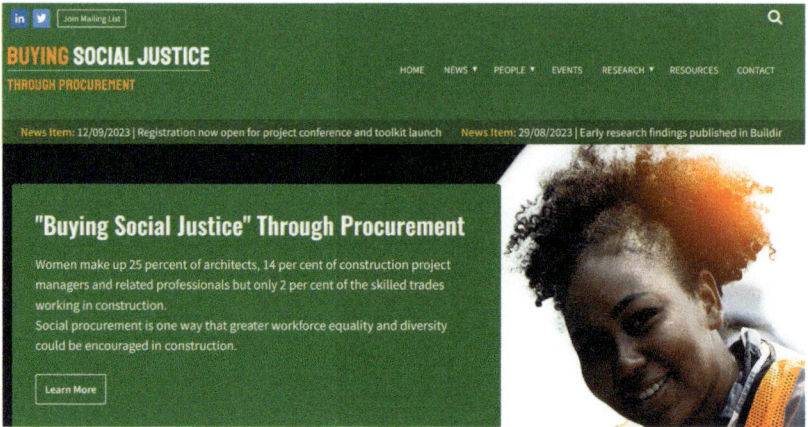

Figure 6.2 Buying Social Justice Through Procurement website frontpage.

guidance and insight is to support individuals in the public sector in their efforts to advance social justice through their procurement activity, with a focus on EDI.

> Although it draws from research conducted on local authorities, housing associations and universities, we believe it can provide valuable insights for a broad spectrum of public organisations. It aims to complement the existing guidance and frameworks on procurement and social value developed for the public sector.

QR Code 6.1:
ACCESS: Buying Social Justice Through Procurement Toolkit.

Construction remains a male-dominated sector, despite many industry efforts to change the gender balance and increase workforce diversity, and public procurement has been identified as a tool for change. While many of the examples in the toolkit focus on the procurement of construction works, the toolkit also covers the purchasing of goods and services and should be of use to those undertaking different forms of procurement. There is a growing need for organisations to prove their economic and social governance (ESG) credentials to clients, investors, and employees.[13]

QR Code 6.2:
ACCESS: Buying
Social Justice Through
Procurement Report.

Whilst the toolkit (see QR Codes 6.1 and 6.2) has been created with the public sector in mind, there's no reason why the principles can't be applied to other businesses and third sector organisations in order to deliver on social justice objectives. It is freely available and anyone reading this book can download it right away to start applying its principles.

CASE STUDY: Delivering Social Value

Russell Curtis, Founding Director, RCKa

How do you start to build social value into a project?

We finished a building ten years ago, the TNG Youth and Community centre in Lewisham (see Figure 6.3). It's very deprived in some areas, but also very affluent in some respects. The reason we are looking back at it now, ten years, is we can start to measure some of the outputs.

That project was the product of a very intense and inclusive engagement process. We ran a series of workshops with young people from the estate in collaboration with – as it was then – the Stephen Lawrence Charitable Trust.

With the so-called more 'difficult to reach' young people, we talked about their experiences and what it was like to live in the area. It was like the site analysis bit, but social site analysis. We discovered the social ley lines that we were trying to understand.

We can go to the site and we can walk around and take photographs of stuff, but we don't know where the gang boundaries are and where the druggies hang out and where the homeless guy sleeps, and so on.

These things are all part of that social context.

Figure 6.3 TNG Youth and Community Centre in Lewisham. Photograph by Jim Stephenson.

How did you engage the community?

Then we did some spatial exercises getting them to think spatially about some of their experiences. We started to talk about the brief itself and the kind of spaces that they needed, where they were comfortable and what sort of spaces they felt thought were uncomfortable and what was welcoming and what wasn't.

And that process engaged them in thinking about the built environment and gave them a voice, being able to question whether the built environment is designed for them or not. It gave agency over it.

We co-designed the building.

But our key motivation for doing the building, and the key metrics of success for us, were understanding the social challenges and then how we might address those.

What were the outcomes?

The Centre has leisure spaces, a climbing wall, an event space (see Figure 6.4). It's got a recording studio, but it's also got sexual health clinics in it. So kids can go there, and they can go on the climbing wall, but they can also learn how to write a CV and they have access to healthcare. So key metrics we were looking at were things like, can this building help address sort out some of the social challenges? Things like underage pregnancies or anti-social behaviour.

We knew some of the existing data around that site; there was an existing youth centre on the site, it closed because the building was unsafe, and there was a spike in anti-social behaviour when it closed down. We could see this measure because we had the statistics. So we could also measure the impact of the building once it had opened.

Ten years on, we could look back on it, and we know that every single young person that was involved in the design workshops then went on to education, employment or training. And some of the kids that were involved in that design process are now working at the Centre.

You can look back on it with a bit of distance and see how well it's performed against these metrics.

It won some architectural awards, but the thing we were interested in was the outputs of the building. Both the process itself and the building had positive social outcomes.

This is something that we are interested in across all of our projects; the ways that we can achieve these sorts of social outcomes.

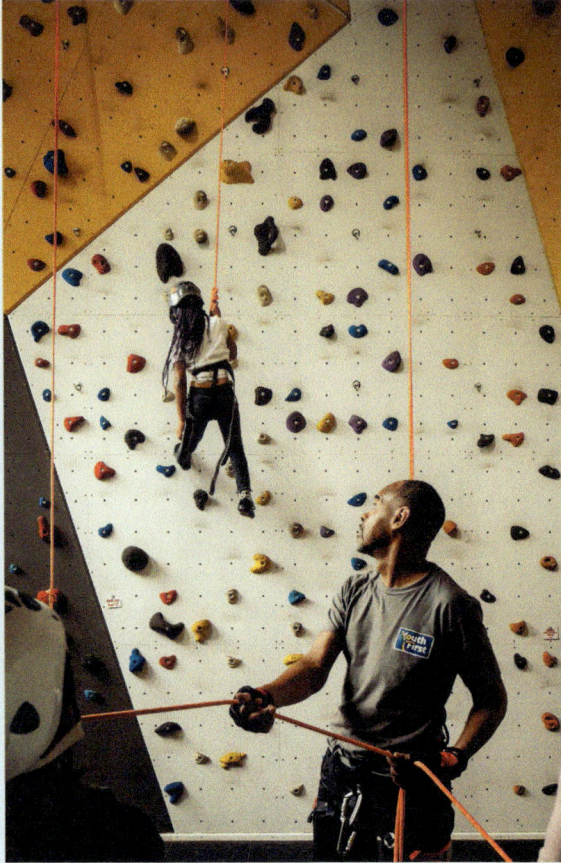

Figure 6.4 TNG Youth and Community Centre in Lewisham. Photograph by Jim Stephenson.

BEHAVIOURAL ANALYSIS

DRIVE: Delivering social value can activate both your intrinsic and extrinsic motivators – dig into both to see what you can draw upon that would compel you to deliver long-term outcomes like these.

KNOWLEDGE: Listen keenly to those you need to by going into their space at their time with their permission to gain trust to thoughtfully deliver this kind of work.

STRATEGY: Plan carefully, recognising that lifestyles and experiences may be very different to your own. Make no assumptions about why people live the way they do currently and be aware of your own privilege to ensure that you can effectively engage with communities.

ACTION: Work with local teams in a collaborative way to give back for the long term.

KEY TAKEAWAYS

- Micro and SMEs proportionally make up almost all businesses and a disproportionately large number qualify as diverse suppliers, because there are more opportunities in running your own business than working within male-dominated white-led organisations.
- Smaller businesses are agile and invariably meet or exceed delivery expectations.
- Perceptions of risk are often unfounded, and are rooted in bias.
- Develop and support existing frameworks which champion supplier diversity.
- Amount of spend as well as number of complaints are useful data trackers.
- Don't be tokenistic and approach or use EMBs to make your competition entry or procurement bid look like you're doing the right thing. Properly engage and understand why using, for example, an EMB is worthwhile.
- If scoring or entering a competition or procurement bid, consider the table as a useful way of systemically addressing EDI.
- Suppliers, as well as procurers, need to demonstrate EDI.
- The Buying Social Justice Through Procurement toolkit exists to help you with this.

NOTES

1 Linda Scott, *The Double X Economy: The Epic Potential of Empowering Women*, Faber & Faber, 2020, p. 5.
2 MSDUK Report on Inclusive Procurement. See www.msduk.org.uk/static/The-Road-to-Inclusive-Procurement.pdf [Accessed 29 November 2023].
3 UK Government, *Business Population Estimates for the UK and Regions 2022: Statistical Release*. See www.gov.uk/government/statistics/business-population-estimates-2022/business-population-estimates-for-the-uk-and-regions-2022-statistical-release-html [Accessed 29 November 2023].

4   MSDUK-CIPS, *Supplier Diversity White Paper*, 2023. See https://sand-msduk.optimiser. site/resources/CIPS-SD-whitepaper-2023.pdf [Accessed 29 November 2023].

5   McKinsey, *Expand Diversity among Your Suppliers—and Add Value to Your Organization*. See www. mckinsey.com/capabilities/operations/our-insights/expand-diversity-among-your-suppliers-and-add-value-to-your-organization [Accessed 29 November 2023].

6   Charlie Edmonds, *From Power to Freedom: On the Future of Organising Architectural Workers*, For the Love of Power, AfterParti Zine #01.

7   Hackett Group's *Supplier Diversity Survey*. See www.thehackettgroup.com/podcast/ supplier-diversity/ [Accessed 29 November 2023].

8   *Supplier Diversity & Inclusion Code of Conduct*. See https://media-weconnectinternational-org.s3.amazonaws.com/2020/08/supplier-inclusion-code-of-conduct-supporters-code.pdf [Accessed 29 November 2023].

9   ISO 30415:2021, Human resource management: diversity and inclusion. See www. iso.org/standard/71164.html [Accessed 29 November 2023].

10 Richard Waite, 'How can we go beyond box-ticking on diversity in architecture?', *Architects' Journal*, 19 May 2021. See   www.architectsjournal.co.uk/news/how-can-we-go-beyond-box-ticking-on-diversity-in-architecture [Accessed 29 November 2023].

11 See buyingsocialjustice.org.uk [Accessed 29 November 2023].

12 F. McAndrew, H. Conley, J. Mamode, E. K. Sarter and T. Wright, *Buying Social Justice Through Procurement: An Equality and Diversity Toolkit*, Queen Mary University of London, 2023. See https://buyingsocialjustice.org.uk/toolkit/ [Accessed 29 November 2023].

13 Ibid.

ENGAGE

Chapter Seven

We need to give the unheard voice a place to speak.

Me, 2013

I had been interviewed for a job, in my broadcasting days, and I'd not got it. I'd come second – again. (This is a bit of a running joke in my family.) However, I'd impressed one of the panellists and he suggested we went for a coffee.

I remember it clearly. We met at The Mailbox in Birmingham where BBC Midlands is currently situated. I was trying to influence him around the need for us to approach our newsgathering more inclusively. Earlier in my career I was heavily involved in creating and implementing community engagement strategies, divining, and experimenting with media literacy projects and empowering communities to tell their stories the way they wanted them told. The feedback from those communities was immense, be they environmentalists, Eastern European economic migrants, Muslim women, abusive men trying to change their ways – they valued, not only being heard about things that mattered to them, but having the chance to do so on a prominent platform, like BBC outlets. It was a vital stepping-stone to them reaching out in future to share more. I have to say, I did love my job.

In this conversation over this coffee, I was getting a bit frustrated, and I blurted out, 'We need to give the unheard voice a place to speak!' He responded, 'That's a great line'. I retorted that it wasn't a line, it's what I believed. And in that moment, having articulated it in that way, I realised it's what I'd always believed, and it was my true purpose. It's why I named my consultancy Unheard Voice – the work has always had the Voice as the focus and my service to it, as the mission. As I moved across to RIBA, I was always clear, I wasn't just there for the Institute's members, I was there to support and help with strategies to improve the whole profession in the widest sense, and for those it impacted,

DOI: 10.4324/9781003435747-12

especially those underrepresented within it working to advance architecture by demonstrating public benefit and promoting excellence in it. Something I continue to do.

In the early days of my career, I did work at BBC Pebble Mill and witnessed the move to The Mailbox, so, I'm excited to see how the plans will shape up for the next BBC Midlands move to the old Typhoo Factory in Digbeth, Birmingham, which Glenn Howells will lead.[1] As all households (are supposed to) pay the licence fee, and the future of audiences is so crucial to an organisation like the BBC, I hope the unheard voice will have a say.

Listening to the unheard voice is a crucial approach the built environment needs to take in its work, in order to be inclusive. A fundamental rethink is necessary, because core, especially to a lot of the education of those in architecture, is the sense that The Architect has to be indelibly part of the design process, and it's very much all about The Architect, and The Architect's name should be over the metaphorical door, and The Architect should be able to drive by with pride and say they made their indelible mark and left a legacy.

Rather, we need to embrace Einstein's new type of thinking, and reframe significantly.

The starting question needs to be different. Responding to space and context has to start with listening, learning and reflecting. No pen should touch any paper until people, place and planet have been consulted. The question for the architect and principal planner[2] is can they relinquish self in the process, and can they educate their clients, to do the same?

Whether you're working on a public sector project, or someone's home, inclusion and sustainability should be the foundational underpins, and overarching principles.

The final area for inclusion implementation is that of how we engage external stakeholders; clients, communities and other users.

TESTIMONIAL

If the client who writes the brief isn't an organisation from the communities that the brief will affect, then it's bound to represent the client's interests only – I think it doesn't matter then if a Black architect delivers that brief or not. It just makes it a more palatable face, it's really cosmetic; it goes only so deep, it's not enough. Just because you have a Black architecture practice delivering whatever project for whatever borough, it doesn't necessarily mean that the project is therefore not hugely problematic and marginalising. A lot of Black architects, people from BME backgrounds want to think about these things and think about them differently.

COMMUNITY CONSULTATION

At the moment in the UK, there is a housing crisis. This chapter won't solve this problem, but it may help with navigating some of the 'Not In My Back Yard' (NIMBY) isms which can halt development before it's even started, especially when referencing development that won't impact green space detrimentally.

Community can be defined as quite similar to culture, as in some respects, as it is about a group with shared backgrounds and beliefs. In this case it's a group of people with diverse characteristics who are linked by social ties, share common perspectives, and engage in joint action in geographical locations or settings.

I would consider **community engagement** in the context of built environment discussions to be a combination of commitment to the placemaking process and its values, plus a willingness to help out others in the process. There's an element of active participation, taking an interest and feeling like a stakeholder in outcomes.

The UK government website mentions public consultation in the following context: 'After a local planning authority has received a planning application, it will undertake a period of consultation where views on the proposed development can be expressed. The formal con-sultation period will normally last for 21 days, and the local planning authority will identify and consult a number of different groups.'[3]

It is at this stage – planning – that we've traditionally seen developers engage with communities.

The government guidance on these matters has the direction that the guidance 'sets out the process for efficient and inclusive consultation of planning applications'.

I'd like to draw your attention to a number of elements here which would question the inclusiveness of the guidance.

- The word 'after'.
- The fact the development 'has been proposed'.

- The length of time to gather information – three weeks.
- And who is identifying who could be consulted.
- This is not engagement, it is considered consultation.

In the course of researching this matter, I noted the paragraph, further down the page, headed 'Why are consultees' views important?' has been deleted (see Figure 7.1). It was removed in 2019.

This paragraph originally said:

> It is important that local planning authorities identify and consider all relevant planning issues associated with a proposed development. Consultees may be able to offer particular insights or detailed information which is relevant to the consideration of the application.

The reason why I alert you to this deletion is to impress upon you that taking community engagement seriously in development and placemaking won't necessarily be driven by current legislation or statutory process, depending on where you are in the UK. This is done differently elsewhere in the world, where a dedication to the UN Sustainable Development Goals (SDGs) is very much about listening, and acting on what we hear. The relevant SDGs when considering inclusive consultation are:

- GOAL 8: Decent work and economic growth.
- GOAL 9: Building resilient infrastructure, promoting inclusive and sustainable industrialisation and fostering innovation.
- GOAL 10: Reducing inequalities within countries.
- GOAL 11: Making cities and human settlements inclusive, safe, resilient and sustainable.

As a result, the guidance and documentation on these matters provided by the UN is plentiful.

Why are consultees' views important?

Paragraph deleted.

Paragraph: 007 Reference ID: 15-007-20190722

Revision date: 23 07 2019 See previous version

Figure 7.1 Screenshot of gov.uk guidance on public consultation.

As professionals, you must hold yourselves to this higher bar, if you want to progress community engagement and consultation effectively, and not just look to the government guidance – certainly in England (Scotland is brilliant at this)[4] – because, not only will it not necessarily help you get to the outcomes you want, given this deletion, and it doesn't appear to be cross-referenced with a different part of the guidance, and appears to have been removed, you could conclude, therefore, it is not considered relevant information. My advice is that better practice would be to consider engagement with consultees of paramount importance, for all the reasons I'll now go on to describe.

Community consultation currently follows the guidance which says:

> **After** a local planning authority has received a planning application, it will undertake a period of consultation where views on the **proposed development** can be expressed. The formal consultation period will normally **last for 21 days**, and the **local planning authority will identify** and consult a number of different groups.

'After': At planning is far too late to be asking communities about development.

'Proposed development': If communities are being asked about what they're essentially being told might happen to them, that doesn't tend to go down well. Even if it's the most beautiful, thought-out scheme, from your point of view. This is a very paternalistic approach – which must be tackled for different outcomes.

'21 days': Three weeks is not enough, given people can go away, and, for example, work a number of jobs.

'The local authority will identify': For the local authority to do the identification of who is worth listening to, this is also an issue that needs addressing. It's not always the most civically active that you need to engage with.

Remember the Einstein quote, 'we need a new type of thinking', and so a reframe of all these elements would suggest that **inclusive community engagement** would be:

> **Before, during and after** a local planning authority receives a planning application, you should undertake a period of **engagement** where views on **developing the area** can be expressed. The informal engagement

period should normally last for (**timed as suitable**), and **seek local intelligence to identify all groups who need to be heard**.

These discussions, and potentially participatory design, should feed into a proposal which is then submitted to planning.

TESTIMONAL: Deaf Architecture Front

Chris Laing

Deaf Architecture Front (DAF) is a platform that forms a bridge between the deaf community and architecture.

When we think about inclusion and what it means, we should think about access for all. DAF was established due to the absence of equal access for deaf people, both in experiencing the built environment and the lack of opportunities to voice our views relating to how our neighbourhoods and public spaces are built. Currently there is no process for deaf people to have access to and engage in public consultations. In addition, the government also has no access budget for BSL interpreters in work experience settings, which means people considering a career in architecture have less opportunities.

Architecture needs to adopt deaf space resources within design and at the early stages of the process. DAF, once registered as a charity, will apply for funding to create resources into BSL accessible formats, this includes expanding the Signstrokes glossary, which, at time of writing, is paused due to funding, but will require ongoing support.

DAF will establish the roles of a *mediator* and *DAF consultant* who will work between the deaf community and the built environment with the aim to form a Deaf Space Lab. We are in the process of addressing the issues relating to work experience and access to public consultations, by providing an intermediary BSL access budget.

INCLUSIVE ENGAGEMENT ISSUES

Money: It does cost time and money to invest upfront in good community engagement strategies. The point is, if you engage properly upfront you'll save yourself time and money down the line. Accessing these funds can be tricky when the value is perceived to be after planning consent has been given, but you need to fashion a different argument for the client, that says it'll cost x now, or x+y later if we don't do this correctly and invest properly, now.

Again, it comes down to a fundamental rethink about how we avoid the constant NIMBY outcomes which planners and developers are constantly fighting when we have a housing shortage and the potential to do something about it. If there isn't an overhaul of the process, how would you expect to reach different outcomes? And an overhaul would require funding to be present at a different stage to now.

Trust: 'It arrives on foot and disappears on horseback', is the saying, and when it comes to 'authority figures', previous experience and rumours about how development decisions are made means communities have no reason to believe or trust what you're saying. You need to work on three things: integrity – show that you do what you say, and say what you do; credibility – you're competent and will organise engagement sessions well; intimate – and this is about displaying humanity and vulnerability, listening, learning, reflecting and resolving to do things differently when fed back to. All of this will be undermined with the slightest hint of self-orientation. Of course, you're there because you want to develop, but always have in the back of your mind that there is the possibility 'Hmmm – maybe it's not the right thing to develop in the way we were originally thinking here and now'. Even if you think you've done this, it's an ongoing effort to build, retain and maintain trust.

Access: Who gets to hear about what's going on and how can they engage with the process; well, there are a number of issues here, from access to technology to language barriers – what about the d/Deaf community and blind people, how are you engaging with them? Are you aware of the cultural considerations that come with managing these approaches? Digital poverty is a real thing, if you're expecting someone to download an app or use a website, some might choose not to use their data in that way. If you're doing in-person events or going onto high streets, remember that just like you may not stop for people handing out leaflets, are they likely to stop and talk to you?

Gatekeepers: These are the loudest voices and self-appointed community leaders. I can't tell you the number of times I've been into communities and people have said to me, 'that's not my community leader – they don't speak for me' – even if they might have the same cultural or faith background. Gatekeepers can take the form of residents' associations, so beware of these groups, and choosing only to consult with them, and the amount of power you give them in the process.

Motivation: This is both yours and theirs to engage. It's not easy and can be very fraught engaging with communities that aren't your usual crowd. Doing it well often means doing so on evenings and weekends. You can get third parties to do this, but it's important, however, that if you are working with them, that they're good ones, and that you listen keenly to the responses that you're being given by the engagement partners you use. There is a lot of malaise around these kinds of engagement activities – people who don't usually have a voice can't be bothered to give you their time – this isn't just about trust, it's about weariness and previous experience. You only have to look around you to see how the marginalised are generally treated by policies, which embed inequality. So you have to work hard to reach groups you don't normally engage with – there's a lot of unseen baggage.

TESTIMONIAL: Challenging Community Apathy

Sandra Hedblad, Built Environment Trust

My work at the Built Environment Trust (BET) explores communities' attitudes towards the built environment. What I'm discovering is how little we all notice and reflect on what is around us. We take our children the same route to school even though we arrive feeling stressed and frustrated about the traffic, we don't use the local park in the winter after 4pm when it's too dark, etc. We are passive users of our spaces, letting them dictate our behaviours, instead of seeking out positive solutions or leading change. Why is that?

The BET's work focuses on turning passive users to active users and passionate advocates for the importance of our built environment, we work across audiences on projects raising awareness of how the built environment makes us feel and behave.

Over the years our habits and understanding of the importance of healthy eating and recycling have changed due to persistent and impactful campaigns, the time is now here to also look at the impact that the built environment has on our health and wellbeing. This knowledge and appreciation of its impact on our lives will be the key to getting the general public to take more notice of developments in their areas and increase their desires to have a say.

Assumptions: Be in no doubt that you will make assumptions about every single person and group you engage with. Sadly, in some cases, such assumptions are deadly – in the book *Show Me the Bodies* by Peter Apps about Grenfell, assumptions made about people who live in social housing and their alleged propensity for anti-social behaviour meant that straightforward emergency measures in lifts were removed.[5] Unhelpful bias can be activated by difference, and it's so important to mitigate this with specific procedures.

RECOGNISING NEEDS

Recognise the needs, expectations and interests of ALL the communities impacted in the wider context of the development, and relate those back to the EDI principles of your organisation.

If you don't have EDI principles, you need to get in some help to shape them with you, because social value doesn't exist without principles of inclusion baked into them.

People are the experts of their own experience, and it's your job to deeply and empathetically understand what their experience is.

Alice Brownfield, when speaking of Kiln Place in Camden, a project for Peter Barber Architects, described that one of the first things they did was a couple of estate walkarounds with residents to understand where the open space was, where there were problems, and if there were areas where anti-social behaviour might happen. Whether green spaces were valued? And through this they identified some significant social value improvements that would help people's day-to-day lives, and the delivered those changes ahead of and alongside the project.

Get to know local businesses, shop there, spend time there. You'll start to meet regulars and hear stories, go to parish meetings, go to town halls, go to gatherings. Before you start knocking on doors, it's important to build those relationships by showing up in public and meeting people. And through that, you'll get to understand who the real community influencers are, and they'll understand who you are before you/you company are introduced.

When you're in a place where a community doesn't appear to exist, possibly because of cutbacks to cultural activities, local businesses would be a good place to engage, and be thoughtful about how your development could literally provide a change to the cultural landscape too.

We often fail to recognise that there is a whole history of the neighbourhood and sometimes that history has been challenging. There can be a trust deficit that we need to work to overcome. You do that by showing up to things that are already happening in the community so that you are then able to move on to the next step.

Using EqIAs

As I mentioned in Chapter 3, Equality Impact Assessments (EqIAs) can be used as a tool for community engagement too. Traditionally used in public sector organisations to manage change and to indicate how change could have a disproportionate impact on protected characteristics, the same principle could be applied in a built environment setting.

Looking at key population groups and gathering a narrative about needs and impacts of certain changes can help determine a way forward that will seek to address the community context.

Age, languages, caring needs, mobility, access to public or private transport, students, tourists, and so on – some of these things are not 'protected characteristics', but they need to be taken into account when placemaking.

Properly assessing the situation on the ground of how a space is used will help you create a dataset that would be useful, so you can build a relevant assessment to clearly and objectively discuss impact.

CASE STUDY: Community Engagement

Neil Onions, Founder Director, Beyond the Box CIC

What's the issue you try to solve with your community engagement approach?

For all of our projects we approach our methodology, which is, community engagement or stakeholder engagement, social value or social impact, and then equality, diversity and inclusion (EDI). The issue that we're trying to address is layered. If we are working with a developer and an architectural practice or a local authority approaches us, it's how do you engage, but then how do you engage equitably?

Who is it that's sitting around that table? Who is it that gets the invitation? We're talking about the stakeholders but also about the diversity of the team or the practice. So, if it's a public procurement framework, we get approached by architectural practices who ask for, do you know any diverse-led practices that we should be bringing into the team to help on the bid and to help with procurement.

How do you do it?

We do a lot of advisory work with practices there, helping pull a team together so that collaboratively you have that diversity of thought, knowledge, insight, perspective.

We carry that through the whole process. It's the same for the stakeholders and the engagement. It's the same for the people who are being invited. But the social impact that we create throughout that process starts at the very beginning.

We create social impact, social value outcomes for every workshop we deliver. For example, we commissioned some young architectural students to come in for one of the workshops and live illustrate the findings that were coming out from the creatives in the workshop. We're creating this social impact, this social value outcome at the same time as getting insights about findings from different stakeholders.

What's the positives of doing that? If you imagine that on a local housing estate project, those young people that we are creating a social value with, and it is primarily young people, we're directly connecting them to what is happening in their community in terms of the built environment. But we're doing it through a creative lens. Through that creative engagement, through them having paid skills, we then slowly start to integrate them with the design team. They start feeding into the process, but with agency and power.

That model is always that the engagement should not sit separately to the social impact. It should be intrinsically linked, and it should always have EDI as its focus. And you'll find that if we end up working with a community whose resident association board has been established for a couple of decades, but they're all primarily white males, how do we then start to engage younger people who are interested, but the narrative of always 'they're not interested', but how do you create an environment that's fun and engaging as a way for them, build their skills whilst influencing what's happening in the process (see Figure 7.2).

Figure 7.2 Community engagement process with Beyond the Box. Photograph by Kirin Saul.

Can you provide a specific example?

Convent Way was a collaborative project with Bell Philip Architects in Hounslow. We were approached to work with the community to do community engagement and social impact. We designed a whole series of stakeholder engagement workshops, but within the master plan there was a desire to have a new community centre.

There was already an existing community centre in the middle of the estate. There was some green belt that was being included in the master plan that they would like to have built some housing on. But to do that, they wanted to offer something to give back to the community, which was a new community centre. I'm not an architect, but all my background is community, I already knew that a lot of community centres get built and opened and then there's no thought about the infrastructure and who runs them and who operates them. They usually go to a private operator and you have this cycle of 'we need to build something for the community. Let's build X without finding out what they really want'. And then, guess what? The community centre is not used.

As well as designing the community engagement workshops and theming those, we employed some community champions. They're all paid London Living Wage. We made sure they were representative in terms of age, race, gender. And it was working with them to look at, and testing and piloting, a number of different community events on the estate that would help gather insights from the residents. At the same time, we were teaching them how to apply for funding, how to manage events, how to do risk assessments, all the infrastructure that you would need, that if you have a new community centre, the community and the skills and the knowledge it sits within that local community.

Culturally, coming back to the EDI and cultural awareness, that community knew what kinds of events would bring out the community to come and see designs.

We had elders in the community who just said I wouldn't have come if you weren't having a cooking, knowledge exchange session. Using significant foods through the large South Asian community that lived there that we just wouldn't have known to do that. There's this constant link and feedback throughout the process.

There's a reason that there's such low engagement, particularly when it comes to racial diversity of people turning up. We look at creative ways in which we can get people to come out whilst – and I always talk short, medium, and long term – the value of what you're doing can't just be when it's all finished, in eight or 10 years' time. It just can't. People who live or work or study whatever the project might be right now, need to have benefits from this project.

Through the engagement process, we found out nobody wanted the community centre to move because parents said, 'It's just close enough for me to send my kid to [whichever activity]. I could see them from the window and I feel safe'. Some of the elders said, 'It's just about close enough for me to walk to, but if you move it to your new proposed location it won't be'. They were planning the move because they were taking over a part of the green belt and they thought we need to give something back. The intention was there, but it was only through the engagement we discovered that they wanted the community centre to remain in the centre. And when they went to planning, and again, but no one really understands the value of what we're doing until the very end.

They went to planning, presented the architectural designs. At the end, they gave over our work and said this is also what we've also been doing. We highlighted the people. We'd done resident profiles. How do people move around the estate? How do they operate? What bus do they get off? Is it safe for them to cross the road? How does that impact the design? All of the social impact, all of the training and the skills provided.

The planner said, 'You should have led with this. Why didn't you lead with this? This brings the thing alive. Why did you not put this at the front of your presentation?'

Architects tend to have this pride in wanting to share their creativity, but sometimes they get lost in who you're centring.

Let's tell the story of who this is for. Yes, it's additional affordable homes. Who are those homes for?

What are your learnings and reflections from that as you move forward to other projects?

Every project is really a test and pilot, because every community is different. So, you know, there might be a strand within your methodology, which is, you know, localised context that could be encompassing. But for us there's such nuances with every community. So just because that worked in Hounslow and the local authority liked it, we wouldn't have just blueprinted. Even though sometimes the local authority thinks, 'well that works, that's great, let's do it again'. I say no. The whole idea is 'what works for *that* community?'

The feedback we had from the Hounslow residents, even we were like moved by. Things like: 'You taught us to dream big'. That's such a huge thing for someone to say in their sixties who has lived on the estate for 40 years.

We always say don't underestimate the value of the people that work in the engagement space. We continue to provide job references for people two years later.

Community doesn't need to stop when we have to stop.

There is value in us being in pre-app meetings. That's a very practical thing. Sometimes people like to keep engagement consultants out of the pre-application meetings. I think engagement consultants should be in that room, but there should also be a mechanism where people who represent and live in that community are also a part of some of those pre-app applications.

When someone approaches us to work on a project, I will go into a lot more detail, ask 'How much influence can the community have? Let's be really specific on what the scope is. Let's not tell people they can design the entire estate if that's not what they can do. Where is the area of influence? Where is the scope of influence?'

We don't just take the community on the journey. We often take the design team with us.

We ask everybody, 'What's your experience with co-design? What does it mean to you?' Because we started to realise that you're just in a room saying words that mean something different to everyone. We know you are the designer, and we're not saying that we want the community to design absolutely everything. Of course, you are the expert in the room from a design point of view. No one's taking that away. But you will be able to design based upon need, and lived experience, and understanding, that will create a much more successful project.

BEHAVIOURAL ANALYSIS

DRIVE: Having the confidence to work with communities may not be your skillset, so consider working with partners who can facilitate it well.

KNOWLEDGE: Recognise the expertise of the partners you are working with and foreground their input alongside design when going through planning.

STRATEGY: Be aware of how you feel when working with others regarding participation. If you feel you're giving away too much of your agency in the process, ask yourself if this isn't for the greater good.

ACTION: Listen and iterate differently for every project to ensure it's truly rooted in local context, rather than simply trying to replicate something that worked before.

When conducting this work you have to ask who is already here, who has been here before, who's showing up at your meetings at 'city hall', who's responding to requests to meet and who's not.

It's not about just listening to the loudest voices and you have to seek out those you're not hearing from. Being able to gather demographic data on who is engaging will help you see where there are gaps in terms of age, racial background, gender.

In my conversation with Alice Brownfield of Peter Barber Architects about their community engagement activity generally for this book. For one of their projects, she said the resident's association was very powerful, and it's on reflection they realised that it's those who had the time who run them, who spent time on engagement activities.

When a group is organised, it is very tempting to spend a lot of time listening to them, because your life is made easier, but it is not necessarily the best way to get as full a slate of engagement as you can. Examine who you are listening to and what are the risks in doing so? Who does it mean you may not hear?

Be clear why you might prioritise a group or certain groups and be transparent about the process.

Community exists everywhere, even in places that don't outwardly seem like it. It is our job to ask and find out where do people gather, where are the informal gathering places, where are the formal gathering places and ask people about the neighbourhood. Have a chat with them about their community. And you know, it might sound obvious, but you'd be surprised how many times it's heard from developers, in hindsight, 'Oh, the big lesson we learned was that we should've actually talked to people and got them involved in the whole process'. It's like people assume, or maybe it just feels easier to send out letters saying, 'Hey, we're having this community thing', but then hardly anyone from the community shows up – or maybe just a specific group does.

OUTREACH ACTIVITIES

Inclusion requires you to answer these questions with a variety of answers:

When? Morning, noon, evening, night, online, in person.
How? Meetings, mailing, surveys, market stalls, family fun events/fairs,
for example, literally put on a community event, where there's food,

music, activities, and then at a fixed point you can get up on a little stage and talk about the engagement piece, and encourage people to come to you, *and* go around talking to people.

What way? Food is very important, and not tea, scones or cake for some communities. Be very cognisant of what kinds of food and drink will draw people in – and make sure that there are proper amounts of it. Use a local supplier. Have child-friendly activities also to hand.

Methods? Sometimes technology helps, sometimes people like paper and pen. Have recording devices for those who want to share verbally. Find out if there are d/Deaf people who would need a sign-language interpreter, and *then* book one for events. Consider visual aids for both those who have vision impairments and those who struggle to read.

The list of how you can do this is not exhaustive and I'd urge you to be as creative as you can, because doing so demonstrates commitment to wanting to hear from everyone.

Communicating EDI Principles

The more you're out and about in the community, the more people will start recognising you. You can have chats that might begin small, but with time they can grow, allowing you to discuss the project you're involved in. It's not a formula, it's more of an art, knowing when and how to bring up your project during other people's events. Sometimes it's just not the right moment. Maybe you're in a community space, an event, or attending someone else's gathering. At those times, it's crucial to be mindful of the context, just like you'd want the same respect if they were attending your event.

Going back to the most basic way of building relationships, friendships and communicating – it's about spending time, understanding what drives them, what matters to them, and what challenges them. Through those conversations, your project naturally becomes a part of the discussion, and they'll start linking you with it. Another aspect we haven't covered much, which depends on where you're based, is if you have the chance to kick off with a pre-development activation of an empty space or a temporary event on an unused lot. This can start creating a sense of place on the site you want to develop.

This way, people will start associating these pop-up events and activities with your site, your company, or your specific project, depending on how you decide to present it. This approach accomplishes three things:

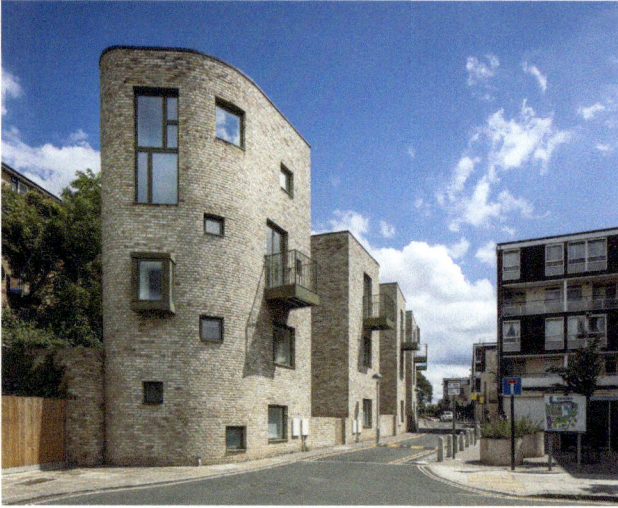

Figure 7.3 Kiln Place, Peter Barber Architects. Photograph by Morley von Stenberg.

1. It brings life to the site and benefits the community positively.
2. It begins to establish a sense of place.
3. It serves as a method of community engagement. This creative approach lets you seek real-time feedback, input, and ideas while sharing your own plans and actions.

You receive immediate input on your project. Having a tangible location where you can organise a pop-up, activation, or engagement focused on public design and participatory design is among the key methods to achieve this.

When speaking to Alice Brownfield, she advocated for the use of physical models. She said from her experiences at Kiln Place (see Figure 7.3), a housing development in Camden, that people being able to see and hold and move around a real thing in their hands really helps people who are unfamiliar with architecture to understand the process.

Reviewing and Evaluating

If the community provides substantial input, and some of it contradicts the developer's initial intentions, dealing with that can be tricky. A significant aspect revolves around being truthful and open about your capabilities and limitations, what you can and cannot achieve. Community engagement is not without challenges; it may not always yield input that aligns with your objectives or that proves helpful. Sometimes, the input received may even challenge your fundamental beliefs, vision or mission. It isn't about incorporating every piece of input, but rather understanding how to respond effectively both to the input and to the community.

Transparent communication is paramount in addressing these dynamics. Establishing a community engagement process allows you to foster relationships with neighbours, community members and leaders. When faced with tough questions or objections, your ability to respond in a manner that demonstrates respect and attentiveness becomes essential. This reciprocity showcases that you've valued their input, and they, in turn, exhibit respect by understanding and accepting your responses.

However, it's important to acknowledge that the process is not as straightforward or easy as described. Undoubtedly, you've encountered complex projects where developers and communities remain at odds. Often missing in such scenarios is the effort and time invested upfront to cultivate respectful relationships. The second crucial element is honest communication about your capabilities and limitations, along with transparent explanations for the feasibility of certain actions.

Many challenges stem from historical exclusion of communities in these processes. While this can't fully rectify past injustices, a primary step is to build these respectful relationships and acknowledge the existing trust deficit. Overcoming this deficit requires engaging in conversations, actively listening and providing space for concerns to be voiced.

Maintaining connection is a vital consideration, extending beyond immediate needs. Frequently, developers only reach out to communities when seeking public support during hearings, for example. Creativity and consistency are pivotal components of successful community engagement. Regular engagement meetings should be held, with a creative approach to their format. Conventional public input sessions often fall short, being inconvenient and lacking substantial discussion or imaginative input.

Several principles are key to guide your approach:

1. **Purposeful engagement**: Understand the intention behind your community meetings. Are you merely fulfilling a requirement, or are you genuinely committed to enhancing your placemaking process through community engagement?

2. **Regenerative approach**: Shift towards practices that are not only generative but also regenerative for communities. Depart from historically extractive development methods.
3. **Respect and trust**: Prioritise respect and trust within the community, which in turn will foster mutual respect and trust towards you.

In practice, this can manifest in various ways:

- Clearly define the purpose of your community meetings logistically. Why are you gathering people and asking for their time?
- Embrace a philosophical stance that treats community members as experts in their own experiences and their locality.
- Co-creation should extend beyond physical space ideas to encompass community goals, success measures and rules of engagement. Co-creating these benchmarks promotes trust, respect and shared accountability for a smoother process.

CLIENT PUSHBACK

Simply speaking, if you cannot convince your client that you should have a different approach to your usual tactics around community engagement, ask them to suggest how they propose to sail through planning using the same methodology. Ask them to reflect on how much it has cost developing a project only to have it refused. Ask if they have the appetite for that battle again, or if there is value in exploring this alternative approach, which should yield better results.

Co-creation and greater participatory engagement have been shown to be far more effective at resulting in better outcomes. That in turn would benefit us all in easing the pressures on housing, wider costs and the macro economy.

CASE STUDY: Managing Client Relationships, Africa Centre

Jonathan Hagos, Freehaus

What is the issue you were trying to solve?

What we were able to do in the competition to win this work was to demonstrate that we understood the complexity of The Africa Centre's brief and set out strategies for how we would work with

Figure 7.4 The Africa Centre. Photograph by Taran Wilkhu.

them to deliver that. And I think we framed that in a way which was non-architectural. We tried to use language to demonstrate to the client that we understood what their ambition was (see Figure 7.4).

We were talking about the role The Africa Centre might have as an organisation, what their mission statement was, how architecture and how the working in the built environment can help an organisation establish its identity.

I think we tried to show how architecture's only one piece of it, and as a team, we would help join them and work with them to address and support other broader issues as well.

But I suppose the core element of the brief was that The Africa Centre had slightly lost its way as an organisation.

When we were brought onto a project, we inherited a deep conversation about that. Our brief was to create something that was unmistakably African.

But having won the competition, we had inherited some pre-existing ideas and a design, and we had to challenge those and then reframe them for the client.

How did you do that?

If you embrace it and lean into what you inherit, it can be a really powerful, a design parameter.

If I go back to my training as an architect, I think there was a sense a lot around ego and around this idea of authorship and masculine genius. I don't think it was very inclusive in terms of the idea that to achieve appropriate design, that that could be shared.

When I talk about authorship and inheritance, part of me is: 'of course'. But there's also a part: 'no, that's not what I was taught. I was taught that it should be mine and there should be this "thing", a product that we look at and that we create'.

There was a previous architect involved who took the organisation up to RIBA stage two: concept design for the purposes of seeking funding.

I completely understand why you would need an architect to do that. An architect in that situation, probably to get to planning permission, as quick and as cheaply as possible. Normally doesn't allow for engagement. Broader conversations were needed to understand operational needs to further inform the design.

What perhaps wasn't anticipated by the client was that we couldn't come in at RIBA stage three and take it on, and a revisit would be needed. So although that was our brief and we pitched against that, which was 'we'll pick up the project and move forward', we did say in our ambition, we needed to go back as well, and we needed to speak with all those people who informed the initial design because we recognise that this inheritance is a responsibility.

The programme and budget didn't allow for that. But we were insistent that we really need to do this. That we needed to meet with the previous architect and that we need to meet with the interim director who wasn't in his role anymore. We need to have conversations with these people, otherwise we have no idea what we're inheriting and we're going to make incorrect assumptions, and that won't serve you in the long term. We put forward a small nominal fee for the revisit, and we demonstrated how we could do that in tandem with the programme.

Those conversations were hugely important. We met with the previous architects a couple of times to understand the rationale for why certain decisions were made, super informative conversations.

We were able to kind of sidestep ourselves a little bit and some of our initial throwaway responses to the brief, to deeply understand why certain decisions had been made.

It gave us a bit of agency to challenge as well. By having those conversations, we could ask the right questions (see Figure 7.5).

The organisation had expected us to run with the existing design. Actually, it meant that we had to go back into planning again.

We had really powerful conversations about placemaking. We did a series of drawings of the organisation, elevations to say, 'if we deliver the consent scheme, this is what you'll get, i.e. there are no proposed transformations to the external facades and there is also no budgeting for this'.

We had to walk them through step-by-step. We had to use lots of non-traditional drawing methods, collage, sketches, really simple visuals to explain that, because when they were seeing an elevation, which they put in for planning, not consent, they were seeing one thing, but when we showed them, this is what that means, they started to understand. A lot of that process of inheritance, revisiting, unpicking, needed to happen alongside the client as well. We were fortunate to have champions for this process amongst the client team which helped.

Figure 7.5 Freehaus working with The Africa Centre leadership. Photograph by Freehaus.

What were the outcomes from that?

The majority of the client group understood that we needed to go through a slightly slower process than envisaged, but there was a little bit of tension because not everyone appreciated, (a) the importance of this process, or (b) that part of their funding requirements was that they should engage in this way. So, there were a lot of conversations we needed to have to explain quite carefully to the client that there was a responsibility here.

We had to change the perception of architecture from being a product that is delivered, to a process, a very unique process, and bespoke journey that has to be traversed and to demonstrate why it has value.

Overall, I believe the client is very happy with what they've got. There were some challenges, one being that the pandemic put a huge obstacle in their way from being able to obtain external funding to support some of the other aspects of the project that they wanted to do. So, we had to phase the project quite significantly.

Resultantly The Africa Centre that we delivered isn't The Africa Centre that we designed; it's Phase One only, a phase which focuses mostly on income generating opportunities, which is really important to the organisation and its longevity. It's the restaurant, the cafe, the bar and the exhibition space.

Phase 2 will include a learning space and a space for African startups, which will expand the centre's socio-cultural offer.

What are your reflections on the process?

In a way, The Africa Centre may be perceived now through the lens of its bar and restaurant and perhaps therefore commerce. We had this idea that a welcome to a space, a cultural institution shouldn't feel like your being there is predicated on a commercial transaction. But in a way, because of the focus on income generating opportunities, it has shifted this way.

But what they are able to do now, looking at the positives, is that they were able to start off with a much smaller operational output and expenditure, and they've been able to grow into the building.

I think what maybe architects don't recognise is that you're also sitting side by side with a client who needs to grow into the building that you're designing for them. And often that isn't a discussion that is had. Often I think we can take a brief as being verbatim, and deliver it without questioning whether the client is able to meet the operational demands of that building.

I personally put myself in a position where I was advocating for these conversations and highlighting these gaps. By asking these questions and I wouldn't say I was being perceived as a 'troublemaker' but I'm sure it came across as slightly antagonising, because my point was, how do we design a restaurant if there is no one around the table to tell us what is needed? By asking, who needs to be around the table, we were kind of pushing them towards that.

We could we have been slightly quicker to recognise that maybe concurrent conversations needed to be had to support the strategic brief. This view might be coming from a position of how we could have avoided tension, but ultimately construction is incredibly stressful, and as best as you can, sometimes it does happen, and we need to recognise that you need to be quite adaptive to work through it.

BEHAVIOURAL ANALYSIS

DRIVE: Recognise what your fears might be when wanting to push back against a client. Reflect on why you might be fearful or defensive regarding doing so and find the motivators you need in order to do the right thing for them, for people, place and planet, and for your craft.

KNOWLEDGE: Have you done the homework and digging to demonstrate the value of your understanding of their full context, especially if it is one you haven't worked in before, so you can do so authentically?

STRATEGY: Plan carefully how you will approach the conversations with possible different outcomes in mind. Rehearse those conversations with an ally in the client organisation/context. Check any assumptions you might have are true, or be prepared to dispel them.

ACTION: Adapt your communication style to the ones that would suit your client best. Flex the mode of communication, pace and tone, as well as your body language.

THE SPRAWLING OCTOPUS: WHEN CHALLENGING THE CLIENT SAVED A CITY

> This group of seven architects were actually teaching the Corporation how to deal with the cities problems, and in the end, the Corporation listened.[6]

'The sprawling octopus of an elevated highway'[7] is Michelle Delea's telling of an extraordinary story:[8] how Cork City in Ireland was nearly enveloped, indeed, suffocated, by a concrete collar, a 'Spaghetti Junction' ring of roads (see Figure 7.6), but was shelved – after planning had been approved for it – due to the tenacity of a journalist (Leland) and a group called the City Seventy Planning Group. This group was born of a pioneering RIBA-approved architecture course at the Crawford School of Art in Cork, in the 1960s.

In 1968, a council report recommended the construction of an elevated three-lane dual carriageway and to widen existing inner-city streets into four-lane, undivided roads. To cater for the estimated 54,000 private vehicles expected to be registered by 1986 (compared to 11,000 in 1968), the provision of 18,000 parking spaces was recommended. To accommodate this road on one level, approximately 90 acres or 22 per cent of the central area of Cork City would be required. This was known as the BKS Plan, after the company that came up with the idea. It was clear this was to prioritise the car, over all else.

Figure 7.6 A modern impression of the BKS Traffic Plan looming over the city of Cork. Sketches. Digital modelling by Viktor Gekker.

Horrified at the potential impact of the BKS Plan, Gerald McCarthy presented these findings to his peers in the City Seventy Planning Group, and they began to devise a counter proposal. A series of drawings produced by Des Heffernan proved crucial to the success of the campaign. Sketches of key affected areas were drawn from both aerial and pedestrian perspectives, illustrating the impact of the proposed road network for the first time.

Reflecting on the story, Mary states that "there were no plans, no drawings, no models ... if Des Heffernan hadn't produced his sketches, nobody could actually visualise what this really meant, least of all, the people who had to decide – and did decide – to take it on".[9]

The early career architects set about campaigning to stop the proposal with a variety of reports, proposals for alternative – public transport – schemes and ideas to address the issues of the city, pushing back against those who could ultimately determine the trajectory of their burgeoning careers. However, they wanted only the best for where they lived and grew up. Mary Leland referenced John Ruskin, calling this 'social affection', saying she wished people could be fonder of where they live.

MEANINGFUL PARTICIPATION

To address both Sandra Hedblad's point (in the testimonial above) and Mary Leland's observation, there are a couple of tools to help you help communities really engage with where they live.

The Toward Spatial Justice RIBA Plan of Work overlay: *A Guide for Achieving Meaningful Participation in Co-design Processes*[10] 'concisely captures the key co-design concepts and themes with signposts to relevant resources for further reading'. One of the key audiences for the guide, as identified by the authors, is the individual and community groups, aware that language needs to be defined, and people need to feel it's an accessible document to help them understand and deal with the process of placemaking.

The Association of Collaborative Design (ACD) (see QR Code 7.1) – which was also involved in the above – have taken this further, producing a technical document, the RIBA Plan of Work overlay for Community Engagement.[11] At time of writing it was being finalised but not yet published. It seeks to answer how can we create better engagement with the built environment at systemic level for practitioners to facilitate it.

KEY RESOURCE: The RIBA Community Engagement Overlay to the Plan of Work

Sarah Jones-Morris, Co-CEO, The Association of Collaborative Design

What is the problem you're trying to solve with the overlay?

We started with the question, why is there no benchmark on what engagement is? There is a tiny percentage of people doing excellent work. However, the majority is minimal at best. In Scotland, they have engagement national standards and they have done for 20 years. They also have a Community Empowerment Act and community engagement is far more embedded within government than other parts of the UK. It is just standard. When speaking to Scottish collaborators they were surprised it was a conversation, as it already existed for them, but it's not UK universal.

I do a lot of design panels and review, experience in the built environment industry for 25 years and the vast majority of projects do not have any form of engagement. Clients can get overwhelmed by the prospect of trying to follow the way of exemplar projects, lack of resources and funding, so they don't do it at all. Professionals lack skills and experience and do not know where to begin. We felt we needed to provide a technical framework that raised the standard from nothing, to at least *something*, to keep it manageable.

When we embarked on exploring the issue, we didn't know it would end up as an overlay – at times we did wonder what we were doing and why we were bothering!

How did you create it?

In a call out we discovered that Sustrans Scotland are highly involved in community engagement and there are national community engagement standards there. We formed a partnership with them and held a collaborative workshop with over 40 participants from over 25 organisations from across the UK. We then approached RIBA who were excited and encouraged by this new and much needed overlay. They have sponsored us, help developed and 'host' the overlay.

We tested what were areas of commonality and at what RIBA stage of work the engagement was happening. We discovered that pre-Stage 3 was critical, but also that it wasn't done often enough.

We examined a lot of issues, including what does it mean to use the term stakeholder. So, we've not only created an overlay, but there is glossary of terms akin to the RIBA Plan of Works, including co-design, participation and community. The language got ripped apart, and then put back together again.

For example, empowerment is a word we've deliberately chosen not to use. Following research in to the spectrum or levels of engagement we refer and use the International Association for Public Participation[12] internationally recognised definitions. The UK legislation does not enable empowerment. The IAPP are an important organisation; recommend looking at their code of ethics, code conduct, all about public participation.

A lot of people say they're doing co-design, but they're not. They're doing participatory design because co-design is a collective creative approach to sharing power and decision-making.

When we were doing this, we realised we needed a multidisciplinary approach too. We know this needs to reach out to other professional institutions like the Landscape Institute who have endorsed this overlay.

What do you hope the outcomes of its use will be?

That people who do not work in any form of engagement currently, feel confident to try *some* at least. That the process that seems manageable and seems clear.

That people benchmark against it and can see what good engagement is. That they capture data in a transparent, meaningful way, and it's clear as to why, how, what, where, when.

We tried to create something that's not too onerous but gives people a good framework to base things around and to refer to.

What we'd like to see is for people to have ownership of it and feel confident to use it in my future. That it's providing people the tools and the confidence that they can do engagement without feeling like it's this massive unknown.

QR Code 7.1:
ACCESS: The Association for Collaborative Design Resources.

Our communities are the reason we must have inclusion in the built environment, at all levels, at all stages of design, and all parts of the process.

Dr Devorah Block, whose passion for place literacy for all and in education has led her to create a project for this purpose,[13] says:

The built environment is an incredibly complex ecosystem which can be very difficult to understand as a layperson. This is a big part of why so many of us are passive recipients of our built environments. Place literacy invites us to engage critically with the places we live, work, and play in a holistic way. Rather than separating out buildings and streets, environments, and people – or even deciders, designers, and participants – speaking about place recognises the complex ways in which all these pieces and experiences are woven together.

Places hold our experiences – past, present, and imagined. When we dive into the understanding of a place, learn to read its languages, and query its stories, we learn about how the world works and how our individual lives fit into the spaces we are in. We learn to recognise the ways in which places shape us – who we are and what we dream of – and the agency that we have, as individuals and communities, to shape places.

CASE STUDY: Wolves Lane Community Centre

Pedro Gil, Director, Studio Gil, with Material Cultures

What was the situation you were trying to address?

The Wolves Lane Community Centre is an incredible existing asset, and it's been part of the North London Wood Green community for decades. It has existing greenhouses where food growing takes place. It's also home to lots of community initiatives such as food markets, independent markets, children's parties, and home to growers such as Black Roots, which are a Black run organisation for planting and growing.

We were approached by a consortium client who had just taken on the lease from Harringay Council on peppercorn rent for 25 years. And a consortium consisted of two organisations: Organically, which is a food growers cooperative based in Epping and Ubele, which is a Black run organisation that champions Black businesses, Black charities, Black organisations, across the UK. Those two organisations came together and formed the Wolves Lane Consortium.

The situation was they didn't know what they wanted, and this is where co-creation became very, very useful. We collaborated with Practice Architecture Paloma Gormley's practice that has now been rebranded as Material Cultures. There was collaboration everywhere. The client was a collaboration. The architect's design team was a collaboration, a female led practice, and a global majority led practice in myself. So it was baked into the structure of the project.

How did you go about the co-creation?

What Paloma and I began to do was we began to facilitate conversations and we asked the consortium to put together a list of stakeholders that they wanted around the table to help shape the brief.

There was no brief. There was just a site. There was this incredible community spirit that was already happening on the place. But they did realise that the facilities were not fit for purpose. They just didn't know what the purpose was. It was an overarching community offer, but they didn't know how that translated into an architectural response. This is where architects add a lot of value.

We talked about identifying priorities wants, needs, nice to haves, and luxuries.

The steering group then came up with a set of activities that they wanted to take place. We took that away, reshaped that into what might then be a very, very early room accommodation schedule.

We shared that with the client at a separate event; testing what they felt was working, what wasn't, re-establishing the priorities.

It was about having open and non-predetermined conversations. And from those conversations, we got to four building typologies. Building A is a community hall. Because from that we gleaned that strong need for a multi-use space (see Figure 7.7)

Building B was the administrative space – that was really a strong requirement. Building C became a fruit and vegetable processing facility. So all of the amazing food grown that takes place on the site already, that need, that could be harvested somewhere.

So you can see, the brief begins to reveal itself. And rather than predetermining and saying, this is what it's got to be, trusting the process and also trusting the people, which I don't feel architects or sometimes local authorities or developers, they don't, they don't want to trust people.

Building D became overspill space. So as and when the organisation grows and expands, so they could.

That was where codesign and co-creation was really vital, even to this day, even to the start of the project.

Figure 7.7 The Wolves Lane Community Centre. Digital image by studiogil.

How did you ensure that you continue to listen when perhaps your own expertise outstripped the ideas of the client?

The core ideals of the client are about inclusion, knowledge transfer, education, and are about empowerment from both Organically's side and Ubele's side. Regardless of their missions, they share those core ideals.

So legacy is something I talk about often in the practice as we're very brief custodians of the project. Even though our egos and our arrogance lead us somewhere else. It's the people and the communities that are going to be using these buildings. They're the ones that are the real beneficiaries. So the client has been involved in every single RIBA work stage, whether it came to material choices, the architecture, the building. The project must be responsible to the planet and to the place.

We did several projects with young people and upskilling too of locals. It was more than just a co-creation of a particular space. It was the development of a community, the development of a wider idea about how this community could not only be developed for now, but for the future.

What are the outcomes of the project?

The project is on site due for completion in spring 2024. I's going well. The skills and knowledge transfer continue to this day. Seminars, multi-generational seminars are happening from very young children right up to people that want to think about re-skilling or retraining into another sector, adults that might want to retrain. We're very proud of the project.

BEHAVIOURAL ANALYSIS

DRIVE: If daunted by the prospect of a blank sheet of paper approach to a project, consider how to draw on the confidence and purpose of your client.

KNOWLEDGE: Listen keenly, not only what is being said, but also identify what is not being said, so that you can reflect back to them in a useful way and you can strip back the ideas to formulate an effective plan.

STRATEGY: Be prepared to park your ego and be very aware of how it feels to do so. Practice humility in the design process, even when you do not have a client like this one.

ACTION: Think about how the project can create opportunities for your client and the surrounding community to develop a greater understanding of how the built environment shapes lives.

It all comes back, full circle, to who learns about our built environment, how we learn about it, how we can be inspired to work in it, how we can influence its shape – and all of that having a profound impact on how we think, communicate and behave with each other as humans.

Ensuring full and habitual inclusion in how we engage with our communities could start a virtuous cycle for all our lives.

KEY TAKEAWAYS

- Community consultation needs to be more participatory and be an ongoing process.
- Be proactive considering issues with the community engagement process.
- Recognise the needs of different groups and consider an EqIA.
- Provide a variety of engagement opportunities.
- Review and evaluate regularly, iterating processes for different projects.
- Don't be afraid to challenge your clients.
- Adopt a coaching style to reach better outcomes.
- Use the RIBA Community Engagement overlay and access other ACD resources.
- Think about how to encourage 'social affection' and place literacy in your work.

NOTES

1   'Plans for new BBC Birmingham HQ The Tea Factory approved', BBC News, 16 March 2023. See www.bbc.co.uk/news/uk-england-birmingham-64979950 [Accessed 29 November 2023]

2   In an effort to avoid the genderised term master planner, I suggest this term principal planner. I understand that 'to master' also means also to be proficient in something, but the etymology of both meanings is the same. Part of the challenge of this book is to question our acceptance and use of genderised language in the professions.

3   Guidance on consultation and pre-decision matters. See www.gov.uk/guidance/consultation-and-pre-decision-matters#what-local-planning-authority-consultation-takes-place-before-a-planning-application-is-decided-and-with-who [Accessed 23 November 2023].

4   National Standards for Community Engagement, Scottish Community Development Centre. See www.scdc.org.uk/what/national-standards [Accessed 29 November 2023].

5   Peter Apps, *Show Me the Bodies*, OneWorld, 2022, Chapter 1, p. 17.

6   The Sprawling Octopus of an Elevated Highway, directed by Michelle Delea (independent, 2022), 1:14.

7   The Sprawling Newspaper. See www.type.ie/product/the-sprawling-newspaper [Accessed 9 November 2023].

8   Michelle Delea, 'Halting the highway: How the future of Cork was reimagined', *Architecture Ireland*, 2023, 328: 11. See https://www.riai.ie/discover-architecture/architecture-ireland-digital/issue-328 [Accessed 29 November 2023].

9   Ibid.

10 Towards Spatial Justice: A Guide for Achieving Meaningful Participation in Co-Design Processes. See www.dsdha.co.uk/gridfs/645507529b0f42000e91b43b [Accessed 29 November 2023].

11 RIBA Plan of Work Overlay for Community Engagement by The Association of Collaborative Design. See www.theacd.org.uk/research [Accessed 29 November 2023].

12 The International Association for Public Participation. See www.iap2.org/page/IAP2-DEI-English [Accessed 29 November 2023].

13 The Place Literacy Project. See www.placeliteracy.org [Accessed 31 May 2024].

Allow the terror of an unliveable future to be balanced and soothed by the prospect of building something much better than many of us have previously dared to hope.[1]

Did you know that the UK Equality Act of 2010 is more than 200 pages long, and there are only three mentions of the word 'Diversity', all in relation to monitoring? Did you know there is no mention of the word 'Inclusion', and no mention of 'Equity'? In fact, I have wondered if it matters that it doesn't reference 'skin colour' when defining race. Simply, 'colour'. It could be referring to eye or hair colour if one wanted to be legally pedantic, and therefore is it even properly 'protecting' racial difference? As I was reminded recently, legality isn't a guide to morality: the Holocaust was legal, when hiding Jews was criminalised; slavery was legal, when freeing slaves was criminalised; segregation was legal, and protesting against it was criminalised. And even today, in various places around the world, women not having control over their own bodies is legal, and them campaigning for rights and power is criminalised. At time of writing, there are women in the United States being jailed for miscarrying babies.[2]

'A riot is the language of the unheard', said Martin Luther King Jr. Isn't it better, then, to listen and hear, rather than rely on legislation to guide you?

Here, in this book, there are tens of thousands of words, and yet I know there was so much more I could have written about every aspect of inclusion, lived experiences, backgrounds and cultures. About how the built environment professions are so key to bringing about inclusive change; safety for women, accessibility for disabled people, progression for racialised groups, a voice for younger people. About how we need to hold ourselves to a higher bar, a better standard, and not just tick the box around 'necessity' in some legislation, which, quite often, is lacking in so many ways. And, constantly, constantly asking you: what is it about you, your team, your organisation that needs to change, so it can be more inclusive of all; and, providing you with the tools to do so.

DOI: 10.4324/9781003435747-13

Don't be under the impression either, however, that this is the 'be all, and end all' on the subject of EDI practice in architecture and the built environment. I wouldn't be so arrogant as to suggest it. There are so many other great generic practical guides and tools to delivering this work, from Lily Zheng,[3] to David Livermore,[4] to Sheeren Daniels,[5] to name just a few, and more coming out every day.

Show Me The Bodies,[6] Peter Apps' devastating insight into failure after failure leading to the Grenfell disaster, clearly outlines the roles all of us have to play in these professions to inclusively, sustainably, ethically, safely, innovatively, protect life.

But we should be going further. Creating provision, not just so we protect life, but so all can live fully and enjoy it, based on what is inclusive and appropriate for that community and context.

In the way we create our built environment presently, overwhelmingly, this is not the case. It is your job to use a guide like this one, also armed with ethics,[7] safety,[8] and climate[9] guides, to deliver and influence society for the better, not just by using design, but through how you behave.

Ask, whose vision are we uplifting? Who is being inspired? Who is finding it delightful? Whose lives are we transforming?

How deep are you thinking? To what standards are you measuring quality? Whose input has gone into the detail? How would the swing of the door affect different groups? What can be considered about the position of a window?

This approach to perceiving value in people and planet, how we create 'place', for whom and why, how we predict, manage and mitigate impact on climate and neighbourhood, all must be rooted in those inclusive behaviours, delivering on developing your cultural intelligence, formulating those procedures, policies and practices, implementing them and enforcing their use, adaptively and fairly.

Answer those questions with help from this book using the Action Plan template at the back; take responsibility for answering with humility and good conscience. Slow down to acknowledge and mitigate your bias. Be an agent of change.

There are no magic wands, no silver bullets, no quick fixes in order to deliver successful EDI outcomes – only deliberate, considered conscious chipping away at the systems that cause discrimination.

And strip away with vigour where you can, ripping the paper-thin veneer covering over the status quo.

Inclusive change in the built environment is not optional. It's a personal and leadership obligation. A comprehensive approach, as outlined in this book, which provides workable solutions and case studies of them in action, should provide us with the optimism we need to start to combat societal ills made manifest in our organisations and institutions, across the sector, and then embodied in the built environment we create.

EDI work is an opportunity. An opportunity to join an effort to build a better workplace, a better society, a better world. This is a chance to fulfil that obligation and drive forward towards an alternative future.

I acknowledge that the scale of the task can seem scary. Naomi Klein says:

> Fear is a survival response … But we need somewhere to run *to*. Without that, the fear is only paralysing … Allow the terror of an unliveable future to be balanced and soothed by the prospect of building something much better than many of us have previously dared to hope.[10]

I've tried to give you somewhere to run *to*. Something better to build. Develop your inclusion fitness and strive to reach elite levels, through practice, practice, practice.

And hope. It's in your hands to create hope.

'We need to fight more and hope less', said Professor Chelsea Watego,[11] following the defeat of the Yes campaign to give indigenous people a constitutional voice in an Australian referendum in October 2023. And, following that vote, I felt like agreeing with her. On hearing the news, my heart plummeted and I wept. It's at those times, I have to force myself to believe though, as always, it can't be 'either/or', it has to be 'this/and': fight and hope. Hope: stronger than fear or hate. Hope: stronger than division or intransigence. Hope: the fuel which inspires our fight for justice – spatial, racial and otherwise.

At time of writing, amongst other conflicts, war continues to blight Ukraine in the struggle with Russia. In amongst the devastation, debris and disaster, I received an email:

> I humbly write to you in the hope that you would agree to honor us, a group of Ukrainian architects and professionals in related fields, by delivering a lecture on inclusiveness and implementing its global practices.
>
> First, let me explain why this matter is crucial for us.

> Our main goal as a development company is to help rebuild Ukraine after the war. However, this process has already started: our veterans who are already returning from the frontline and civilians who survived missile attacks now have life-changing injuries and disabilities. They have already paid too high a price for us not to make our country a more convenient place for them to live. It's an opportunity for Ukraine to be a better place, and we need your help to start acting now.
>
> Your expertise in equity, diversity, and inclusion genuinely impresses us. Your experience and knowledge greatly inspire us, people who strive to make a difference just like you do.

I could hardly breathe on receipt of this and with the responsibility of such a task, but found myself in a virtual room with nearly 100 Ukrainian professionals, trying to speak a bit of Ukrainian to show some solidarity, and utterly, utterly in awe that with the background of war, Ukrainians are seeking to do this work when so many of us who don't have to deal with that challenging context aren't always willing to engage with it.

So, I called on Amanda Gorman, and her poem 'The Hill We Climb', 'We will rebuild, reconcile and recover …'. I talked to them about the taking of personal responsibility, and her call at the end, to be brave, step up, and step out:

> For there is always light
> If only we're brave enough to see it,
> If only we're brave enough to be it.[12]

If they can welcome such a message, surely, so can you.

There will be challenge. There will be strife. But, with courage, there is also hope. And, with your endeavour, step-by-step, there can be change.

When you take personal responsibility, when you change your world, you change the world.

You can see the light.

Just look in the mirror, and be it.

NOTES

1   Naomi Klein, *This Changes Everything: Capitalism vs the Climate*, Penguin, 2014.

2   'US women are being jailed for having miscarriages', *BBC News*, 12 November 2021. See www.bbc.co.uk/news/world-us-canada-59214544 [Accessed 23 November 2023].

3   Lily Zheng, *Reconstructing DEI: A Practitioner's Workbook*, Berrett-Koehler Publishers, 2023.

4   David Livermore, *Leading with CQ*, HarperCollins, 2024.

5   Shereen Daniels, *The Anti-Racist Organisation*, Wiley, 2022.

6   Peter Apps, *Show Me The Bodies: How We Let Grenfell Happen*, One World Publications Ltd, 2022.

7   Alasdair Ben Dixon and Carys Rowlands, *RIBA Ethical Practice Guide*, RIBA Publishing, 2023.

8   Dieter Bentley-Gockman, *RIBA Health and Safety Guide*, 2nd edn, RIBA Publishing, 2023.

9   Mina Hasman, *RIBA Climate Guide*, RIBA Publishing, 2023.

10 Naomi Klein, *This Changes Everything: Capitalism vs the Climate*, Penguin, 2014.

11 Professor Chelsea Watego, speaking on ABC, responding to Australian Prime Minster on The Voice referendum, as reported on *The Guardian*. See https://bit.ly/3RTHvio [Accessed 23 November 2023].

12 Amanda Gorman, *The Hill We Climb*, from *Anthology Call Us What We Carry*, Chatto & Windus, 2021.

BAME – Black, Asian, and Minority Ethnic a grouping of people who experience racism. Alternatives can include **racialised groups**, **global majority**, or non-white.

Cultural intelligence – this is the capability to function and relate effectively across difference. CQ stands for cultural intelligence quotient, because it is a measure, as well as an improvable skill.

Cultural norms – researched, observed and descriptive terms for a group of people.

Culture – a shared pattern of beliefs, values, assumptions and behaviours that distinguishes one group from another. What is acceptable and familiar to a group.

Diversity – is simply the fact of visible and invisible difference.

Equity – this is equality of access to life/society/opportunities based on individual need and making up for historic imbalance. Equality is about everyone getting the same, which is fine if we're all at the same starting point, but we know that is not the case.

Explicit/conscious bias – attitudes and beliefs we have about a person or group at a conscious level.

Extrinsic motivation – is the behaviour you use to perform tasks and learn new skills because of the promise of reward or to avoid punishment.

Implicit/unconscious bias – subtle and non-conscious thoughts that happen to all of us, all the time.

Inclusion – is the act of creating an environment where people feel that their identities, values, lifestyles are acknowledged, understood and respected.

Intersectionality – the multiple social forces, social identities and ideological instruments through which power and disadvantage are expressed and legitimised. The layered nature of discrimination.

Intrinsic motivation – is doing something that does not have any obvious external rewards. You do it because it's enjoyable and interesting to you.

Microaggression or **microincivility** – a low intensity act which violates the norms of respectful behaviours and whose intent to harm is ambiguous.

Microaffirmation – is an act of allyship which supports someone facing a microaggression. Small, subtle gestures to indicate you have respect for someone and value them as a person and colleague.

Privilege – simplistically, the opposite of intersectionality. The layered nature of advantage through identity or characteristics.

Psychological safety – feeling comfortable sharing concerns and mistakes without fear of embarrassment or retribution.

Stereotype threat – the risk of confirming negative stereotypes about an individual's racial, ethnic, gender or cultural group, which can create high cognitive load and reduce academic focus and performance.

Stereotype threat adjustment behaviour (STAB)/self-shielding – taking particular actions to overtly display that you're not a negative stereotype, and the effort of that.

Stereotypes – oversimplified, judgemental and frequently pejorative descriptor of people as they pertain to a group they might be in.

Underrepresentation – when the demographics of your organisation/process doesn't reflect its societal context

The website www.buildinginclusion.info will serve as a source of updating information to support this work.

The QR codes provided will link directly to resource source, however, I will endeavour to keep the website updated where the QR codes no longer work.

On the website you will find a list of supportive books, websites, talks and podcasts, and people to follow on social media.

QR Code:
ACCESS: www.Building Inclusion.info.

Inclusion Action Plan Template

Start with one thing in each area and build from there. Use the actions described in each chapter, and the Behavioural Analysis in the case studies to assist your thinking.

Do this for yourself as an individual; work on one together as a team; ask leadership to deliver one for your department, if from a larger organisation; and consider several for the organisation as a whole as you deliver different elements of inclusion.

This template can be seen as a holistic strategic approach – a bag of sand. But examining each part is like ripping open the bag, every action is grain, to push forward the agenda in the right direction.

Business areas	Understand Inspiration, Data, Trust	Develop Training, Objectives, KPIs	Role-Model STREAM	Mechanisms Policies, Procedures, Practices
	Behaviours			
Attract	Drive			
	Knowledge			
	Strategy			
	Action			
Retain	Drive			
	Knowledge			
	Strategy			
	Action			
Create	Drive			
	Knowledge			
	Strategy			
	Action			
Engage	Drive			
	Knowledge			
	Strategy			
	Action			

279 **Inclusion Action Plan Template**

Acknowledgements

There are so many people to thank and acknowledge. There's simply no way I could have delivered this book on my own. If I should have acknowledged you and haven't, please forgive me.

Francesca Ford, my editor, has been a wonderful person to work with on this project. So patient, kind and understanding. Fran, you've given fair and constructive feedback and been very gentle with me. It's been great getting to know you – thanks for all your support, and to Hannah Studd, for taking these words and making them into a book! I'd like to extend my thanks to all at Routledge, especially for your patience waiting 'those' four months for me.

But also, I don't want to forget Helen Castle and Clare Holloway who supported the initial idea and drafts for this book. It wouldn't have made it this far if it wasn't for you in the first place. I know you believed in this project and I remain grateful for your efforts getting it off the ground.

Ilona McKie, thanks for all that time-saving support! Your help with those last minute bits and pieces really eased my pulling together the manuscript at the end!

All my case study participants who took the time to speak to me about their amazing work. You are doing fantastic work! Those who feel like an island in your own organisations, keep doing what you do – we need you! I hope by role-modelling and being featured here will make a difference to the support you get. To all those who I spoke to and wanted to feature, hopefully we will have future editions, I'm so grateful for your backing and interest.

To those who provided testimonials, I am eternally grateful. Black Females in Architecture and Pooja Agrawal and Joseph Henry of Sound Advice; I'm here to support and amplify your voice and your work. For all the underrepresented whose voices and experiences reverberate, this work is for you, in the hope that within, people will check their behaviours unwilling to be the ones responsible for such outcomes, so that you and others like you need suffer less and, then, hopefully, not at all in future.

In the beginning there was Mel Mayfield. Your support in those first two years in the profession was everything for me. Figuratively, helping me find my voice in it, authenticating it, encouraging me to use it. And then, literally, giving me the pen, bidding me: 'Spread the word'. I'll never forget – you provided me with strength, insight, laughs and motivation when I needed it. I really hope you remain proud of that. Always. No regrets.

Sumita Singha OBE and the Architects for Change, doing this work long before I arrived on the scene and continuing still – thank you for all the support you have shown me. I hope this book serves as a useful tool to support you in an ongoing way for the profession.

Dr Devorah Block – where have you been all my [built environment] life?! Although we're late to each other's party, I've hugely valued your arrival. Dr Neal Shasore has a lot to answer for in delaying our introduction. Both of you are incredible champions of everything that can be achieved in the sector, and the three of us should have written this book together. Second edition?!

A huge, HUGE, thank you to Nick Cunningham of Gowling WLG, an incredibly generous man with his time and expertise. If it wasn't for him, I would not have been able to deliver this book.

The wider architecture and built environment collective of colleagues, acquaintances and friends, who convinced me of the value of this work and that I should stay in the sector when I have been compelled to abandon this project and leave – thanks for your encouragement and support. Machel Bogues, Mark Harrison, Sybil Taunton, Louise Duggan – for supporting me and my work from a professional standpoint, in your roles with your organisations, and from a personal one, as fantastic people, useful challengers and friends.

Rebecca Lovelace, partner in crime trying to do this work and battling the forces that seek to derail, together. Building People CIC, your dot-joining entity, is vital in this work, and long may it continue in whatever guise it finds itself. The network you have brought together is powerful, and I hope this book can serve as a tool to support its work.

Katie Neeves, for your kind patience explaining language around trans lives and identity. I know you and other trans people put yourselves out there to much ridicule and pain, and march on regardless. I, for one, am so grateful that you persevere, and I hope I, and this work, can be a useful ally in your endeavours.

Dr Pragya Agarwal, everything you do and contribute towards the knowledge to understand, and delivery of, the social justice space is invaluable. Thank you for being such an inspiration, for the writing encouragement from afar and the check-ins with my progress.

David Livermore PhD, 'The Godfather of CQ!', always on hand for an encouraging word and support for this project when it was just an idea, and for me, personally, too. And the wider cultural intelligence family – so many of you. Your support for this project and support of me is always so precious and valued.

The O'Sullivans: Louise – that lift into Macroom! Norma – you know how you helped! All of you taking an active interest, and supporting my Irish writing retreat, go raibh milé maith agat.

My cheeky, cheery, wonderfully intelligent girls, Tara and Naomi, I am so proud of you and the women you're becoming. You keep it real for me every day, checking my bias, and your patience allowed me to complete this task. I hope that this work will support your journey in the Big (Bad) World, and that you might consider how to take up a similar mantle.

And, my mum, Oma, for the hot meals and warm bed throughout my life! Forgive me for appearing to take for granted my London BnB. I know you're proud of me and this work is dedicated to you.

Last, but absolutely, never least, my ever supportive, forgiving and boundlessly generous husband, Peadar; there are not enough words to express everything I think and feel for you and everything you do for me; for understanding, appreciating and loving the Whole Me – beidh mé de shíor, go hiomlán i ngrá leat.

Index

*For Product Safety Concerns and Information please contact
our EU representative GPSR@taylorandfrancis.com Taylor & Francis
Verlag GmbH, Kaufingerstraße 24, 80331 München, Germany*

T - #0137 - 060525 - C320 - 234/156/19 - PB - 9781032564838 - Gloss Lamination